1014

THE CHRISTIAN SACRAMENTS

THE CHRISTIAN SACRAMENTS

BY

OLIVER CHASE QUICK

M.A.

CANON OF CARLISLE CATHEDRAL

London
NISBET & CO. LTD.
22 BERNERS STREET, W.1

First Published September 1927
Reprinted . . . January 1928
Reprinted . . . March 1929
New Edition . September 1932

Printed in Great Britain at
The Mayflower Press, Plymouth.   William Brendon & Son, Ltd.

TO

BERTRAM KEIR CUNNINGHAM
PRINCIPAL OF WESTCOTT HOUSE
CAMBRIDGE

WITH GRATITUDE AND AFFECTION

FROM HIS PUPIL

AND FELLOW-MEMBER OF THE

FARNHAM BROTHERHOOD

GENERAL INTRODUCTION

THE Editors of this series are convinced that the
Christian Church as a whole is confronted with a
great though largely silent crisis, and also with an un-
paralleled opportunity. They have a common mind
concerning the way in which this crisis and opportunity
should be met. The time has gone by when " apologetics "
could be of any great value. Something more is needed
than a defence of propositions already accepted on
authority, for the present spiritual crisis is essentially a
questioning of authority if not a revolt against it. It
may be predicted that the number of people who are
content simply to rest their religion on the authority of
the Bible or the Church is steadily diminishing, and with
the growing effectiveness of popular education will continue to diminish. We shall not therefore meet the need,
if we have rightly diagnosed it, by dissertations, however
learned, on the interpretation of the Bible or the history
of Christian doctrine. Nothing less is required than a
candid, courageous and well-informed effort to think out
anew, in the light of modern knowledge, the foundation
affirmations of our common Christianity. This is the aim
of every writer in this series.

A further agreement is, we hope, characteristic of the
books which will be published in the series. The authors
have a common mind not only with regard to the problem

but also with regard to the starting-point of reconstruction. They desire to lay stress upon the value and validity of religious experience and to develop their theology on the basis of the religious consciousness. In so doing they claim to be in harmony with modern thought. The massive achievements of the nineteenth and twentieth centuries have been built up on the method of observation and experiment, on experience, not on abstract *a priori* reasoning. Our contention is that the moral and spiritual experience of mankind has the right to be considered, and demands to be understood.

Many distinguished thinkers might be quoted in support of the assertion that philosophers are now prepared in a greater measure than formerly to consider religious experience as among the most significant of their data. One of the greatest has said, " There is nothing more real than what comes in religion. To compare facts such as these with what is given to us in outward existence would be to trifle with the subject. The man who demands a reality more solid than that of the religious consciousness, seeks he does not know what."[1] Nor does this estimate of religious experience come only from idealist thinkers. A philosopher who writes from the standpoint of mathematics and natural science has expressed the same thought in even more forcible language. " The fact of religious vision, and its history of persistent expansion, is our one ground for optimism. Apart from it, human life is a flash of occasional enjoyments lighting up a mass of pain and misery, a bagatelle of transient experience."[2]

[1] F. H. Bradley, *Appearance and Reality*, p. 449.
[2] A. N. Whitehead, *Science and the Modern World*, p. 275.

The conviction that religious experience is to be taken as the starting-point of theological reconstruction does not, of course, imply that we are absolved from the labour of thought. On the contrary, it should serve as the stimulus to thought. No experience can be taken at its face value ; it must be criticised and interpreted. Just as natural science could not exist without experience and the thought concerning experience, so theology cannot exist without the religious consciousness and reflection upon it. Nor do we mean by " experience " anything less than the whole experience of the human race, so far as it has shared in the Christian consciousness. As Mazzini finely said, " Tradition and conscience are the two wings given to the human soul to reach the truth."

It has been the aim of the writers and the Editors of the series to produce studies of the main aspects of Christianity which will be intelligible and interesting to the general reader and at the same time may be worthy of the attention of the specialist. After all, in religion we are dealing with a subject-matter which is open to all and the plan of the works does not require that they shall delve very deeply into questions of minute scholarship We have had the ambition to produce volumes which might find a useful place on the shelves of the clergyman and minister, and no less on those of the intelligent layman. Perhaps we may have done something to bridge the gulf which too often separates the pulpit from the pew.

Naturally, the plan of our series has led us to give the utmost freedom to the authors of the books to work out their own lines of thought, and our part has been strictly calling these ultimate, I mean that they are not further analysable, and that each is distinct from the other. Consider any spoken sentence, e.g. " Shakspere is the greatest of all dramatists." If I say that, the words of my utterance in their proper order are symbolic or significant, and they have a twofold relation of significance, (1) towards Shakspere himself and his position among dramatists, and (2) towards my thought of Shakspere and his position. Thus the saying may be said to signify (indicate) something about Shakspere, and also to signify (express) some thought in my mind. But the saying stands in a relation of *instrumentality* to the particular purpose with which on a given occasion I utter it. The saying is then both symbol and instrument, both signs and means. But in order to have value as a means (i.e. in order to be efficacious) it must *first* have value as a sign, i.e. it must be *understood*. In other words, in this case the efficacy is dependent on the significance.

Is this true also of sacraments ? Surely in all cases the value or function proper to a sign consists in the presentation of something signified to the mind. And if the " causality " of sacraments is limited to that which is proper to signs, their action on the soul must follow this same law : they can have their effect only by presenting to the mind that which they signify. In other words, a sacrament will be effective only in the same general way as a sermon. Just as the hearer of a sermon can say more or less how much good he may reasonably suppose himself to have derived from it, so the partaker of a sacrament must be able to say more or less how much grace on this occasion he may reasonably suppose himself to have received from it. The meaning of sermon and sacrament is sometimes more, sometimes less, vividly impressed on the mind ; and (if we leave out of account the case of disagreement or conscious rejection) according to the vividness of the impression the good or grace received is roughly to be measured. Just in the same way the sight of a flag may stir different degrees of patriotic feeling in different minds, or in the same mind on different occasions. The same general law applies, *mutatis mutandis*, to the effect of music, art, literature and natural beauty. The effect of all these on the soul is measured by the impression produced in the mind through its understanding or appreciation of what the outward things in each case signify or express.

And yet I venture to think that no Catholic, and only few Evangelicals, would really be satisfied by an account of sacramental efficacy given strictly in these terms. Does it not, rather absurdly, seek to circumscribe the power of God in His sacraments, and explain away the characteristic element of mystery which belongs to their very nature ? If it is an irrational limitation of God's love and power to suppose that God does not bestow His spiritual gifts outside sacramental rites, is it not equally an irrational limitation to suppose that He does not bestow His gifts in those rites except through the causality which they possess *as signs ?* If in the former case we seek to limit God by the forms of institutional religion, in the latter case are we not seeking to limit Him no less really by the feeble flickering light of human consciousness ? For my own part, I should desire to affirm that, given a faithful humble disposition of the will towards receiving God's gifts, God may and does, both through sacraments and apart from them, bestow much more on the soul than anything of which its consciousness can be aware. Such efficacy remains essentially mysterious ; but I cannot see that it is either irrational or unintelligible or miraculous ; or that to believe in it is superstition.

Nor do I think that to emphasize the possibility that signs may impress the *subconscious* mind really helps us to understand the characteristic operation of sacraments as signs. Signs act on the subconscious most effectually, when the main attention of the mind is so far directed elsewhere as to make it incapable of criticism, and most of all, when the mind is in a " hypnoidal " state. Hence the efficacy of advertisements, of hymn-book theology, and stained-glass windows. But I hope no Christian will wish to add, " Hence also the special efficacy of sacraments." No doubt, in considering the accessory details of cere-monial, first importance must be given to their probable influence on the subconsciousness. But this is precisely because such things are not intended to occupy the main attention of the conscious mind.

It may, however, be said that I am ignoring the most important analogy to sacraments, namely, the formal acts connected with legal and institutional ceremonies—inves-titures, the conferring of honours, offices and the like. In these, it is urged, the appointed actions clearly have the nature of signs, and yet they do convey something actual to the recipient beyond what lies in the vividness of his appreciation of the thing signified. But, granted that it be so, what is that something ? If we think accurately, it is not the actual enjoyment or possession of the office or honour or property in question ; it is the acknowledged *right* or *title* to such possession or enjoy-ment. Is then what the sacraments confer nothing but an acknowledged right or title to the grace of God ? Passing over the objection that to speak of a *right* or *title* to *grace* involves a contradiction in terms, I still find it almost impossible to believe that any devout worshipper in receiving the sacraments can really think of their operation in that way, whatever dialectical exigencies may lead

The conviction that religious experience is to be taken as the starting-point of theological reconstruction does not, of course, imply that we are absolved from the labour of thought. On the contrary, it should serve as the stimulus to thought. No experience can be taken at its face value ; it must be criticised and interpreted. Just as natural science could not exist without experience and the thought concerning experience, so theology cannot exist without the religious consciousness and reflection upon it. Nor do we mean by " experience " anything less than the whole experience of the human race, so far as it has shared in the Christian consciousness. As Mazzini finely said, " Tradition and conscience are the two wings given to the human soul to reach the truth."

It has been the aim of the writers and the Editors of the series to produce studies of the main aspects of Christianity which will be intelligible and interesting to the general reader and at the same time may be worthy of the attention of the specialist. After all, in religion we are dealing with a subject-matter which is open to all and the plan of the works does not require that they shall delve very deeply into questions of minute scholarship We have had the ambition to produce volumes which might find a useful place on the shelves of the clergyman and minister, and no less on those of the intelligent lay- man. Perhaps we may have done something to bridge the gulf which too often separates the pulpit from the pew.

Naturally, the plan of our series has led us to give the utmost freedom to the authors of the books to work out their own lines of thought, and our part has been strictly confined to the invitation to contribute, and to suggestions concerning the mode of presentation. We hope that the series will contribute something useful to the great debate on religion which is proceeding in secret in the mind of our age, and we humbly pray that their endeavours and ours may be blessed by the Spirit of Truth for the building up of Christ's Universal Church.

PREFACE TO THE FOURTH EDITION

THE appearance of a new edition of this book gives me a welcome opportunity for making clearer the bearing of its main argument upon one or two points frequently raised in current discussions of sacramental theology. Such discussions indicate that there is a real basis of unity in the different doctrines put forward by various "schools of thought" both within and without the Anglican Communion. But I cannot think that the true basis of unity is to be found in a hasty assumption that all fundamental problems are solved if we agree that sacraments operate and have efficacy only as signs or symbols of the grace of God. This principle of doctrine is indeed welcomed by Evangelicals, and it has been exactly stated and defended by the great Jesuit theologian, Cardinal Billot, who declares that *sacramentum, cum sit signum, habere nequit causalitatem quae praetergrediatur rationem signi.* And yet I cannot think that this proposition ought to be assented to without further question. The argument of this book is directed to the conclusion that, in a true philosophy of sacraments, efficacy cannot be made to depend wholly on significance, but that both aspects of sacramental reality are equally primary, as well as inseparable from each other.

Reflection leads me to conclude that there are two and only two positive and ultimate relations between things "outward" or "material" and things "inward" or "spiritual," viz., *significance* and *instrumentality.* By

a

xi

calling these ultimate, I mean that they are not further
analysable, and that each is distinct from the other.
Consider any spoken sentence, e.g. " Shakspere is the
greatest of all dramatists." If I say that, the words of
my utterance in their proper order are symbolic or
significant, and they have a twofold relation of significance,
(1) towards Shakspere himself and his position among
dramatists, and (2) towards my thought of Shakspere and
his position. Thus the saying may be said to signify
(indicate) something about Shakspere, and also to signify
(express) some thought in my mind. But the saying
stands in a relation of *instrumentality* to the particular
purpose with which on a given occasion I utter it. The
saying is then both symbol and instrument, both signs
and means. But in order to have value as a means
(i.e. in order to be efficacious) it must *first* have value as
a sign, i.e. it must be *understood*. In other words, in this
case the efficacy is dependent on the significance.

Is this true also of sacraments ? Surely in all cases the
value or function proper to a sign consists in the presentation of something signified to the mind. And if the
" causality " of sacraments is limited to that which is
proper to signs, their action on the soul must follow this
same law : they can have their effect only by presenting
to the mind that which they signify. In other words, a
sacrament will be effective only in the same general way
as a sermon. Just as the hearer of a sermon can say
more or less how much good he may reasonably suppose
himself to have derived from it, so the partaker of a sacrament must be able to say more or less how much grace
on this occasion he may reasonably suppose himself to
have received from it. The meaning of sermon and
sacrament is sometimes more, sometimes less, vividly
impressed on the mind ; and (if we leave out of account

him subsequently to allege. It is, of course, evident that some sacraments do confer what we may call *status* or office. Baptism makes the recipient a member of Christ's Church, and ordination gives him an office and authority within that body. But this function of the sacraments is something distinguishable from their operation as actual means of grace, which is here in question. The conferring of a status or office or right is essentially a different thing from the bestowal of the powers or qualities which enable the recipient to exercise it worthily. And it is such powers or qualities, rather than the status itself, which constitute the grace given in every sacrament.

The fact is, surely, that it is irrational to suppose that any analogy can enable us clearly to understand or conceive God's action upon us either within or without sacraments. At every moment God's presence is upholding the soul in life, and no finite consciousness can clearly present to itself all the methods of His most intimate interaction with every thought and deed and feeling. " Closer is He than breathing, nearer than hands and feet." Why then should we not suppose that God uses an appointed sacramental action so as to be, not only the sign of a presence and gift to be realized through conscious appreciation of what the sign signifies, but also the direct means of a bestowal, the reality of which *makes* the sacramental action significant ? In other words, I would suggest that it is not more true to say that the efficacy of a sacrament depends on its significance than that its significance is dependent on its efficacy. Certainly I should affirm that it is partly because the ritual of Holy Communion means and suggests so much to my mind that I believe that in it I receive the inflowing presence and power of my Lord. But I should equally affirm that

it is partly because I believe that in the Holy Communion
I receive that presence and power, more really than my
consciousness can ever testify, that the sacrament is to me
so deeply significant.   And so again, when the question is
of the baptism of infants, I find no intellectual scandal
in believing that in the baptism God actually receives and
blesses an unconscious child, and sows the seed of
spiritual life in its nascent soul.   Why should we *confine*
the effect of the sacrament on the child to that formal
incorporation into the Church, in respect of which the
sacrament is in principle no more of a mystery than any
other ceremony of admission ?   All such limitations seem
to be the result of a strict logic which starts from a
questionable principle, viz. *sacramentum, cum sit signum,
habere nequit causalitatem quae praetergrediatur rationem
signi.*

Perhaps I may add a few words about the special
problem of the eucharistic presence.   How are we to understand the words " This (bread) is My Body ? " in the light,
not only of what actually happened in the Upper Room,
but also of what the words have been found to mean in
Christian experience down the centuries ?   I do not
think it helps us to affirm that the words are " symbolically true."   The word symbol is really synonymous with
the word sign ;   and every truth is necessarily symbolic
in so far as it is significant of a reality.   The words " This is
My Body " necessarily symbolize or signify some relation
between the Lord's Body and the bread.   No doubt what
is meant by affirming that their truth is symbolic is that
the relation asserted between the bread and the Body is
itself one of symbolization or significance, so that the
words are really equivalent to " This symbolizes or signifies
My Body."   But even this does not take us much further
by itself.   Significance is of two kinds, *indicative* and

expressive.[1] It is indicative when, and in so far as, the
sign is separate from the thing signified. It is expressive
when, and in so far as, the thing signified is inherent in the
sign. For instance, in what we call a plain statement of
fact, the significance is simply indicative. In great
literature, on the other hand," the word is one with what
it tells of," and the significance therefore tends to become
expressive. Or again, if in teaching a subject, say,
physiology, I use an illustration drawn from a quite
different subject, the significance of the illustration is
indicative ; but if I exhibit to the class an actual living
organism to illustrate my teaching, the significance of
this illustration is expressive. For in this case the thing
signified is actually present in the sign.

Now it is no doubt possible to hold that in His words
and acts at the Last Supper our Lord was simply, as it
were, *indicating* pictorially the sacrifice which was to be
expressed in fact on Calvary, and was to issue in a new
spiritual communion between God and His people. And

[1] It is a most unfortunate obstacle to clear thinking that in English
the word *significance* stands equally for the " act " or relation of
signifying (*significatio*), and for the thing signified (*significatum*).
Similar ambiguity besets the meaning of such words as *revelation*, as
well as of the word *meaning* itself. I have tried to be consistent in using
the word significance as equivalent to *significatio* only, except in cases
where the context leaves no doubt as to the meaning. With this
ambiguity in mind I now think the distinction between indicative
and expressive significance is much clearer and more useful than the
common distinction between " literal " and " metaphorical " or " symbolic." Where this latter distinction is not arbitrary, it nearly always
reduces itself on reflection to a distinction, not in the significance or
truth of language, but in the things signified or referred to. Thus, if
I talk about " crossing the Rubicon," I may refer either to the actual
crossing of a river (literal), or to a critical and decisive step (metaphorical). But obviously the difference resides entirely in the thing
signified, and not in the significance. Again, poetry seems to me different
from prose, not in being more " metaphorical " or " symbolic," but
because the significance of poetry is more expressive and less indicative
than that of prose.

we may then go on to teach that what is done with the bread and wine in the Eucharist is, strictly speaking, a piece of indicative symbolism, merely illustrating realities that belong to another sphere, whether the past facts of our Lord's Crucifixion, or the present spiritual communion between God and faithful souls through Jesus Christ. We should thus reach one definite type of Eucharistic doctrine that is current among Evangelicals.

On the other hand it is impossible to see how, at the Last Supper at any rate, the broken bread could symbolize the Lord's Body *expressively*. For if the thing symbolized was the Body, then clearly it was not present in the symbol. And great difficulty remains in the Eucharist, if we try to think of the consecrated species as symbolizing the Body in such a way that the Body is really present *in it*.

But there is another line of interpretation possible. In every human organism the material body is essentially the expressive symbol and actual instrument of the inward spirit or soul or personality. And it is that relation of expressiveness and instrumentality towards the spirit which makes the material " flesh and blood " to be the very body of the person. May we not then interpret the affirmation that " this is the Lord's Body " to mean that this bread broken and distributed in the Eucharist is in very truth the expressive symbol and instrument of our Lord's spiritual presence and action towards us, and is therefore related to Him as His Body ? In that case the consecrated species does not symbolize the Body ; but it *is* the Body, because it is the expressive symbol and instrument of Himself. Analogically, the Church is the Body of Christ, because it also stands in this same relation to Him.

This is how I should seek to interpret and restate for

myself the essence of Catholic belief concerning the Real Presence. In sacramental communion the outward action is an act of giving and receiving the consecrated element. This act both expresses and effects the imparting of the Lord's presence and gifts to the soul, in so far as the disposition of the recipient's will is such as to make that imparting possible. Therefore the communicant's faith is entitled to rely, not just on his consciousness of spiritual benefit received, but on the thing done, the *opus operatum*. If so, he is bound to identify, spiritually and really, the outward thing given and received, the consecrated bread with the Lord's Body, the sign-and-instrument of the Lord's presence or coming. The Body is not in or under the consecrated species ; the consecrated bread is here identified with the Body, as the outward medium by which the Lord Himself acts and expresses Himself. I should hold at this point to the words of St. Thomas Aquinas : *per hoc quod dicimus ipsum esse sub hoc sacramento, significatur quaedam habitudo ejus ad hoc sacramentum.*[1] That relation (*habitudo*), I suggest, is what we denote by that saying that the consecrated bread is the Body. Clearly the relation is spiritual, not physical. The bread is the Body spiritually and not physically. Our Lord was physically related to His earthly flesh and blood in the days of His Incarnation. He is spiritually related to the Eucharistic bread and wine. But both relations are real ; and since both earthly flesh and Eucharistic bread are really means of His self-expression and action, the term *body* is properly applied to both.

One word more. The whole notion that the consecrated species must remain continuously identified with the Lord's Body until its material entity is dissolved seems to me to depend implicitly on the assumption that the

---

[1] Summa III, Q. 76, Art. 6.

relation between the consecrated species and the Lord's presence is of a quasi-physical sort. This assumption I do find abhorrent ; and it is evident that the abhorrence is shared by those who attach the highest value to extra-liturgical devotions, although they do not draw the conclusion which I feel bound to draw, that the consecrated bread may only be identified with the Lord's Body within the outward and visible context of the Eucharistic rite.

Finally, I ought perhaps to add a word in explanation of the fact that Appendix C on Eucharistic Presence and Devotion, which appeared in previous editions of this book, has now been omitted. It consisted merely of a criticism of a particular theory of Mr. Spens. Mr. Spens has expounded his views more fully since the criticism was written, and nothing in it seemed to be worth reprinting.

OLIVER C. QUICK.

1 AMEN COURT,
   ST. PAUL'S, LONDON,
      Augnst, 1932.

PREFACE TO FIRST EDITION

IN offering to the public this essay in the philosophy of sacraments I may perhaps be allowed to emphasise the fact that I have not attempted to approach the subject from the standpoint of historical scholarship. I could not indeed have undertaken the task which, by the invitation of the Editors of this series, was proposed to me, if I had not made some effort to acquaint myself with the main systems of thought and the broad lines of argument from which current modes of presenting sacramental doctrine have been derived. But I make no claim to pass any authoritative judgment of my own upon controversial matters of history, in which decision rightly belongs to the historical expert.

The point of view which I have tried to take up may be said to be that both of philosophy and of general experience. And it may be that this method of approach has a value of its own. In certain respects the statement and discussion of the substance of doctrines may be freer and clearer, when precise questions of authorship and origin are frankly left in the background. Such at any rate must be the excuse for my presumption. And I am encouraged to offer it by observing that, with rare exceptions, modern theology of the sacraments seems to live and move in a distinctly antiquarian atmosphere.

A word as to the plan which I have followed. Chapters I to III lay a general foundation of philosophy. Chapters III and IV represent the historical Incarnation and Atonement as the supreme sacrament and the fount of all others. The remaining chapters deal with the sacraments themselves. I have taken some pains to make the first three chapters as generally readable and as free from technicality as I could. But I am aware that there are some to whom all philosophical argument is distasteful, not because they cannot understand it, but because the expression of such abstract thought as is the essence of philosophy stirs in them only feelings of irritation and impatience. I believe that a reader who is interested in sacramental doctrine, but cannot tolerate what he would call metaphysics, will find the argument of this book substantially clear, if he begins his perusal of it at Chapter IV. In the subsequent chapters matters involving subtle points of theological dialectic have been as far as possible confined to footnotes and notes appended at the ends of chapters.

The pages discussing the Resurrection at the end of Chapter V contain a certain amount of material derived from an article of mine in the *Anglican Theological Review* for October, 1925, and from a chapter on the Resurrection which I contributed to *An Outline of Christianity*. I am indebted to the courtesy of the Editor of the *Review* and English publishers of the *Outline* for permission to make use of this material. A similar acknowledgement is due to the Society for Promoting Christian Knowledge for leave to incorporate in Chapter IX certain paragraphs of a paper which I contributed to the Farnham Conference on *Reservation*.

Finally, I should like to express my warmest thanks to Dr. W. R. Matthews, one of the Editors of the Series, who gave much time and trouble to going through the whole of my original draft. At many points the form of the argument owes much to his sympathetic criticism and suggestions. My colleague, Canon H. N. Bate, has been a deeply valued counsellor, and an epistolary discussion with Dr. J. K. Mozley also greatly helped me to clarify the argument of Chapter IX. Obligations in smaller points of detail are too numerous to mention.

CONTENTS

xxiii

Contents

XXV

CHAPTER IX

PAGE

THE EUCHARIST 185–228

Eucharist and Baptism contrasted, 185. The Institution, 188. The canon of truth in doctrine, 193. The Eucharistic Sacrifice, 196. The Eucharistic Presence, its connexion with offering, 204. Established theories and their confusion in modern thought, 205. Historical grounds for objection to Real Presence, 209. Defect of Receptionism, 212. A mediating theory criticised, 214. Devotions before the Reserved Sacrament, 220. Constructive suggestions, 223.

CHAPTER X

WORSHIP AND MORALS 229–244

Illustrations of the principle of synthesis through antithesis, 229. Origin and opposition of religion and ethics, 232. Attempts at reconciliation, 235. The Christian way in theory, 238. In practice, 241.

APPENDICES

A. A MODERN THEORY OF EUCHARISTIC SACRIFICE . 245–248

B. THE MEANING OF TRANSUBSTANTIATION . . . 248–255

INDEX 257

THE CHRISTIAN SACRAMENTS

CHAPTER I

SYMBOLS AND INSTRUMENTS

IN giving general instructions about sacraments most teachers are wont to start from the fact that throughout human experience the outward and the inward, the material and the spiritual, are found to be inseparably linked. We ourselves are souls or minds in bodies. We use material instruments to achieve our mentally conceived purposes, and outwardly spoken or written words to express our thoughts. Nay more, the language which we use in order to signify the most spiritual of realities is inevitably language which has also a material meaning— as when we speak of God as *above*. And conversely, no spiritually disposed person can meditate long upon the most commonplace of material objects without finding there some suggestion of a parable which carries the mind back from the outward to the inward. By dwelling on such obvious facts as these the teacher endeavours to elicit in his pupil's mind the notion of a world sacramentally ordered ; so that in the context of that great idea he may render more intelligible what the Christian believes concerning God's use of outward things in His plan of salvation through Christ.

That this method of exposition is based upon a precious and vital truth, few Christians would deny. It is there-

B

fore the more remarkable that so little effort seems to
be made by modern theologians to determine more precisely what that truth may be, what exactly we mean
by speaking of a sacramental world, and how we are
led thereby to conceive the nature of the events or things
or rites called sacramental in the special sense. Popular
teaching is obliged to be vague in its use of terms, and,
when not checked by more exact methods of thought, is
apt to transform the profoundest verity into the half-
truth which is the most dangerous of errors. Our object,
then, must be to examine afresh the first principles of
a Christian philosophy of sacraments.

The first problem that confronts us is to define the
difference between "outward" and "inward". The
most obvious definition that presents itself is to say that
the outward consists of everything that can be apprehended
by the bodily senses, and the inward of everything that
cannot. But the ambiguity of this statement is familiar
to physicists. There exist particles of matter too minute
to be apprehended by human touch or sight, colours
beyond the range of the visible spectrum, notes of music
too high or too low on the scale to be recorded by the
human ear. Are these things then inward, or do they
approximate to the nature of the spiritual ? Surely not ;
yet there seems to be some confusion on this point. For
many enthusiasts for the reality of spirit seem to imagine
that physicists are necessarily in some way spiritualising
matter, whenever they reduce it to elements which are
imperceptible by the human body. If we are to avoid this
absurdity, we must affirm at least that there may be outward things which are in fact imperceptible.

A second conceivable definition is to say that the outward is that which occupies time or space, the inward
that which does not. This is much better, and may

ultimately stand ; but it certainly leads to other difficulties at first sight not less serious. Our thoughts
certainly occupy time. Are they then to be classed as
outward ? It would really be little use to evade this
question by suggesting that what is properly outward
must occupy both space and time, and that what occupies
time alone is really inward. For, even apart from the
doubt raised by the modern theory of relativity, whether
time and space are themselves separable from one another,
it seems at least undeniable that we do in some sense
connect the operations of our minds with the places at
which our bodies are, and that therefore even mental
processes are in some vague and partial way localised.

In fact, the more deeply we consider, the harder we
find the task of seeing clearly any hard and fast distinction between the two great kinds of reality which constitute our essentially dual experience. Perhaps we shall
be laying the best foundation for subsequent discussions,
if we determine that in general, when we speak of outward things or realities, we shall be referring to those
which both occupy space and time and are in principle,
though possibly not in fact, perceptible by bodily senses ;
while we denote as inward things or realities those which
fail to satisfy both these conditions of outwardness.
According to this definition the minutest particles and
the most rapid vibrations of matter may still be classed
as outward, since they occupy space and time and would
be perceptible to bodily senses which were either more
acute than ours or assisted by more powerful instruments
than we possess ; and we may still classify thoughts as
inward, since, though they occupy time and are in a
vaguer sense connected with place, it is not conceivable
that they should ever become objects of physical sight
or touch or hearing.

From this very method of division, however, we may
draw an important suggestion, the truth of which will
appear more plainly as our discussion proceeds ; namely,
that any rigid line drawn between what is inward and
what is outward in our experience is bound to be more or
less arbitrary, that we cannot classify the objects of our
experience into some things which are purely inward and
others which are purely outward, but can only say that
some things are certainly more inward or more outward
than others. Thus, within the domain of the inward, as
we have just defined it, a thought, considered as an act
of thinking, would seem to be less completely inward than
an ideal or even a general law, considered as an object of
thought. For the thought itself is certainly an event
which occurs in time, and so far partakes of the nature of
the outward, whereas the ideal or general law, which is
thought about, does not occur anywhen or anywhere,
and cannot be said to occupy space or time at all. And
again, within the domain of the outward, colours would
seem to be less definitely outward than the " primary "
qualities of material things which are perceptible by touch.
For it is always the coloured object rather than the colour
itself which occupies space ; and that which in the spatial
object gives rise to our perception of it as coloured, turns
out on examination to be a kind of vibration which is not
in itself colour. Finally, there are, of course, many
realities commonly denoted by single words, which appear
in reference to our present classification to have an in-
tricately mixed character. For instance, what we call
an external act, such as that of walking or writing, includes both a series of events perceptible to the senses
in space and time, and also a certain volitional activity
which cannot be so perceived.

Without entering further upon the intricate problems

of metaphysics and epistemology just indicated, we will accept as a working arrangement the definition of the difference between outward and inward things which has been given. But we shall bear constantly in mind that the whole distinction between outward and inward may turn out to be relative to our point of view. Thus an act of my thinking, when compared with a movement of my hand or a modification of my brain-cells, is certainly inward ; but, when referred to the value of my whole character, it seems to be rather outward, inasmuch as it is an embodiment of that value within a particular temporal event. Ultimately, and in an absolute sense, any occupation of space or time seems to be a mark of " outwardness ".

We have now to consider the possible relations which may connect outward realities with inward. It will simplify the problem if we take first for our outward realities the material objects constructed by man's own craft. Considered in relation to his inward or mental life they divide themselves at once into two classes. Some take their character from what is done with them ; and these we will call instruments. Others take their character from what is known by them ; and these we will call symbols. Thus, a violin is properly called an instrument, because it exists to be played upon ; but a musical score we should call a symbol, because it exists to inform the musician what he is to play. Or again, a machine-gun is an instrument, because it is a weapon to be fought with ; but a flag is a symbol, because its use is to convey information or to suggest certain ideas to the mind.

An important complication is introduced into this distinction when it is recognised that every instrument is also a symbol, and every symbol also an instrument. Thus the sight of a violin is bound to suggest to the mind at least the thought of music, and may be charged with much more specific meaning. In the same way weapons are suggestive of fighting. Conversely, a score is part of the apparatus which makes it possible for a piece of music to be played, and a system of signalling by flags is essential to the conduct of naval operations. Just as there are things to be known by instruments, so there are things to be done with symbols. Yet our distinction remains valid. For an instrument only becomes a symbol because it is first an instrument. A violin only suggests music because it is suitable for playing on. And a symbol only becomes an instrument because it is first a symbol. A musical score is useful in the playing of music because it signifies certain notes and rhythms to the mind of the player. We may still therefore differentiate between instruments and symbols by saying that an instrument takes its character from what is done with it, while a symbol takes its character from what is known by it.

What then can we learn further concerning the two relations of instrumentality and significance themselves ?

Instruments are made what they are by their usefulness in human action directed to an end. Now the immediate organ of human action is man's own body and limbs. But it is characteristic of the human animal to widen its range of activity by fashioning tools and machinery of all kinds, which serve as extensions of the bodily equipment belonging to its own natural physiology. The hand is man's natural instrument ; the violin, the axe or the umbrella held in the hand is his artificial instrument. But the instrumentality of both consists in their forming part of the outward or material element with which man acts in doing that which he wants to have done. Again, that upon which man works with his instruments or tools is made instrumental in his purposive activity, if it can properly be regarded as part of that with which he does something. If I use an axe for chopping wood to light a fire, the wood as well as the axe becomes my instrument, in so far as it is regarded as part of that with which I act in achieving my purpose of lighting a fire. If I put up an umbrella to keep off the rain, the rain does not become my instrument, since the rain itself can hardly be regarded as part of that with which I act in order to shelter myself from the rain.

Now all the things with which I act have some existence and reality apart from my use of them. The things therefore which we call instruments are not mere instruments, or at least they are, as things, separable from their instrumentality. But, when we reflect further, we find that in action instrumentality itself seems to be, as it were, embodied and made concrete. If I desire that something should come to pass, the moment my desire becomes a purpose, I start on some action as a means to bring it to pass. If there were no purposes or ends in the world, there could be no means, and no actions properly so called. On the other hand all that is really means to end, is related thereby to action as part of that with which something is done. And no action could have any being or existence whatever apart from its function as a means or instrument in bringing something to pass. Indeed, in our observation of what goes on in the world outside us, we habitually distinguish what we hold to be actions from other events, by noting that these events appear to happen and to be what they are, solely because they are instruments in the realisation of some end or purpose. The moment the behaviour of some insect or lower organism seems to be only intelligible as a means to some end, such as the preservation of its life or the propagation of its species, we begin to think and speak of it as acting in the proper sense of the word, and thereby to contrast its behaviour with that of inanimate objects which is wholly expressible as the result of what happens to them.

At this point it may be worth while to note that the essential connexion between instrumentality and purposive action may be obscured by our ambiguous use of the terms "mechanism" and "mechanical". Machines properly so-called are artificial instruments of man; they are artificial extensions of man's natural organs of activity. Whenever, therefore, we see a machine at work, we are entitled to infer that it is directed by some governing purpose, and that it is essentially connected with the action proper to it. But, on the other hand, a machine is specially effective for human purposes, just because it is elaborately constructed so as to work, in a relative sense, "by itself" and apart from human action; and, therefore, attending exclusively to this relative independence of the machine, we often use the term "mechanical" to denote those processes in nature which seem to have nothing to do with any purpose at all, and are certainly unaffected by any purpose of man or any interest of living creatures. Thus, we may say that the heat of the sun evaporates water "mechanically", and we may even speak of nature or the universe as a "mechanism", in order to express the view that its processes are not really or ultimately instrumental to any purpose at all. This use of terms is of course quite legitimate, if we remember that it is strictly metaphorical. If nature is conceived as a proper or instrumental mechanism, it must owe its being and character to purposive action of some kind.

As a definition of instrumentality we therefore offer the following. Instrumentality is primarily the relation of act to purpose, and is extended to include the relation to purpose of anything with which action is performed.

When we turn from instruments to symbols, we find that the task of arriving at the essential character of symbolic nature, or significance, is more difficult. We have already remarked that all man's instruments are also symbols, and all man's symbols also instruments. Just as everything with which anything is done also signifies something, so also everything which signifies anything is also a means by which something is done. We have now to qualify this statement by another. So long at least as we confine our attention to things specially constructed to be either instruments or symbols, it seems truer to say that a symbol is necessarily an instrument, than that an instrument is necessarily a symbol. It is possible to conceive instruments having no significance ; it is not possible to conceive symbols having no instrumentality.[1] For a symbol is essentially a means of expression. If living creatures had never acted so as to express their knowledge or to convey information one to another, symbols could never have been invented. Every constructed symbol has been an instrument from the first. On the other hand, the usefulness of an instrument does not in the same way depend upon its being a symbol also. For instance, primitive man when he fashions a club does not necessarily mean anything by it, except in the sense that he " means " to knock someone on the head. And the effectiveness of the instrument certainly does not depend upon its symbolising anything, however significant it may prove to the wary foe who perceives his danger in time to take precautions. Indeed the inevitably significant character of weapons is often a hindrance to

[1] This is implied by St. Thomas Aquinas : *Signum est per quod aliquis devenit in cognitionem alterius* (Summa III, Q. 60, Art. 4).

their effective use—a fact which is the origin of camou-
flage and disguise in warfare.

It is not therefore altogether surprising that some philosophers should have attempted to reduce the relation of
significance itself to a certain form or type of instrumentality. Thus, it is suggested that, when we say that
certain words signify a certain reality, we mean that these
words are used in order to present a certain reality to
someone's mind, and are significant only as means of
fulfilling this purpose. Now this may be true so far as it
goes ; but nevertheless it is quite insufficient as an
analysis of the nature of meaning. For it ignores the
fact that the relation of the words to that which they
signify is radically different from their relation to the
purpose of the mind which uses them as significant.
We have here two radically distinct kinds of relation
involved ; and no dialectics can overcome the duality.
And, if we must attempt the impossible task of framing
a general definition of significance, we can hardly do better
than say that it consists in that relation which language,
or anything taken as the equivalent of language, bears
to that which it brings into the consciousness of the minds
which use it.[1] Thus, while action is the essential embodiment of instrumentality, language is the essential vehicle
of significance. And, although it be true that the utterance of language is a kind of action, and all symbols
must be related to a purposive activity which uses
them as symbolic, it is also true nevertheless that this

---

[1] It would be more accurate to borrow a technical term from Dr.
Alexander, and say " that which is compresent with it in the minds
which use it ". The definition is, of course, circular. Significance is
defined in terms of language and language in terms of significance.
St. Thomas in adopting St. Augustine's definition of a sign does not
attempt to define the relation of significance : *Signum est quod praeter
speciem quam ingerit sensibus facit aliquid aliud in cognitionem venire*
(Summa III, Q. 60, Art. 4, ad. 1).

symbolic character or significance consists in a relation
of things to mind, or of things to one another in mind,
which is certainly not instrumental.

Let us consider the point further. Long before man
arrived upon the scene of evolution and invented language,
rudimentary forms of the relation of significance existed
in the natural expressiveness of bodily posture, facial
movement, inarticulate cries and the like. For instance,
the animal baring its teeth before its enemy is undoubtedly initiating action instrumental to its combative purpose ; but it is also suggesting to its enemy what is in
its mind, and, in so far as it does so, its facial contortions
are something other than instrumental to its purpose,
they are also expressive of it. Suppose this expression
to be itself instrumental to the purpose, because designed,
whether consciously or not, to strike terror into the foe ;
nevertheless even in this case the instrumentality depends
upon the expressiveness, and the expressiveness consists
in a relation of the facial contortion to the rage and
combative purpose within, which is different from instrumentality. Bared teeth do express and signify rage. You
may say truly that they express rage because they are
instrumental to its purpose ; and again truly, that they
are instrumental to its purpose because they express it.
But you cannot identify the expressiveness with the
instrumentality.

Now man, as we have seen, is distinguished from "lower"
animals by his ability to construct artificial instruments
in order to extend the range of the action of which the
natural instruments are the limbs of his body. In the
same way, he invents systems of artificial symbols, of
which spoken and written language is chief, in order to
extend the range of the significance which is naturally
inherent in the changes of his face and posture. True,

these artificial symbols are a special class of instruments, since they are designed to serve a definite and very practical purpose in communicating knowledge. But still the symbols are instruments of this purpose, only because there is already established and recognised a relation of a distinct and peculiar kind between symbol and thing symbolised. Thus, if I say to you " The rain has stopped and the sun is shining ", the words have a relation of instrumentality to my purpose of conveying to you information about the weather, but they have a relation of significance towards the state of the weather itself, and, incidentally, also towards the state of my mind as I speak. Regarded as instruments, the spoken words effect my purpose and affect your mind. Regarded as symbols, they neither effect nor affect anything whatever ; they signify the fineness of the weather, and, incidentally, also what is in my mind, in so far as you conjecture from them my reason for speaking. Hence language, considered as a system of artificial symbols, extends enormously the range of what can be signified and so known, just as language, considered as an artificial instrument, extends enormously the range of what we can do in signifying things, and so in communicating and increasing our knowledge.

Thus, the essential difference between instrumentality and significance gradually emerges. Instrumentality is the relation of a thing to that which is effected by it ; significance the relation of a thing to that which is suggested by it. Instrumentality is the special property of acts, extended to cover that with which action is performed. Significance is the special property of language, extended to cover all that is used as expressive.

This difference has more abstract and general implications. We may say that instrumentality relates its terms in time, whereas significance relates its terms timelessly. This important distinction is not perhaps immediately obvious, but it follows from the foregoing analysis. Effects or results either follow in time the means taken to produce them, or else are strictly simultaneous with the completion of the means. To produce violin-music it is necessary that the violin should be played. For the achievement of this purpose it is required that a whole series of instrumental actions should be performed, the last of which is the drawing of the bow across the strings by a skilled violin player ; *then* immediately, and not till then, there is the music. In the same way, if I desire to convey to you certain information, it is necessary that I express myself in intelligible language, and, when I have gone through the series of instrumental acts required, then, and not till then, you understand me, and the purpose is achieved. On the other hand, the relation of the words which I speak to that which is signified by them is essentially timeless, or time-transcending. I may be informing you about an event which is either past or future. But in either case my words must make it, still as past or as future, yet present in your mind. And this is possible, because words spoken at one time can be understood to refer timelessly to an event which has occurred or will occur at another time. The relation of significance is precisely that whereby in common experience the separations of time are overcome and transcended. Indeed, it is evident that I can only make a general assertion, say, about the eighteenth century, because I am able to treat the successive years of that century as together making up a unity which is simultaneously present both to your mind and mine. It is the relation of significance which makes this possible.

Once more, it follows that instrumentality is in itself a more " outward " relation than significance. Instrumentality, in the strict sense, connects a conceived purpose through action in time with its effected achievement, whether that achievement be realised in wholly outward things or in a state of mind. Instrumentality therefore necessarily relates its terms temporally, and, so far, outwardly, if we have agreed to regard occupation of time as marking at least a certain degree of " outwardness ". Significance on the other hand may relate two quite outward things, e.g. spoken or written words and a past event, but it relates them altogether inwardly and timelessly. For instance, if the words assert that William the Conqueror landed in England in 1066, the signifying words are present, and the event signified is past, but the relation of significance between them bridges, as it were, the gap of time, just because it is itself not in time.

Hitherto, we have been trying to apprehend more clearly the nature of instrumentality and of significance, by considering them mainly, if not exclusively, in connexion with human action and means of expression. And this procedure is justified, because undoubtedly man uses his own experience of the instruments and symbols, which he more or less fully controls, in order to interpret to himself and master more completely that world of surrounding nature, the order of which is beyond him.

But this order presents a puzzle. In part, though man did not fashion it, it seems to have been expressly fashioned so as to serve man's purposes. He lives and acts and is successful in his aims, only because the necessities of life and action, food, warmth and the like, lie more or less ready at his need. And he is able to know, only because everything that presents itself to his mind through his bodily senses comes to him charged with a significance which relates it to something beyond that which at the particular moment is directly perceived. Man finds sun and rain most useful for his practical purposes in life. And he knows them to be such, and can make this assertion about them, because each experience he has of sunlight and rainfall is significant to him of other similar experiences, and thus enables him to make generalisations about sunlight and rainfall, and, within limits, to predict their recurrence. Certainly man's knowledge of external nature, as many modern philosophers have pointed out, is largely determined by its possible and actual usefulness to his practical ends. But certainly also this usefulness in turn depends on the fact that everything which man perceives has to him a meaning which in itself is not usefulness. Thus once more we find instrumentality and significance interdependent, yet radically distinct.

But all that we have stated in the last paragraph makes up only one side of the picture. The nature, which up to a point so faithfully ministers to human life, is nevertheless perpetually destroying it, and may finally abolish it altogether. The world, which up to a point so readily reveals itself to man's enquiry, is nevertheless perpetually upsetting his calculations, and in some minds, such as that of the author of Ecclesiastes, stirs a deeper scepticism by its very regularity. What is to be the inference? Is the universe itself purposeless? Or is it in some sense the instrument of a vaster purpose to which man himself is but a means? Is the universe itself meaningless? Or is it wholly significant of something which surpasses man's understanding?

Such are the questions which from time immemorial

man's metaphysical theology has been trying to answer. We are not concerned to examine or to appraise the merits of the various answers which have been given. What is germane to our discussion, is to note that those answers which are in a broad sense theistic may be divided into two classes, according as they incline to take either instrumentality or significance to be the fundamental type of relation which unites the world to God. In the view of some the "outward" world of space and time appears primarily as the instrument whereby God is effecting some cosmic purpose. In the view of others this world appears primarily as the symbol in and through which God is signifying and expressing His eternal nature to those who have eyes to see.

This central difference of thought works itself out in many long familiar divergences of opinion and belief. The one philosophy pictures God chiefly as acting on, or doing something with, the world; the other pictures God chiefly as revealing Himself within it. The one thinks of "heaven" chiefly as a future state, the other as the inward reality of things. The one finds the main source of evil in disobedience, the other in error or illusion. The one attaches relatively greater value to moral effort, the other to mystical experience; and so forth.

The vexed problem of the divine transcendence and immanence is the occasion of a rather interesting cross division among theologians of the two schools. He who inclines to think of the world rather as God's "artificial" instrument (after the analogy of a piece of machinery) tends to deism, and therefore exaggerates the divine transcendence. He who thinks of the world as God's "natural" instrument (after the analogy of the human body) finds God acting everywhere in the processes of nature, and therefore conceives Him as immanent. This immanence is still more strongly stressed by those theologians of the opposite school who think of the world as God's "natural" self-expression, comparing it to the body as expressing the mind of man. On the other hand not a few have regarded the world rather as an "artificial" symbol of the divine, using, perhaps unconsciously, the analogy of language which signifies a reality infinitely remote from what in itself it is; and along this road of thought we approach the "negative" mysticism which pushes the doctrine of divine transcendence to the verge of absurdity, if not beyond it.[1]

Both these types of theology or philosophy, if we except negative mysticism, may be thoroughly sacramental, but each in a different way. We may express the difference by saying that the first tends rather to value sacraments, the second to value sacramentalism. The theologian who thinks in terms of instrumentality will emphasise the truth that in some particular sacrament God really acts and does something; while he who thinks in terms of significance will teach rather that in particular sacraments God's universal presence and activity are more readily apprehended and made known.

Again, when we think of the relation of the world to God as a relation of significance, it is easier to conceive His omnipresence and eternity, just because the relation of significance is "inward", and does not involve connexion in space or time. Omnipresence and eternity seem much more difficult when we think in terms of instrumentality, because instrumentality is an inherently temporal relation, and to think of God as working out a purpose is to regard Him as within the time-series, and

---

[1] It seems paradoxical, but not inconceivable, that those who insist most strongly on the complete ineffability of the divine nature should have been led to this conclusion partly by relying to excess on the analogy of language for interpreting the relation of the world to God.

c

as producing effects at particular times and places. On
the other hand, to him who holds by significance, the
being of God is apt to become a too purely static perfection. The notion of God as really active comes much more
readily to the instrumentalist.

CHAPTER II

ÆSTHETIC SACRAMENTALISM

WE must now revert to the distinction, roughly indicated at the beginning of the last chapter, between the outward and the inward element in our experience. We there suggested that, if the distinction were ultimately best understood as discriminating realities which occupy space and time from those which do not, many at least, and conceivably all, of the objects of our experience would be found to partake of both natures in different manners and degrees. Possibly no concrete reality known to us can be classed either as purely outward or as purely inward. But certainly some are much more outward, and some much more inward, than others.

Our next task is to argue that the realities which, judged by this standard, seem to be least outward and most inward are our ideals of absolute goodness or value.

When we compare ideals with thoughts, or acts of thinking, the case is fairly plain. Granted that neither are in space, our ideals do not occupy time in as great a degree as our thoughts. For at least our thoughts occur as actual events in the time-series of our consciousness; whereas our ideals, as such do not. If, for instance, I ponder over some concept or image of perfect goodness, my thoughts are existing in time, but not necessarily the goodness about which I think ; and yet the goodness is no merely " unreal " figment—on the contrary it may

19

impress me with all the weight of the most absolute
authority I know.

Even in cases of what we may call realised or embodied
goodness, the sublime work of art, the heroic action, the
illuminating utterance of wisdom and insight, the goodness, though it here determines and orders things or
events which are in space and time, does not itself form
part of that which is spatio-temporal. Plato's philosophy,
for instance, in so far as it is really or ideally true at all,
is as true for our time as for his, and was equally true
before he discovered it ; no dialectical knots can tie down
the occurrence or existence of the truth itself to any
particular time or place. Again, the self-sacrifice of
St. Francis of Assisi certainly took place during the
particular years of his life and at the particular places where
he lived : yet we call it morally heroic, just because we
recognise in it the embodiment of an ideal of goodness,
which, as an ideal, was real before St. Francis was born,
and speaks to all generations with more cogent authority
because of the witness which he bore to it. The beauty
of some symphony of Beethoven, or of a Madonna of
Bellini, perhaps approaches more nearly to a goodness
which as such exists in space and time, and perishes
with its outward vesture. And yet we call these things
truly beautiful, only because they express and reveal to
us something of a goodness which is assuredly not altogether comprised or included in a particular series of
harmonious sounds or in a particular scheme of line and
colour. Beauty ranges free over the world of things and
events, being itself neither event nor thing ; although
the creation of a beautiful thing involves one series of
events, and the appreciation of it another.

The more inward reality of ideals is perhaps less apparent when we compare them with general ideas or

scientific laws. Consider, for instance, the law that the angles of a triangle are together equal to two right angles. This law certainly does not occur or exist anywhere in space or time : it is purely an object of thought. True ; and yet it can only describe a property of all triangles which do exist in space and time ; apart from them it has no truth or reality whatever. Neither, it may be replied, has beauty any reality apart from particular things which are beautiful. But the analogy will not altogether hold. For the beauty of a great work of art is essentially the cause of its existence ; the work was created, because it was beautiful, and, existing as beautiful, its existence is explained. On the other hand, it would be nonsense to say that the law, that the angles of a triangle are equal to two right angles, is the explanatory cause of the existence of triangles. Now, that which is the cause of a thing must in a sense be real *before* the thing itself can exist. We may say, therefore, that beauty must be real, before beautiful things can exist. On the other hand it is only the existence of triangular things which makes the laws of triangularity real. We do, therefore, rightly attribute to creative ideals of goodness an inward reality of their own, superior to that of merely general laws.

The point may be further illustrated by comparing the common antithesis between making and creating. To make, it is said, is human ; to create is divine. And the difference is found in the fact that whereas man can only refashion already existing material, God " creates out of nothing ". Whatever be the metaphysical value of this distinction, it does point to a significant difference in our use of terms. What seems to be true is this : that, whereas " to make " means to fashion pre-existing material to a new value or use, " to create " means to embody a pre-existing value or ideal in a new material. When

we speak of " making ", our minds are attending to the
previous existence of the " matter " and the newness of
the " form " : when we speak of " creating ", our minds
are attending to the previous reality of the " form "
and the newness of the " matter ". Thus the great artist
is relatively a " creator ", in so far as he freshly embodies
ideals of value previously real : the great inventor is
relatively a " maker," in so far as he adapts to a new value
a material which already exists. If God is a Creator in
the absolute sense, it is because He brought into being
a new matter in which to embody the ideals which have
been in His own nature from eternity.

On the whole, therefore, it is not surprising that
modern theology, which has learned during recent centuries to adhere ever more closely to the spirituality or
" inwardness " of the divine nature, should find the means
of conceiving that nature in the reality of goodness or
" absolute value ". It is indeed dangerous and often
very misleading to affirm without qualification that the
reality of divine being is the reality of the ideal.[1] For
we commonly use the term " ideal " to connote the double
fact, that absolute goodness is somehow the object of
our thought, and yet is nowhere found completely
embodied in the " external " world. Thus we are apt to
think of the ideal as something which exists only in our
minds. But plainly our very imperfect minds cannot
be that in which any absolute good actually exists at all.
And the very notion of the ideal carries with it an authority

[1] Many of Prof. Pringle-Pattison's statements, especially those contained in the last paragraph of his article in *The Spirit* (ed. by B. H.
Streeter), seem to me to illustrate this danger. By so constantly
insisting that the human ideal of perfection is the only true notion of
Godhead, he seems at times to entangle us with the suggestion that
Godhead is in itself an ideal of ours, though, of course, he does not
mean to imply anything of the kind.

of goodness the source of which is felt to be in a reality beyond the merely human. If, therefore, we think of the divine nature as that ground of being in which the ideal has its eternal reality, or as that being in which ideal and reality, goodness and existence, are one, we are no longer liable to the charge of making the divine a merely human notion, when we assert that the divine has the reality of the ideal.

Certainly the apologetic for theism most convincing on the whole to the modern mind is that which argues that human ideals of beauty, truth and goodness must have their origin and end in some reality not born or perishing between the dawn and sunset of man's little day upon the earth. In them above all else we hold direct communion with the spirituality of God, which indeed works in the world of space and time, but is assuredly not of it. And, therefore, if we would penetrate to the meaning and truth of sacramental religion, it is through the consideration of outward things as expressions and instruments of *goodness* that the way lies most promisingly open.

If the general result of the distinctions drawn in Chapter I be accepted, it will be evident that outward things may stand towards spiritual goodness in two positive relations ; they may be either instruments which it uses or symbols in which it is signified or expressed ; and the fact that the two relations may always imply each other does not interfere with their essential distinctness. We will take the second of the two relations, that of significance, for further discussion in this chapter.

But first we must say a few words about the kinds of absolute goodness or value, which are commonly distinguished in philosophical discussion. These are generally accepted as three, truth, beauty and moral goodness,

Without seeking to condemn this classification, or wasting time in lengthy criticism of it, we propose to follow a different scheme for our present purposes ; and we must briefly and dogmatically explain our reasons for doing so.

Truth, as an absolute value, we propose to omit from our discussion altogether. Its meaning is incurably ambiguous. Most commonly perhaps it is used to denote what is more properly called reality, or reality considered as a rational order. Thus, when we say that Plato's philosophy expresses a time-transcending *truth*, we mean that it expresses an aspect of the ever-real order of things. On the other hand, in a more strict and proper sense, truth is a property or quality which belongs only to judgments or assertions. In this sense, truth consists in the positive value of the relation of significance. In other words, that is *true* which well or rightly signifies or expresses something. In this case the value or goodness of what is expressed has clearly nothing to do with the truth of what expresses it. Crimes and follies, delusions and trivialities, may be as capable of expression as anything else. But it does not follow that they are necessarily worth expressing. There may be things better not expressed at all, as well as " things which would have been better expressed differently ". In this sense of the word, therefore, it is difficult to see that truth is an *absolute* good at all. In fact, it seems to stand to the relation of significance, exactly as usefulness stands to the relation of instrumentality. The real *good* of the truth depends upon the value of the knowledge which it records or communicates, just as the real good of the usefulness depends upon the value of the aim which it achieves. With these brief remarks we shall hold ourselves excused from further discussions of the vexed questions which concern the nature of truth.

Beauty and moral goodness are the terms which we shall use, in not quite their ordinary senses, to cover, as it were, the whole area of the absolute good. Beauty, in this broad meaning, we shall take to be goodness expressed, or goodness in its expression. Moral goodness we shall take to be goodness active, or goodness in act, towards the achievement of purpose.

The important point is this, that wherever beauty is outwardly embodied, the outward seems to be united to the inward by a relation of significance or expression, whereas, in everything to which we attribute strictly moral value, that which is outward seems to be united to the inward goodness primarily by a relation of instrumentality. For example, a heroic action, when considered as *expressing* the goodness of the agent, is regarded, according to our present use of terms, as beautiful, while its properly moral value consists in its being a means towards the achievement of some good purpose. On the other hand a work of art, the beauty of which lies in its expression of some goodness present in the world and felt in the soul, takes on a moral value also in so far as it is a means of stimulating good dispositions in the minds of those who appreciate it.

On the whole it seems less confusing in the end thus to distinguish the beautiful from the morally good by the different relation to goodness characteristic of each, than by attempting to see in each a specific and different kind of goodness. Every instrumental process which is directed towards producing good of any kind, whether it be the training and labour of the artist, or the reformer's plans and efforts to establish a happier condition of life in human society, may be justly regarded as having moral worth. On the other hand, everything which expresses any goodness known and felt as real has the essential

quality of beauty, whether that goodness be itself a moral
activity or the still less definable harmony of which both
art and nature seem at times to be eloquent and prophetic.
The more deeply we ponder the nature of the good, the
more it appears that there are not many kinds but only
one goodness, which, in so far as it is positively related
to what is outward at all, is either striving or won, either
desiring or enjoyed, either planning or manifesting plan.
In the first aspect it appears as what we call moral goodness, working by outward instruments towards its end ;
in the second aspect, it appears as what we call beauty,
goodness realised, embodied, satisfactorily expressed.
The aim of moral effort passes into beauty as soon as it
is achieved.

We must now address ourselves to the consideration of
that type of sacramental philosophy which is primarily
interested in beauty and concerns itself more or less
exclusively with the significance or expressiveness of the
outward.

So far we have been using the terms "signify" and
"express" as though they were almost synonymous
and interchangeable. But at this point it is time to
indicate a certain relative distinction between them.
When I use words to convey information to another it
seems natural to say that I am expressing my mind or
thoughts, but that I am signifying that of which I wish to
inform my auditor. Thus, if I say "The day is fine", I
am expressing something in my mind, and signifying
something about the weather. The difference seems to be
this, that what is expressed is more intimately inherent
or immanent in the outward words used, than what is,
so to speak, unexpressively signified by them. Expression
comes nearer to embodiment, whereas signification may

refer to something quite remote from that which signifies. Thus, the natural symbolism of the body, the mien and posture of the limbs, is both significant and expressive, whereas the artificially constructed symbolism of language may be significant only.

This distinction is of importance, as soon as we begin to analyse the connexion of beauty with its outward signs. At first sight the beauty of nature, pictorial art and music seems to be expressed beauty, while that of literature is only signified. For in a sunset, a picture or a symphony, the beauty is as closely immanent in its external medium, as is the beauty of the human form in its material structure. The printed page of a book cannot surely express beauty in at all the same way. Rather, it signifies to the reader's mind the objects of thought or imagination wherein the real beauty inheres.

No doubt further reflection makes the contrast appear less clearly defined and absolute. There is a definite type of music, sometimes called programme-music, which would be meaningless apart from the quite definite images and ideas of things outside itself, which it conveys to the mind. There is much pictorial art which gains its effect partly at least through suggesting to the reflective mind objects quite remote from what it presents to the eye. Pictures like those by G. F. Watts, which can definitely be called allegorical, belong to this class. Thus in some degree the outward element in the beauty of art may have the character more properly belonging to verbal language. On the other hand there certainly is poetry in which the words and sentences, taken as such, seem to mean but little, and where the value of the whole resides largely in the feeling expressed by the rhythm and sound. Poe's poem *The Bells* and Southey's *The Cataract of Lodore* furnish obvious but crude instances of this type, and

Tennyson's *Frater Ave Atque Vale* one much more subtle and delicate. Here poetry approaches music ; and no doubt all poetry must in some degree be musical.

Still, when all such admissions have been fully made, it may seem to be broadly true that while nature, pictorial art and music are mainly and characteristically expressive of beauty immanent in them, literature is significant of a beauty outside itself, and must in greater or less degree dispense with expressiveness in order to signify.

And yet, as soon as we penetrate beyond first impressions, we are bound to recognise that the distinction between expressiveness and significance does not really hold in reference to beauty, and that the outward, as related to beauty, must always *express*. The reason appears to be this, that it is impossible really to signify any value or goodness *in its essential character*, without at the same time expressing it. I may of course baldly state that a deed done at a certain date and place and in certain circumstances was heroic. I am then signifying the occurrence of certain facts. But I am not really signifying the heroism of the deed, unless my description makes you feel it ; and, if my description does make you feel the heroism, it has become expressive, the heroism lives again through my words.

Consider, for instance, the series of events connected with the murder of Julius Cæsar. The bare facts may be signified in language which really expresses nothing, or almost nothing. And for this purpose of signifying facts, the exact form of the words matters very little ; the rhythm of the sentences is quite unimportant, and the word assassination will do quite as well as the word murder. But if we are to apprehend, not just the bare facts, but the whole tragedy and grandeur of the story, the words in which the story is told must express those values. For that purpose the telling of the story must be a work of literary or rhetorical art, and forthwith the choice of language becomes a matter of vital moment. The substitution of the word assassination for the word murder may impair the meaning of a sentence by destroying its rhythm ; while translation into another tongue will make a grave difference to what the story conveys. For values, in order to be really conveyed or made known to the mind, must themselves enter into and determine that which expresses them.[1] And, if so, it is possible that in certain respects Shakspere may give us truer history than Mommsen ; and both of them truer history than the most complete list of bare facts and dates, which might enable us to convict both those authors of error.

And we must notice more exactly why all this is so. The original events connected with Cæsar's death express a tragic value which Shakspere's mind discerns and re-expresses in dramatic art. We, as we appreciate his drama, experience in ourselves by sympathy the play of human character and the action of moral and emotional forces, which constitute the value of the events both as they occurred (supposing Shakspere's interpretation to be substantially true) and as Shakspere understood them. Thus, Shakspere's drama, as vehicle or embodiment of beauty, is found to express, first the minds and characters of Cæsar, Brutus, Cassius and the rest, secondly Shakspere's mind and character, and thirdly our own. For mind can only appreciate the values inherent in other minds and lives, in so far as it recognises in itself a nature somehow akin to theirs, and finds in their expression an

---

[1] In this paragraph I am especially aware that I am only restating considerations which have been much more fully and clearly discussed by the Bishop of Manchester (Dr. Temple) in *Mens Creatrix*, chapter x.

expression also of itself. It is because Shakspere's characters so wonderfully express us to ourselves, that we recognise in him the greatest of all playwriters.

The same principle, that the outward vesture of beauty always expresses an immanent and spiritual goodness, and can only therefore be appreciated by spiritual sympathy, holds good also of pictorial art, music and nature. We cannot appreciate a painting or a symphony, unless we enter to some extent into the mind and vision of the artist or composer, and find therein something which appeals to *us*. And it is hard not to believe that something similar is true of the beauty of nature also. We instinctively expect a beautiful face to be the expression of a spiritual beauty within, not alien from our own ideal ; and, when our expectation is disappointed, we experience a shock of disillusionment which is sometimes almost intolerable. And as we view the glories of mountain and sea and sky, often it is only by a severe effort of the intellect that we can refrain from affirming that they are expressing to us the very mind of some spirit, beautiful beyond imagination, whose touch we have already felt within our souls.

The essential connexion of beauty with expression is sometimes pushed to extremes in the doctrine that beauty is nothing but expressiveness.[1] Anything, it is maintained, in which we recognise an expression of our own feelings is to us beautiful ; and thus we may be said in a sense to make for ourselves the beauty of everything we admire, since it is beautiful to us, in so far as we express ourselves

---

[1] Of course, I have here in mind one aspect of the theory put forward in Croce's *Æsthetic ;* but I have not attempted to expound it adequately. For a fuller discussion, I would refer the reader to the chapter in *Mens Creatrix* already mentioned, and to E. F. Carritt's *The Theory of Beauty,* a most interesting study which goes a very long way with Croce.

in it. The activity of the aesthetic sense in appreciating
the beauty of an object is thus the same in spiritual kind
and essence as the activity of the artist who creates an
object of beauty. Rudyard Kipling, though not himself a
theorist in aesthetics, has with deep insight indicated the
truth of this thought in the lines on Sussex :

> God gave all men all earth to love ;
> But, since man's heart is small,
> Ordain'd for each one spot should prove
> Beloved over all,
> That, as He watch'd creation's birth,
> So we in God-like mood
> Might of our love create our earth,
> And see that it is good.

In other words, if we may translate the idea from the
language of religious verse into that of philosophical
prose, each loves above all one spot in the world,
because he expresses himself in it as his home ; and thus
his love for it becomes a creative act which makes it
beautiful.

This is both true and important as far as it goes. But
it is not the whole truth, and it is turned to falsehood
when the philosophical theorist goes on to declare that
the beauty is *nothing but* the projection of our own feelings
and the result of our own creative act. For we are not
able to express ourselves in beautiful things apart from
the consideration of what a reality beyond ourselves is
expressing to us in them. The Sussex man would not feel
himself expressed in the beauty of the Sussex downs, if
he did not feel that it was made *for* him as well as *by* him.
His mood would not be so God-like, if it did not also
humble him to the dust even through the very sense of
his unity and sympathy with a reality so infinitely
greater than himself. There is an opposite, but at least

equally important, truth about beauty expressed in the
verse :

> Now all the heavenly splendour
> Breaks forth in starlight tender
> From myriad worlds unknown ;
> And man, the marvel seeing,
> Forgets his selfish being
> For joy of beauty not his own.[1]

And, again, we must not suffer the inward reality which
is expressed in beautiful things to be divorced from goodness in its " objective " or " absolute " nature. True, it
may be necessary to the beauty of a drama that I should
feel myself sympathising with characters in it which are
mean, selfish or cruel. But the beauty is gone, if I am
not made at the same time to feel the repulsiveness of
the evil with which I sympathise. Or again, it may be
essential to the terrible beauty of some ghastly war-
picture that I should shrink from the sight of what it
portrays. But beauty is only there, if I feel that the artist
has been struggling to express to me his own feelings of
horror or pity or revolt at such abominations. If the
feeling expressed were ghoulish delight in giving pain, or
sordid desire to win applause by outraging convention,
beauty would be far from that painting, however skilful
its execution.[2]

[1] English Hymnal No. 278.
[2] Doubtless at this point I shall be accused of " the moralistic
fallacy ". But I have affirmed no more than a necessary consequence
of the theistic assumption, that there is an absolute standard of goodness, realised in a supreme being, from whose nature our notions of
value are derived. If this is so, we apprehend beauty *truly* only when
the self-expression of the divine expresses also our own feelings ; and
no divine self-expression could confuse the distinction between moral
good and evil. Moreover, I do not believe that as a fact anyone finds
beauty in what outrages his own moral *perception ;* and it is most
important to remember that conscience is itself perceptive and æsthetic.
Mr. Carritt (op. cit., p. 337) discusses why the horrors of J. E. Flecker's
Hassan appear to be bad art, while those of *King Lear* do not. Does

It is by no means necessary to great and beautiful art that the good should appear in it as victorious or successful. Indeed in great art, as in life, failure is the most usual portion of what is best. But it is necessary to the beauty of art, that it should make us feel the intrinsic majesty and authority of goodness, and the inherent pitiableness of evil, and feel them only the more acutely because good is worsted and evil wins the day.

" A Shaksperean tragedy," writes Professor Bradley, " is never, like some miscalled tragedies, depressing. No one ever closes the book with the feeling that man is a poor mean creature. He may be wretched and he may be awful, but he is not small. His lot may be heart-rending and mysterious, but it is not contemptible. The most confirmed of cynics ceases to be a cynic while he reads these plays. And with this greatness of the tragic hero (which is not always confined to him) is connected, secondly, what I venture to describe as the centre of the tragic impression. This central feeling is the impression of waste. With Shakspere, at any rate, the pity and fear which are stirred by the tragic story seem to unite with, and even to merge in, a profound sense of sadness and mystery, which is due to the impression of waste. ' What a piece of work is man ', we cry ; ' so much more beautiful and so much more terrible than we knew ! Why should he be so if this beauty and greatness only tortures itself and throws itself away ? ' We seem to have before us a type of the mystery of the whole world, the tragic fact which extends far beyond the limits of tragedy. Everywhere, from the crushed rocks beneath our feet to the soul of man, we see power, intelligence, life and glory,

not Mr. Carritt himself supply the true answer when he writes of modern poets, " They want to make our flesh creep " ? Shakspere was absorbed in the *truth*.

D

which astound us and seem to call for our worship. And
everywhere we see them perishing, devouring one another
and destroying themselves, often with dreadful pain, as
though they came into being for no other end. Tragedy
is the typical form of this mystery, because that greatness
of soul which it exhibits as oppressed, conflicting and destroyed, is the highest existence in our view. It forces
the mystery upon us, and it makes us realise so vividly
the worth of that which is wasted that we cannot
possibly seek comfort in the reflection that all is
vanity."[1]

In tragic beauty we " vividly realise the worth of that
which is wasted ". Were it otherwise, were the artist
suggesting to us, for instance, that self-sacrifice is a
ridiculous thing or only superficially different from selfish-
ness, the essential condition of beauty would be lacking
from his work. He might be expressing to us what he
thought he believed, but there would be no beauty in the
expression, except in so far as it might still reveal his
personal sincerity. It is never the representation of good
failing or defeated which mars beauty in art, but only the
confusing of the good with the evil. Compare *Androcles
and the Lion* with *Saint Joan.*

So far, then, in discussing the nature of beauty as
expressed goodness we have reached three main conclusions : (1) that beauty moves freely over time and
space ; (2) that it is closely immanent in whatever expresses or embodies it ; (3) that beautiful things are the
created self-expression of a mind or spirit which itself
has the inward quality of the goodness thus expressed,
and they are truly appreciated only by a mind or spirit
which recognises in them its own self-expression within

---

[1] *Shakespearean Tragedy*, p. 23. The Bishop of Manchester develops the same theme in *Mens Creatrix*, chapter xi.

that of their creator, but not its own self-expression and nothing more.

If, therefore, works of art are beautiful, because they express a mind's appreciation of goodness, and if they are themselves appreciated because other minds sympathise with the mind of their creator, it is not irrational that religious faith should see in all the beauty of the world, natural as well as artistic, the expression of a Mind of goodness, closely immanent everywhere in its expressions, and in them apprehended by the sympathy of the finite minds that somehow reflect its own nature. In this direction, as we have already noticed, point the feelings which the contemplation of beauty in nature has often aroused and quickened till they pass over into convictions. Surely, we may argue, it is a narrow philosophy which, because it sees that beauty resides in expressions of mind, and yet rejects the thought of a divine Mind, is obliged either to deny the beauty of nature altogether, or else to contend that nature is only beautiful, in so far as human minds make it an expression of themselves. Persistently from Plato onwards a great school of human philosophy has been persuaded that somehow the whole world is the symbol of a great principle of goodness, which is itself eternal beyond space and time, and yet expresses its own nature in what is spatial and temporal; and that the highest aim of the human soul is to penetrate to the fuller contemplation of the goodness so expressed, until the soul itself be made partaker of eternity. Thus ultimately it is the divine nature which permeates all space and time, which is immanent wherever goodness is expressed in beauty, and which is recognised by that divine insight which itself bestows upon the soul of man.

Such is the fundamental belief underlying what may be called æsthetic sacramentalism. To many it has appeared to be sufficient foundation for a Christian philosophy of sacraments. Yet it has obvious difficulties to contend with ; and its attempts to overcome them not seldom seem to bring it into conflict with the Christian faith.

Of course the main objection to æsthetic sacramentalism as a philosophy arises from the fact that the world of our experience appears to express goodness in such a very limited degree. The limitations seem to have a twofold cause. In the first place there is the element of what may be called " positive " or " active " evil, which comes into the world with natural life, is seen in the wastefulness and cruelty of the evolutionary struggle, and reaches a climax in the evil will of man. In the second place, there is the inherent incapacity of that which occupies space and time to embody a beauty which can permanently satisfy man's spiritual need. Indeed, it is the very characteristic of the greatest works of human art that they make us feel the artist's and our own dissatisfaction with what he has achieved—he has dimly guessed and striven after something more than he has actually succeeded in expressing. In the same way, it is the greatest systems of philosophy which make us most aware that they have not said all that they meant, or tried to mean. And even in the contemplation of some intensely beautiful scene or form in nature there is often almost as much pain as pleasure, because the beauty there present by the very force of its own quality makes us long after the beauty which cannot be there or anywhere else, and yet is known as inwardly real because it is desired. Though nature and art and philosophy have taught us what beauty is, they cry with one voice " It is not in us ", as soon as we have learned their lesson. It is always the ideal which alone is ultimately good and divine, and it is the ideal which never wholly exists in the things of space and time—" Why callest thou me good ? None is good save one " ; that is the message of all. And here it matters not what kind of beauty we are considering, whether the beauty of reason or holiness, or social happiness, or of schemes of line and colour, or of harmonious sound.

From such perplexities the philosophy which we are considering has two possible means of escape. (1) It may suppose that there exists, behind and beyond the phenomena of space and time, a world of perfect reality and real perfection, wherein goodness is fully expressed, and whereof " this world " is either a defective copy or representation, or else a more or less illusory semblance. (2) On the other hand, it may assume that the defect lies, not in the being of the spatio-temporal world itself, but only in our partial apprehension of it, and that, if we could but see the whole, everything that now apears to conflict with goodness would be found to fit into its place and be justified in the total scheme.

The first alternative is that more usually associated with Platonism ; and certainly the notion of the already perfect other-world, separate from that in which we live and move and exercise our senses, is indicated in many Platonic and Platonistic writings, and has had an enduring influence upon human thought. Of course, in proportion as the self-subsistent completeness and eternal perfection of the other-world are emphasised, this world of space and time falls outside and apart from it. Thus the immanence of the eternal goodness in temporal phenomena tends to become inconceivable ; the outward can no longer express the inward, but at best can very remotely signify it. Along this line of thought we pass easily, as not a few Platonists have passed, into the mysticism of the *via negativa*, which declares the one true and divine reality to be altogether ineffable.

We are not here concerned with the many metaphysical objections and difficulties which always beset this type of philosophy. It has really no answer to the question, how is it conceivable that the spatio-temporal copy or illusory appearance of the eternal reality should ever have come to be at all ? But it is enough for our purpose to point out that the religion which goes with such a philosophy must in the end part from sacramentalism altogether. According to it the truest and purest form of religious experience is always to be found in escaping and withdrawing from what is outward rather than in penetrating towards deeper knowledge of it. The very knowledge of the other world which it attains makes this world unknowable to it, just as the knowledge of this world attained by some makes them agnostic of eternity. Of course, even the negative mystic is obliged to find in the outward at least the starting-point of his quest, but he can give no intelligible account of the positive value which he thus perforce ascribes to it.

The second resource open to the æsthetic sacramentalist is to maintain that the one true and full goodness is that expressed in the whole, and that it is only the finiteness of our vision which prevents us from beholding it. Subsequent chapters will, we hope, make it evident that in this suggestion we have a truth which is really fundamental to any sound doctrine of sacraments. All the same, taken by itself, it is incomplete even as a foundation. And our first task must be one of criticism.

We have already observed that there appear on the surface to be two hindrances to the perfect expression of goodness in the world, (1) the " positive " evil which is in actual conflict with the moral will, and (2) the incapacity of what occupies space and time for the embodiment of perfection. Now, the doctrine that goodness is perfectly expressed in the whole is apt to suggest that what we call positive evil is really an illusion, and that what we call moral good, and the evil which conflicts with it, alike have their true being only as imperfectly apprehended parts of a reality which, seen as whole, perfectly embodies a goodness transcending both. And exactly the same principle of explanation covers also what seems to be the incapacity for perfection of that which exists in space and time. The defect of what is spatio-temporal is real in a sense, but ultimately it is a defect only in our limited point of view, the limitations of which we can and ought in some measure to transcend. If we could but widen the range of our contemplation so as to behold what is in space and time, no longer as fragmentary, but as it really is in the context of the eternal whole which includes it, then we should be satisfied with beauty. And even though the fulness of such a vision be for ever impossible for finite minds, yet the faith that it is eternally present to the infinite mind of God may still afford us a principle of reconciliation.

The fundamental objection to such a solution of the problem is this, that it is conceived in terms which are too exclusively æsthetic, and therefore fails to satisfy the demands of our moral nature. It suggests that evil things are harmonised with goodness in the whole, in a manner analogous to that in which a discord is justified in a musical sequence,[1] or some crime or disaster fits into the total significance of a drama. But this analogy offends the conscience. In drama a crime is justified in the plan of the whole, so long as it is seen as a crime, in true æsthetic contrast with an ideal of goodness which the contrast defines. In drama, therefore, there need be no

---

[1] " The discord as such disappears, if the harmony is made wide enough " (F. H. Bradley, *Appearance and Reality*, p. 202).

conquest of evil or actual victory of good—indeed such a victory would more often than not ruin the play by foisting upon it an alien "moral". But this is so, exactly because the essential value of a drama is and ought to be not moral but æsthetic : good and evil must be clearly distinguished in it, but the practical issue of the conflict is irrelevant. To morality as such, however, the practical issue cannot be irrelevant : it does demand the victory of the right. And if moral values, no less than æsthetic, are grounded in the ultimate reality of the universe, any solution of the problem of good and evil, which is conceived in purely æsthetic terms, is bound to be incomplete.

In its æsthetic attitude the mind is concerned with the beauty of moral goodness. It is enough for it that that goodness should be truly represented or expressed ; and that perhaps may best be achieved by depicting the all but complete triumph of wickedness—as Plato the artist saw so clearly, when he drew his famous portrait of the persecuted righteous man in the *Republic*. In its moral attitude, on the other hand, the mind is concerned with the moral goodness of beauty, and then all that expresses goodness is valued by it only as a means for furthering the actual triumph of goodness in the world. The moralist therefore is ever apt to look with suspicion on art that has no moral—as did Plato the Puritan, when, also in the *Republic*, he expurgated Homer from the schoolrooms of his ideal state.

The æsthetic attitude seems to be strongly characteristic of philosophical idealism in almost all its forms. Inevitably, therefore, it subordinates doing to contemplating, moral goodness to beauty, instrumentality to significance, time to eternity. Metaphysically, perhaps, this subordination may in the end be justified. But the sacramentalism which goes with this philosophy is certainly one-sided. It invites us to see in the world as a whole the sacrament of God's self-expression, and in particular sacraments special arrangements of what is outward whereby that universal self-expression may be made more apparent and appreciable. But its reluctance to exclude anything whatever from being in the last resort an expression of the Godhead gives it a pantheistic tendency, and makes it constantly prone to offend the moral consciousness which apprehends God as fighting victoriously with the good against an evil wholly alien from Himself.

Let us briefly sum up our argument. Beauty we have defined as goodness expressed. The beautiful is created as the self-expression of mind or spirit, and is appreciated in so far as mind or spirit recognises in it the expression of its own ideal. On such foundations the æsthetic sacramentalist builds a philosophy in which he contemplates the world as the self-expression of a divine nature, which nature enters into human mind or spirit far enough to enable it to recognise the divine self-expression as embodying also its own ideals of perfection. He then deals with the manifest imperfections of this present world by supposing that, when viewed in a sufficiently wide context, they can be seen as taken up into the perfection of the whole ; and he interprets particular embodiments of goodness as pointing to this universal consummation. But he cannot regard any change to be wrought in the world as an ultimate ground for the explanation of it. His whole outlook, just because it is so strictly an outlook, that is, an activity of pure contemplation or theory, subtly infects all his thinking with conservatism. Because his aim is to see all things fitted into a whole, he must in a sense justify everything. But, in proportion as his interest is purely æsthetic, he may be satisfied with a purely

æsthetic justification. He may be so intent on simply
seeing the good *revealed* in the universe, that he may not
care about its triumph. He may find the ultimate
solution of his problem in conceiving a *tragic* universe,
where the majesty of goodness is contemplated in its
practical defeat. And this indeed is perhaps the type of
solution really hinted at by those philosophers who, in
pointing us to an ultimate order beyond good and evil,
use language which, taken strictly, seems unintelligible.
Be that as it may, at this point æsthetic philosophy is
forced, in spite of itself, into conflict with the moral sense.
And we must now follow the latter in its line of approach
towards the same metaphysical problem.

CHAPTER III

ETHICAL SACRAMENTALISM

WE have now to consider the general features which characterise another rationale of sacraments. We will call it ethical sacramentalism to distinguish it from the æsthetic type. This sacramentalism naturally follows the lead of a philosophy which holds a different clue to the metaphysical maze. Recent years have made us increasingly familiar with philosophical doctrines which take time and action to be the very stuff of ultimate reality, and incline to interpret the world in terms, not of expressed goodness, but of goodness achieving purpose by practical activity. With the non-theistic or non-Christian forms of this philosophy we are not here concerned. But, within the broad limits of Christian thought, it has certainly served to show that the interpretation of the world as God's self-expression is by itself incomplete, that God, with man's co-operation, is really working out a genuine purpose in space and time, and that we should seek to find in good things and events, not so much symbols of God's eternal nature, but rather instruments whereby He fashions His Kingdom that is to be.

This view of the world naturally includes in itself a distinct type of sacramental doctrine. It values all that is outward less for what it symbolises than for what it effects. If sacraments express God's goodness to man's apprehension, they do so mainly in order that man may co-operate the more efficiently with the divine purpose.

And certainly the value of the sacraments is no more to be limited by their expressiveness, than the value of man's machinery is limited by its power of expressing the minds which invented and use it. The most important thing is what God does to us and with us by means of the outward sign, not what He reveals to us in it. He is, so to speak, primarily interested in using things, so that He may also use us, not in displaying Himself to us in things, so that we may know ourselves also as part of His self-revelation.

Now this kind of sacramentalism, so long as it is accompanied by a strong conviction of the moral character of God and all His operations, is in many ways more congenial to the conscience than the type which we have called æsthetic. For moral goodness, as we have already asserted, is essentially goodness working towards an end. Man, on the strictly moral side of his being, must seek to act or to create rather than to know, to serve the divine goodness rather than to contemplate it, to be at work in building the new Jerusalem, rather than to descry it from far or near. And so the moral consciousness naturally apprehends God as the great Captain or Leader or Master-builder, who both inspires and controls those who labour under Him for the accomplishment of His will.

Much confusion would be introduced into the distinction between the two types of sacramentalism by alleging that the æsthetic tends to emphasise exclusively the divine immanence, the ethical the divine transcendence. For to a man who experiences the divine action and control through outward things, God is at least as immanent in them as He is to a man who sees in them the divine self-expression. A man's own personality is as immanent in the instruments which effect his purpose as in the symbols which express his mind. I can only be immanent in my body because in a sense I transcend it, and I can only transcend it because in a sense I am immanent in it. Immanence and transcendence are correlatives ; and to dispute whether God is immanent or transcendent is little more rational than to dispute whether a given curve is convex or concave. The deism and the negative mysticism, which in different ways deny God's immanence in the outward world, make Him not transcendent of the world, but absent from it. And the pantheism, which denies transcendence wholly, makes immanence equally impossible, since it leaves no room for any distinction between the Godhead and the totality of that in which it dwells.

Ethical sacramentalism, in picturing God as the supreme Agent and Accomplisher of purpose, does not at all seek to place God outside the universe or even outside the world of space and time. Rather, in a sense even more than æsthetic sacramentalism, it apprehends God as intimately connected with that world. For, whenever we think of the outward as God's instrument, He is naturally conceived, so to speak, as actually handling and working with it, and we attach a more definite " here and now " to God's presence, than when we conceive it as expressed in an outward symbol. And, since the very nature of instrumentality and efficient action involves a process of real time, to think of God as producing effects by outward means is necessarily to place His very life within the time-series.

But can ethical sacramentalism really offer us any help in the perplexities of thought into which we were led when we took æsthetic sacramentalism for our only guide ? Or are the two points of view finally incompatible with one another ?

At first sight it may seem that the ethical point of view

can only save us from the difficulties which beset the
æsthetic, by limiting the Godhead, and therefore by for-
bidding us to think of God as the Spirit self-expressed in
the whole of reality. Instead, it offers us an image of God
as Captain of the forces of the good perpetually warring
against evil. Such a dualistic hypothesis, resting on the
idea of a limited God, has been revived and popularised,
as is well known, by a good deal of recent speculation.
And this kind of doctrine certainly meets some of the
characteristic demands of the moral consciousness, in so
far as it enables us to retain in our thought of God at once
the purity of His holiness and the reality of His purposive
action.

Yet an ultimate dualism does not wholly satisfy even the
conscience. If it takes refuge in the thought of an unending struggle, it cannot meet the demand, which our moral
nature does make, for a complete victory of the good as
well as for the reality of warfare. After all, " fighting for
fighting's sake " has never been the gospel of a true soldier.
If, on the other hand, it postulates the completest victory
conceivable merely as a future event in time, after which
all is joy and peace, again the conscience is left ultimately
discontent. For the grandest and most characteristic
acts of moral goodness are found precisely in that heroism
of self-sacrifice, for which there can be no opportunity
after the final victory has been won. Thus, from the
postulated heaven of the future that which we know as
morally best would be shut out.

All these notions, however, of a limited Godhead, an
unending struggle, and of heaven as a purely future event
probably do less than justice to the real postulates of an
ethical sacramentalism. We need a closer and deeper
analysis in order to grasp what the best conscience of
mankind is really contending for.

One difference between an expressive symbol and an instrument seems to be this, that the expressive symbol can hardly be thought of as existing apart from what it expresses, whereas an instrument certainly exists apart from its use, and may be put to an indefinite number of other uses. A masterpiece of painting or of music could hardly be apart from its beauty. But a violin and a paint-brush certainly do exist as things quite apart from their value and may conceivably become instrumental to a large number of different purposes. It is true of course that words, which are symbols, constantly change their meanings. But this happens just in so far as words, even in being significant symbols, are also instruments and adaptable as means to the mind's purpose. Single words, as such, with their conventional associations described in the dictionary, are to the poet or prose-artist what pigments, brushes and canvas are to the painter. And, when the great poet has woven words into the expressive texture of a literary masterpiece, we find that " the word " has become " one with that it tells of ", much as the paints on the artist's finished canvas have become inseparable from their " effect ". Just as this particular meaning, we feel, could not be otherwise signified, so this particular combination of words could never mean anything else, though the words which make it up are, taken separately, instruments, each one of which is capable of entering into an infinite number of combinations devised for an infinite number of different purposes.

Now the principle that the instrumental value of things is separable from the things themselves may be of the utmost importance, when we have to consider the fundamental relations of good and evil in the world. For it implies that the value of all things, in so far as it is in-strumental, may to an unlimited extent be altered or

reversed.[1] And it is indeed, not an abstract possibility,
but a plain fact of experience, that things good in themselves may be put to bad uses, and things evil in themselves
be made to subserve the purposes of good. The noblest
beauty of the human form may be made by the unclean
mind into an instrument of lust ; and, on the other hand,
it is at least as true that " men may rise on stepping-stones
of their dead selves to higher things ". These opposite processes of perversion and conversion are continually going
on in the world, and they affect only the instrumental
value of their objects. No misuse of beauty can prevent
the beautiful thing from essentially expressing goodness.
And on the other hand, if I learn wisdom and virtue
from my own or other men's follies and faults, I do not
make those follies and faults any different in their essential
nature of evil, though, by putting them to good use, I
make them instrumental to goodness. In the same way,
when a terrible disaster, such as a famine or a shipwreck,
leads to acts of heroic self-sacrifice, the disaster is not
made any better a thing in itself, though the activity of
the hero converts it, as it were by force, into a means of
realising goodness.

Along this line of thought we reach a juster notion of
what ethical sacramentalism really desires to contend for.
It is not necessarily demanding either a limited God or an
unending struggle, nor yet a future heaven which is purely
and simply successive to earth. Rather, its fundamental
concept is that of a Deity the power of Whose goodness
is sufficient to convert into the instrument of His good

---

[1] The truth that the past can be changed in value, and its importance for Christian metaphysics, have been brilliantly shown by the
Bishop of Manchester (Dr. Temple) in *Mens Creatrix* (esp. pp. 172 *sqq.*)
and *Christus Veritas* (p. 34 and elsewhere). I have here proposed a
modification of his doctrine by suggesting that it is only instrumental
value which is thus changeable.

purpose all the evil that there is, has been, or ever shall be, in the world. And it does not seem that, at least for theists, such a postulate of faith contains any inherent self-contradiction. It is a matter of experience that the converting power of the good will in action not only make a difference to present and future, but also extends backwards over the past to an indefinite extent. Indeed, all the good that is at work to-day has all the mixed good and evil of the past as its material to work on and to work with ; and it converts that material into the service of goodness, just so far as it succeeds in bringing something good out of it. From this point of view, therefore, as M. Bergson and his followers have been so eager to assure us, the gates of the future are indeed open.

And thus we come upon the real difference in outlook between ethical and æsthetic sacramentalism. Ethical sacramentalism moves in a world of change and action. To it outward things are instruments and therefore the value of none is finally fixed. For the value of everything, being instrumental, depends upon what can ultimately be made out of it, and that we see not yet. The only fixed goodness is that of the divine ideal and of the will which seeks to realise it. And these are not outward, nor are they anywhere fully or strictly expressed in the outward : the good will uses the outward in labour and conflict towards the embodiment of the ideal. If we ask, what of the end ? what of the whole ? the ethical sacramentalist answers that faith indeed is the substance of things hoped for, and that the end in which he believes is victory complete. But things hoped for are things future and not seen, and therein lies the very ground of his hope. For if things must remain as now we see them, there is room for little but despair. There can be no solution for the problem of evil, but in fighting evil. And, as we realise the evil

E

within as well as without us, we may thank God that
we ourselves are rather His potential instruments than
actual expressions of Him, and that therefore our own
value may yet be changed. We are better occupied in
accomplishing that change, in converting and being converted, than in wondering how the world will appear when
its conversion is complete.

Æsthetic sacramentalism on the other hand is bent upon
apprehending a world of expression, a world of values
embodied in outward symbols, which as such are unalter-
able. It does not seek to change anything, but rather to
penetrate towards a fuller knowledge of the reality which
the outward still seems to veil even in revealing. For it
to make demands upon an unknown future to reverse the
values of the present would be rank treachery to its fundamental faith.[1] The whole universe is the embodiment of
one unshaken order manifest at every point to those who
have eyes to see. And the various " changes and chances "
of this world can do no more than afford fresh points of
view which may assist our discernment of what is immanent in all. Nothing that can be done, no violence of
action or conflict, makes any ultimate difference to the
whole which already determines, and is represented in,
all things.

Of course these two types of sacramentalism, as we have
just presented them in sharp antithesis to one another,
are abstractions. No actual mind embraces either quite
wholeheartedly or follows it out to its logical conclusion.
But each of us has his natural bias towards one side or the
other ; and this fact lies at the root of much theological

---

[1] Bosanquet has shown this excellently, especially in *Value and
Destiny of the Individual*, Lecture X, where he criticises severely both
Bergson's belief in an undetermined future and the Pauline conviction
that " the sufferings of this present world are not worthy to be compared——".

and philosophical disputation. There are some who tend to treat every expression of goodness merely as a means towards further endeavour after the good, and to be impatient with those who would bid them pause to contemplate the values already realised in existence. There are others who find in action itself, less a means of effecting something, than a symbol already so full of significance that only a full understanding of it is required in order to realise the goal of every effort. And it is especially in relation to the sacraments of religion, where effective instrumentality and expressive symbolism are so closely linked, that the difference between the two points of view is most acutely felt.

Is reconciliation possible ? Perhaps not fully, at least in intellectual terms. But we may point out that each, in order to achieve its own completeness, is obliged in the end to borrow from the other.

Question the moral consciousness, to which the outward appears as instrument, concerning the end after which it strives. The end is the final conversion of all things to be instruments of goodness. But, when that is accomplished, the good is at once seen as expressed and embodied in the whole of which all the parts have now become instrumental to it. The full success of moral effort can only be the full realisation of beauty. And the beauty so realised incorporates into itself, as essential to its very nature, the process whereby its realisation was worked out. Moreover, if moral endeavour is ever to reach such a consummation, the conscience must believe now in the present reality of a goodness which in the end will be known as almighty, and it must be content to learn how the end is to be pursued from the partial expressions of that goodness which our outward world already affords.

Again, question the æsthetic consciousness as to the

manner of the inclusion of all things in the whole of goodness which they express. One of the most important
elements of the expressed good, all of which are to find their
full meaning in the whole, consists precisely in the heroism
of the moral activity which contends through defeat and
disappointment, in face of appalling odds, for the creation
of the world of its ideal. But, if we suppose that that
activity is either from the beginning unnecessary or in the
end unsuccessful, that is, either that the universe had no
need of the real changes which the moral will strives to
bring about, or that the will cannot bring about those
changes or make any ultimate difference by its action,
then the inevitable conclusion must be that the moral
activity loses even its significance ; it ceases to be in any
intelligible sense a true expression of the ultimate reality.
There must be real changes to be wrought, real conversions
of value to be made, a real victory of goodness to be won,
if the moral ideal is to be more than a delusive dream
which troubles nature's sleep.

In result, the apparent conflict between ethical and
æsthetic sacramentalism turns out to be just one aspect
of the ancient, all-pervading problem of the relation of
eternity to time. When we view the universe from the
standpoint of ethics, we see it in terms of time ; the realisation of the good is in the future, the present outward is
at best instrumental to the moral will, and there is nothing
here and now in which we can rest with satisfaction.
When we view the universe from the æsthetic standpoint,
we see it, so far as we may, as in eternity ; we insist that
the outward does indeed express and embody goodness,
though partially, and would be seen to do so fully, could
we but apprehend the whole. And then, reflecting further,
we remind ourselves that no purely future heaven could
satisfy even the moral consciousness, since the realisation

of goodness which conscience seeks cannot in the end be separated, even by it, from the outward acts in time and space which bring the realisation to pass. And again we remind ourselves that an eternity, which excludes the reality of changes produced by action in time, cannot satisfy even the æsthetic consciousness, since it would deprive of ultimate meaning the moral activity which has somehow to be fitted into the whole.

The only reconciliation, so far as reconciliation is possible at all, lies in asserting that eternity must include time and change, and that both the inclusion, and the time and change included, must be real. There is an eternally ordered whole, and yet the order of the whole would not be fulfilled or complete, were it not worked out through the real evolution and conflict and reconciling sacrifices of which spatio-temporal limitations are the condition.

If it be said that this solution is after all no more than verbal, we must confess that the full and ultimate unity eludes, perhaps for ever, our mental grasp. By the uncertain help of analogies we may feel our way towards it. The analogies of the symphony and the drama are often used, and in the last chapter we dwelt upon their imperfection. Perhaps we may advance a step or two further by reflecting on the nature of the creative and self-expressive act of the artist, by which drama or symphony is composed. In a sense the idea of the whole exists in the artist's mind, before it is embodied in the outward medium. Yet the process whereby he works it out in that medium is indeed a real process, full of difficulties, setbacks, and problems of detail, all of which, being overcome, leave their imprint upon the final work and enhance its value in the end. And, though the constructive effort was so really laborious, yet, when the whole is complete, the artist recognises that this indeed is what he originally had in mind, what directed him throughout, and has also taken up and incorporated into itself every incident and set-back which occurred in the process of construction. Thus the whole completed work is beyond the process at the end, directed it from the beginning, and was immanent in it at every stage. Its unity, original and final, is in the creative mind which both conceived it in idea and carried it out in fact. And at every stage of the work, as yet incomplete, the outward medium has both begun to express the creative idea in the artist's mind, and is the instrument towards its final fulfilment. Lastly, even the set-backs and obstacles, which hindered the creative process, are, when overcome, made instrumental to the whole in which the artist's self-expression is complete.

In some such way, perhaps, we may think of the creation as related to the mind of God. Yet no philosophical argument, or carefully drawn analogy, can help our understanding so much as the consideration of the life of Christ in its double aspect as the supreme self-expression of the Godhead within the created world, and as the supreme instrument whereby that world is brought to its fulfilment in eternity. It is high time now that we should turn from the abstractions of metaphysic to the concreteness of the Christian revelation. We must move away from sacramentalism and towards sacraments. And for Christians the supreme sacrament, apart from which no other has use or meaning, is the life of Jesus Christ.

CHAPTER IV

CHRIST'S LIFE AS A SACRAMENT

(1) THE INCARNATION

IT is probably true that the Christian doctrine of the Incarnation has in modern times received more attention from metaphysical philosophers than that of the Atonement and the Cross. It has been generally assumed that the main significance of the latter is moral and practical. Nevertheless, the metaphysical treatment of the Incarnation, when torn from its context in the whole gospel of Christianity, has been, from a Christian point of view, very far from satisfactory. The doctrine of the Incarnation has been taken as signifying merely a general truth of divine immanence. It has thus been made to support a vaguely optimistic humanism, which virtually identifies Godhead with the ultimate aims and aspirations of human endeavour, and suggests that, because human activity is itself in the whole or in the last resort divine, the Godhead is realising itself in the process of spatio-temporal history. Thus the particular and, in a sense, exclusive association of the Incarnation with the life of Jesus is forgotten or slurred over, and the fact that the life of the Incarnate was on earth rejected and crucified is practically ignored. The metaphysical position thus reached is in the end difficult to distinguish from a form of pantheism or positivism.

While metaphysicians have thus been mainly interested in generalising the doctrine of Incarnation without much reference to its particular source and original meaning, historical critics have tended to ignore its universal aspect altogether, and have treated the orthodox dogma as affording simply a psychological problem concerned with the consciousness and capacities of the man Jesus Christ. Their question runs rather as follows : When theologians identify the Person of Jesus Christ with the Second Person of the Trinity, how exactly do they conceive the difference between the consciousness or powers of Jesus and those of an ordinary man, and how do they relate this difference to the records of fact which the New Testament contains ? The very form of the question demands that the life of Jesus should be considered altogether apart from its total meaning and effect in human experience as a whole.

Thus it happens that in modern thought the doctrine of Incarnation is regarded as having, now an entirely general, now an exclusively particular, reference ; and the Christian vaguely feels that the truth of his faith has somehow slipped out of sight between the two stools on which it is supposed alternately to rest. On the one hand, it is not the universal immanence of God in manhood, but His special and unique immanence in the manhood of Jesus, that he is primarily concerned to maintain ; and, on the other hand, he is at least dimly aware that the fact of that special immanence has its proof and verification in the wide and deep experience of those who take Jesus for their Lord, rather than in difficult and necessarily hypothetical theories of what exactly was the unique element in the consciousness of Jesus Himself during His life on earth. The fact that Jesus Christ has been the light of life to so many cannot fairly be ruled out of consideration when we are trying to answer the question, who and what He was.

Now, if our previous argument as to the general meaning of sacramentalism be accepted, to interpret the life of Jesus as the supreme sacrament is to show that in this outward, historical life lived in space and time there is both uniquely expressed and uniquely operative the highest purpose of goodness which all life and all nature are destined to fulfil. That purpose is in its origin and ultimate reality divine. Its self-revelation or expression in Christ is affirmed by the doctrine of the Incarnation ; its instrumental operation in Christ towards the attainment of its end is affirmed by the doctrine of the Atonement.

At once the sacramental outlook enables us to perceive how it is that both the philosopher and the historical critic are apt to miss the real point of the Christian faith. That faith certainly maintains that the life of Christ is unique among human lives, and unique as being more than human ; but that which is unique in the life does not consist in any separable non-human element which can be discerned in it, but is seen rather in this, that here alone in manhood is completely shown and completely operative the purpose for which God made the human race. If there were any element in the life of Jesus which could be shown to be quite non-human or alien from humanity, men would, so far, be debarred from finding in His life the pattern and explanation of their own. Yet on the other hand, if in the whole of His life, and in it alone, all men can find both the expression of that for which they exist, and the power whereby they can attain to it, it would be quite false to speak of the life of Jesus as having no nature beyond the human. Rather, if the purpose which directs the life of creation to its goal is divine, and if that purpose, so far as it concerns man and his world, is clearly seen and felt in Jesus Christ alone, it is simply a necessity of thought

to affirm that the mind of Jesus Christ is uniquely one
with the mind of God : and the affirmation can be made
and maintained without begging difficult questions which
concern the nature either of the consciousness or of the
superhuman powers possessed by Jesus in His spatio-
temporal existence.

It thus becomes apparent that from our point of view
the ground and justification of Christian dogma concerning the person of Christ are found, not in the life of Jesus
considered simply by itself, nor in any general theory
of divine immanence which neglects the uniqueness of
that life, but in the relation of the life of Jesus to human
experience as a whole. This relation consists in the
capacity of the life of Jesus both to reveal and to make
effective in all our experience the universal purpose of
God's goodness. If through that life we are indeed enabled
to realise how all the world of our present experience is
directed to fulfil the divine goodness, or, in old-fashioned
phrase, to glorify God, then the doctrines of the Incarnation and the Atonement are in their essential and sacramental meaning verified. The fundamental question is
this : is the life of Jesus Christ the uniquely perfect
expression and instrument of those values which constitute the very nature of God and for the fulfilment of
which God made the world ?

Our special subject in this chapter is the Incarnation,
which doctrine we take to present the truth of Christ's life
from the point of view of æsthetic sacramentalism, that
is, to interpret that life as the expression of the divine
goodness. But it may be well to remark at the outset
how closely the doctrines of the Incarnation and the
Atonement, as we regard them, must imply and involve
one another. On the one hand, the life of Chirst can only
enable human souls to play their own little part in working

out God's purpose, if they see in that life, not an instrument of goodness merely, but also the very image of that final and eternal good, in the service of which their own lives are to be spent. Thus, the life of Christ is only a full means of conversion and atonement, if it is also in itself a true incarnation. And, on the other hand, it would not be in space and time a true incarnation, unless, through the exigence of its atoning purpose, it had been brought to an end in space and time, and, passing into the heavenly sphere, had pointed onward to a fuller and universal embodiment of Godhead in a perfect and deathless communion towards which it is itself the way. There is a sense in which the earthly incarnation of the Son of God, just because it is true, cannot be in itself complete. It erects a bridge, so to speak, rather than a home. And yet the bridge must afford a vision of the home, or it is no true bridge.

How then are the divine values, which the world exists to fulfil, really embodied and expressed in the life and mind of Jesus upon earth ? We may first guard against a possible misunderstanding suggested by the statement that " Jesus Christ has the value of God," a statement which in recent years has gained considerable currency as interpreting the truth of the Incarnation.[1] It is an unfortunate statement, only because it is ambiguous. If it means that Jesus Christ has the goodness of God, then it

[1] I feel great sympathy with Mr. H. H. Farmer, when he writes : " It is sometimes urged against certain types of Christological theory that they affirm of Jesus nothing more than that He has the value of God. I can never see the force of this. There is surely an inadequate analysis of the religious consciousness behind the criticism. God confronts us through absolute value " (*Modern Churchman*, December, 1926, and January, 1927, p. 557). The whole article, entitled " The Worship of Jesus Christ," from which these words are taken, is well worth attention as a study in the theology of the Incarnation made from a point of view somewhat similar to that which I have tried to take in this chapter.

does indeed emphasise what must always be taken as the essence of the orthodox dogma. After all, God's goodness is His very self. But if the phrase " has the value of " is taken to mean " is equivalent to ", its effect is very different. It then suggests that we may treat Christ as God, at least for certain purposes, without making up our minds whether He really is God or not. But this is disastrous. For the notion that Jesus Christ can represent God to man, without being really identical in Godhead with the Father, is just as repugnant to the reason as the notion that He can represent men to God, without their being really identified with Him in the inmost nature of their manhood. It would certainly be a strange situation if some theologians, who have been most warm in protest against a vicarious Atonement, should lay themselves open to the charge of teaching a vicarious Incarnation. If our Lord in His self-offering to God cannot be a substitute for man, neither in His self-revelation towards man can He be a substitute for God.

Our task then is to show how Jesus Christ can be said to have the value of God in the full and proper sense of the words, that is, to show how the person and life of Jesus Christ express the goodness which is God's very nature and determines His purpose for His created world. For convenience of discussion we will make use of the threefold division of " absolute " goodness or value which is commonly accepted. We shall speak of Christ's life as manifesting first beauty, secondly moral goodness, and thirdly reason and rationality, which term we prefer to the term " truth " more usually employed. But we shall not forget that here we are treating all these values as having toward the one ultimate good the relation which we have defined as beauty, that is to say, we are considering them, not with reference to their instrumental or active operation in redeeming the world, but rather as they stand realised and embodied in Christ's expression of the Godhead.

(1) First then let us consider the beauty realised in Christ's person, meaning here by the term beauty that form of goodness which people usually have in mind when they speak of the beauty of nature or of art. That our Lord had a deep appreciation of the beauty of nature is indicated in many sayings, and is particularly attested by the discourse upon the lilies of the field. This discourse is a sermon against anxiety. But we miss its point if we fail to see that the quiet naturalness of the faith which our Lord here commends, and which He taught on another occasion by the image of the mustard seed, is in truth a spiritual beauty, of which beautiful things in nature are, after their own kind, a real expression. Solomon's grandeur cannot rival the lily's grace, just because it is elaborate, self-conscious, artificial. The highest achievement of artistic creation is to conceal the labour of the process by which its effect is produced. Unforced, unlaboured naturalness is the very spirit of true beauty. And surely, judged by this standard, the mind and soul of Jesus are seen to be beautiful with a beauty transcending even that of nature, though in intimate communion with it. In moments of calm and of passion, of joy and even of agony, His divine dignity inheres in His supreme simplicity of soul. And no small part of the mystery of His conscious-ness arises from the fact that that perfect poise of the spirit simply defies analysis in terms of the psychical machinery on which, in a sense, it rests. In vain do we try to base His divinity on some unique and definable *consciousness* of Godhead. For in truth just when His words and actions seem divinest, they seem also to have most in common with that quite unconscious grace of

which man, in passing up the ladder of evolution, has lost the secret. It is often not so much the self-consciousness as the unself-consciousness, which declares Jesus to be divine. We feel inclined to alter some famous lines of Wordsworth, and to say :

> His hath been the breathing balm
> And His the silence and the calm
>   Of mute insensate things.
> The floating clouds their state have lent
> To Him ; for Him the willow bent,
>   Nor hath He failed to see
> Even in the motions of the storm
> Grace that can mould the human form
>   By silent sympathy.
> The stars of midnight have been dear
> To Him ; and He hath lent His ear
>   In many a secret place
> Where rivulets dance their wayward round,
> And beauty born of murmuring sound
>   Hath passed into His face.

The very aloofness of natural beauty has its spiritual counterpart in the mind of Jesus, for all His intense sympathy with human sufferings. It is indeed this very aloofness which gives force to such words as " Come unto Me, all ye that labour and are heavy laden, and I will give you rest." And the belief of the disciples that even the winds and the waves obeyed Him, whatever we may think of a particular miracle, may surely attest their intuition that the majesty of His Spirit was mysteriously at home even in the manifestation of the natural forces which are accounted terrible.

Following out this line of thought, we seem led to acknowledge a certain divine perfection in the animal and vegetable and even inanimate creation, which we, personal, struggling, incoherent beings lack. The single-mindedness of the dog or the majesty of the stars, no less than the grace of the flower, may be taken to represent perfections from which man has fallen by the very fact of his evolutionary rise. And perhaps one reason why our Lord seems to us divine is in this, that his love and care for individuals is rooted in, or, if you will, balanced by, a certain tremendous and impersonal detachment from carefulness, which is more effectually mirrored in certain aspects of the order of nature, than in the passionate struggles of the moral will of man. Perhaps one might say that our Lord is divine not only in being perfectly human, but also in being perfectly natural.

Perfectly natural is just what a mere man can never be, just because his nature is neither completely unified in itself, nor thoroughly at one with his surroundings. A human person, as many philosophers have said, is the highest of created beings, because, more than any other being, he is a universe in himself. But he has purchased this finite universality, only by becoming the most isolated and separate of all creatures. The human individual, more than anything else in the world, is discontinuous, incompletely fitted, with its environment. This isolation, considered strictly in itself, is an evil, perhaps the evidence of a " fall ". And the effort of man's moral nature is, through service or unselfishness or whatever name we may give to true virtue, to overcome and break through that isolation, and to make or find an environment, in which he can once more merge himself and be thoroughly natural, free from strain, beautiful. Man's very sins are from one point of view, as has often been pointed out, only misguided efforts after this same end. It is this haunting sense of imperfect adaptation which leads the religious man to acknowledge that on earth he is but a sojourner and a pilgrim. And in Jesus he recognises a personality which brings heaven to earth, because in an indefinable way it

seems to fit in to every natural setting, even in Geth-
semane, or, as the poet fancied, at Charing Cross.[1]

Again, in relation to art, the truth that the very soul of
beauty dwells in the life of Jesus is further illustrated,
when we reflect on the impossibility of dramatising it. It
cannot be dramatised, because the facts, as tested and
verified by sane criticism, are already a greater drama
than any which the imagination could produce. Every
quality of the highest tragedy is to be found in the brief
record of what Jesus Christ did and spoke and suffered.
In the case of other historical tragedies we need the
artist's imagination to elicit for us fully the dramatic
values of the story. We need a Shakspere to interpret a
Julius Cæsar, even at the cost of historical accuracy.
But it is very significant that we feel most intensely the
tragedy of Jesus Christ, not through Luke's literary skill,
nor through John's mystical interpretations, but in the
crude and awkward narrative of Mark. It is the facts
themselves that are here expressive, and the closer we get
to them, the more deeply we appreciate their power. It
is these that enable us to see a meaning even in the saddest
chapters of the record of human failure.

(2) We turn from beauty to moral goodness. Any
incarnation of moral perfection in a single personality,
living under conditions of space and time, must needs
appear, from the point of view of an intellectual logic, to
be self-contradictory. For the ideal of moral life, considered
as an end, is necessarily social ; it consists in a communion
and fellowship of spirits, wherein each enriches the others
by the free, unselfish communication of the values realised
in itself. Such, in its moral aspect, is the Kingdom of God.
It transcends the ideal of distributive justice, wherein

---

[1] I need not quote Thompson's rather hackneyed, but very beautiful,
lines

each has his due, by including it in the ideal of community, wherein each makes his own contribution ; and, in so far as the contribution of any one member is lacking, perfection is still to seek. Nevertheless, finite human souls can only take their final place and part in that community by accomplishing through spatio-temporal experience a sacrifice of self, in which the most truly crucial and characteristic moment is not perhaps even the surrender of outward existence, though that is included, but rather the sense of loneliness and isolation which is always the penalty of unswerving loyalty to moral truth. Love cries out for fellowship and spends itself to create it ; yet its supremest efforts by their own inherent logic drive it into the wilderness. In all the pathos of the gospel-story there is nothing so infinitely touching as the ever-increasing isolation of Him Who called Himself Son of Man in order to emphasise His kinship with all men, Who on the very eve of His foreseen rejection was ready to accept and justify even the uncomprehending plaudits of the mob, and Who was seized by His enemies as He appealed in vain for the sympathy and companionship of His disciples. Yet, indeed, it behoved the anointed Man to suffer and be forsaken, in order that He might become the Head of an eternal fellowship. It is the double movement of separation and of union, which is at once the test of truthful love, and the secret of all abiding moral grandeur.

It is the realisation of this truth, through the life of Christ, that has imparted to the Christian ethic its most characteristic quality, which is creativeness. For the Christian there can be no salvation in merely keeping a Law, though there may be damnation in breaking it. For his whole moral effort is directed towards creating the social order of a community in which Christian fellowship

F

may become the one law and harmony of the whole. He is seeking not so much to discharge a duty or to fulfil a trust as to use his life to bring in a new heaven and a new earth. In a sense, then, the moral value of the Christian life can only be judged by its results, i.e. by the effects of its atoning power. And yet that new order of fellowship, which is the ultimate achievement and justification of Christian living, is indissolubly one in spirit with the heroic and solitary self-surrender on which the ultimate achievement rests : so that we are able to declare, by a true and tremendous paradox, that the spirit of fellowship is never in space and time so gloriously embodied as in the loneliness of the Cross.

We find therefore our Lord's moral perfection, not so much in minutely examining particular acts and sayings by the standard of some generally recognised rule of moral conduct, but rather in considering how the search for, and service of, the spiritually discerned kingdom of goodness governed His whole life as the instrument of that kingdom, and led up to the revelation of its inmost nature in His death. We must not shirk the moral difficulties presented by certain sayings and acts which an unbiased criticism obliges us to accept as genuine. Such difficulties there must be. They arise, not improbably, in part from our ignorance of the complete circumstances of the word or act in question, and in part also from the necessary limitations which time and space impose upon any outwardly expressed perfection. But our broad judgment rests upon the fitness of our Lord's life as a whole to be both the instrument and the expression of that Kingdom of goodness in which, as proclaimed by Him, we divine the satisfaction of our deepest moral need. Even in the very harshness of such a saying as that to the Syro-Phœnician woman we overhear, as it were, not the racial prejudice of the Jew, but the inward struggle of that love which is compelled to restrict its immediate activity, lest it fail in its widest aim. In the flesh Jesus Christ is straitened indeed, and His particular words and deeds must be judged in the light of that coherent plan which determined His whole ministry, just as that plan itself reveals its full moral value as the creative act whereby universal fellowship is made perfect through lonely sacrifice. The conditions of that creative act are the transparent unselfishness of motive and objectivity of judgment, which are perhaps the most obvious and constant characteristics of the mind of Jesus.

Possibly the most serious objection to the moral perfection of Christ is based upon His occasionally extreme severity in denunciation and anathema. Do we not sometimes catch a faint echo of a self-regarding and vengeful animosity against His most obstinate opponents ? The question has to be asked and answered. But a closer examination seems to show that the cases of most vehement condemnation are precisely the exceptions which prove the consuming purity of His love. The key to the understanding of them may be found, if we dare to attribute to our Lord a saying which is often almost, but never quite, recorded of Him, " Damn not, and ye shall not be damned ".[1] The one temper which love finds intrin-

---

[1] It may perhaps be noted in passing that the very " hard saying " contained in Mark IX. 47, 48 is capable of an interpretation somewhat different from that usually given to it. The language about the fire and the worm is, of course, quoted from the last verse of the book of Isaiah ; and in its original context it is meant to suggest an image, not of torture, but of horrible decay. Our Lord's discourse about the cutting off of bodily members which offend has clearly the nature of a parable. And the parable may perhaps be briefly summed up thus : " It is better to undergo a partial disfigurement voluntarily than, by refusing it, to allow the whole body to become a mass of disgusting corruption." No doubt our Lord's words, as they have come down to us, mingle the parable with its application. But Gehenna seems here

sically damnable is that which is content to consign others
to damnation. In denunciation of that temper, whether
manifested in the form of self-satisfied superiority, or
in that of unforgiving vindictiveness, or in that of mere
callous indifference, our Lord's language was certainly
unsparing ; but it is for that temper that His extreme
invective is reserved. Again and again He seems to be
trying to impress upon His hearers the warning that the
only real way to hell is to be content to let others go there.
To reflect deeply on such a truth is not likely to minister
to any honest man's sense of his own security ; and yet for
many a sin-stained soul one of our Lord's anathemas contains surer ground of hope than a thousand ecclesiastical
promises. It is precisely in such matters that moral perfection upsets conventional standards of moral goodness.
Many that are first shall be last, and the last first. And
the ground of the revolution is this, that in Christ moral
perfection is revealed in space and time, not as the keeping
of a prescribed rule, but as the creative unrest of love.

It may be worth while briefly to amplify the last sentence before we pass on. The ethic of the New Testament,
as contrasted both with that of the Old and with that of a
later ecclesiasticism, is essentially adventurous ; it stresses
the value of giving and spending rather than that of
keeping. The notion of the divine covenant in the Old
Testament limits morality to the keeping of a trust and
obedience to a rule ; and the whole discussion of the rival

to stand as a symbol of spiritual decay and death, rather than of
punitive pain. The thought in our Lord's mind seems to be that to
cling to all the goods of temporal life and to refuse the pain of sacrifice
may lead in the end to a spiritual condition fitly symbolised by the
most repulsive forms of bodily dissolution. This is the reverse side of
the truth that real life is won through bearing the cross. In that case
the verses under discussion convey a terrible warning as to the inevitable
consequences of refusing sacrifice. They do not threaten everlasting
torments as a general retribution for self-indulgence.

merits of tutiorism and probabilism breathes an Old Testament atmosphere. But the New Testament finds virtue in the trustfulness which sets sail on uncharted oceans, no less than in the trustworthiness which abides fast in its appointed place. Even the parables of trade and commerce, so frequently on Christ's lips, are used by Him chiefly in order to point the lesson that money must be spent and risked, if anything worth having is to be bought.

How often has the conservative faithfulness of the Church itself been exactly that of the servant who, knowing the strictness of his master, buried his pound in a napkin and thought that in keeping it he would be safe. How often have Christian teachers forgotten that with the words of His first call to His apostles, " I will make you fishers of men ", Christ made morality not a law-abiding impeccability, but an art, a craft and an adventure. It is as the creative craftsman of human goodness, that Christ must be judged to be the embodiment of moral perfection upon earth.

(3) More difficult problems confront us when we pass on to consider in what sense the life of Jesus Christ may be said to embody the further value which philosophers generally call " truth ", but which we will take leave to denote by the names of rationality and reason. First of all the problem or problems must be defined.

By the term rationality we denote that principle of universal order wherein all reality is found ultimately to cohere and to be harmonious. By the term reason we denote the mind's apprehension and appreciation of that coherence and harmony. In God it may be said that reason and rationality are one ; for we cannot affirm either that the divine reason is the apprehension of a rational order *already* real, or that rational order itself is created by the divine reason. The divine being contains within itself both reason and rationality, and its reason created the spatio-temporal world of things and finite minds, in order to embody and fulfil through it its own principle of rationality.

Finite minds may be said to have rationality, in so far as they are members of a rational order. This rationality they possess in common with all else that is ; since everything enters ultimately into the rational order of the whole. Nevertheless all things do not possess rationality in the same degree ; for the rational order of the whole is more fully exhibited in some things than in others. Thus a mind may be said to possess more rationality than a stone or even a plant, though Tennyson claimed that a " flower in the crannied wall " might exhibit the whole order of the universe. Again, there are evil things, which, in so far as they are evil, cannot enter the rational order at all except through ceasing to exist, and there is a sense in which an evil mind may be said to have even less rationality than an inanimate object. Rationality, therefore, pervades all things in different modes and degrees.

Reason, on the other hand, is a characteristic of mind which distinguishes it from other things. Only a mind can apprehend and appreciate rational order ; and, in the case of a finite mind, the rational order appreciated is necessarily beyond the mind itself, and already real independently of its appreciative reason. Moreover, it does not seem to be true that finite minds always possess both reason and rationality in the same degree. The saintly life of some simple-minded peasant may exhibit very much of the whole rational order of the universe in its moral aspect ; but the peasant's appreciation of that order, though real, may be very limited, and apparently less than that of another man, whose life is inferior as an embodiment of goodness. Thus in the existing world reason and rationality fall apart within the rational order of the whole.

By affirming therefore that Jesus Christ incarnates for us the *rationality* of God, we should mean primarily that His life exhibits, with such perfection as spatio-temporal limitations permit, the ultimate order or plan or purpose of the universe as a whole. If such is the true and universal significance to be discerned in the life and death of Jesus, our estimate of His person necessarily makes it one with the divine mind from which the determining order and purpose of the whole have flowed forth. This is the truth which the whole of our present discussion is endeavouring to illustrate, and, so far as is possible, to establish.

Yet there is something more to be considered. Is there not in Jesus Christ the incarnation of the divine *reason* as well as of divine rationality? If He embodies divine beauty and goodness, is it not implied that He possessed also a divine perception and appreciation of the order of reality? And would He conceivably have so exhibited to us the whole rational order of things, if His mind had not been endowed with a corresponding insight into the nature of that order? Certainly the Church has always believed that, in speaking of the person of Jesus as divine, it was attributing to Him in some sense a divine knowledge of what was in man and in the world. The problems here raised are notoriously difficult, but no discussion of the sacramental meaning of the Incarnation can be excused for evading them altogether.

Now nothing is more strikingly characteristic of the mind of Jesus Christ than His unwavering belief in an order of goodness, revealed even in the normal sequences of natural events, and ultimately controlling all things. This belief in order underlies His whole use of parable.

The parables, for the most part,[1] are little word-pictures of some quite normal and ordinary sequence of events in the life of man or of sub-human nature ; and yet Christ's insight elicits from this normal sequence an illustration of the workings of a spiritual order which includes and transcends the natural. More perhaps than any other faithful observer of men and things as they are, He finds one principle of order everywhere, which enables the lower levels of experience to illuminate the higher. The woman naturally rejoices over the recovery of her coin, the shepherd over that of his sheep ; and forthwith we are invited by their help to conceive or imagine the joy of a heavenly owner of property over a soul that had been lost, or had strayed, from the fellowship of its home. The normal methods of trade and commerce and employment of labour, the natural kindliness of parents to their children, the effectiveness of importunate request, the extravagant sacrifice of a connoisseur for the possession of a particularly valuable specimen, the phenomena of growth in plants,— all these, pictured just as they are found to occur in the everyday world, are displayed for us as illustrating in some point the operations of deeper spiritual laws, in which is found the ultimate significance and value of human living. We misinterpret the whole nature of such parables, if we suppose that Christ justifies directly any sequence of events which He thus makes into material for the teaching of spiritual truths. His pictures are drawn from life, from what happens, not necessarily from what ought to happen. And yet throughout there is present the sense of an order, in principle one and good, to which

---

[1] Several of our Lord's utterances which are commonly included among the parables (The Sheep and the Goats, Dives and Lazarus and The Rich Fool) do not answer to this description at all. It would promote a clearer understanding of our Lord's teaching if these exceptional parables were called, not parables at all, but *myths.*

even an unrighteous judge and a dishonest steward may
bear unwilling and unconscious witness. And sometimes
some law of that order is expressed in a brief and pithy
sentence, of which experience is constantly providing
fresh illustrations. " To him that hath shall be given ".
" Seek and ye shall find ". " With what measure ye mete,
it shall be measured to you again ". It is in the long run
profitable, not merely quixotic, to spend oneself for the
Kingdom of heaven, and to rely trustfully upon the power
of its King. Every effort after goodness is supremely
worth while ; none fails of its reward. Thus the moral
adventurousness of Jesus, on which we have already
dwelt, is not incompatible with the profound insight of
His reason into the unshakable order of the universe.

There is, again, another angle from which the rationalism of Jesus Christ may be viewed. So far at least as
the evidence of the Synoptic record is to be accepted, He
consistently refrains from employing any personal claim
to divine or even Messianic authority in order to enforce
the truth of His teaching. Even in the emphatic " But
I say unto you " of the Sermon on the Mount no such
claim is explicitly made the ground of the truth of what
He says. He does not ask His hearers to believe what He
says because it is He that says it, nor to follow Him
because it is He that calls. He prefers that His disciples
should gradually come to recognise His Messiahship for
themselves by following Him, and of any explicit claim to
be more than Messiah there is little direct evidence at all.
Even such a hint as " Behold, a greater than Solomon is
here " conveys a less directly personal reference in the
Greek than in the English. Literally rendered, the words
would appear as " There is something greater than Solomon here ", and the vagueness of the neuter is no mere
accident ; it is the character of the new kingdom rather

than the personal claim of its king, that is mainly in point.

The importance of this negative fact, emphasised by historical criticism, has often proved a stumbling-block to orthodoxy ; and no doubt the fullest reply to those who urge it against the doctrine of the Incarnation is to point out that the whole significance of the Lord's life only emerged gradually through the Resurrection and the experience which followed Pentecost. All the same, even when we consider the earthly life of Jesus by itself, it may be doubted whether His silence concerning Himself and His personal authority is evidence of such a limitation of His human consciousness as is frequently postulated. It may be that so sure was His faith in rationality and so deep the insight of His reason, that He deliberately preferred to wait for men to see the truth by the light of their own reason, rather than to force it upon them prematurely by inducing in them the uncritical acceptance of anything He might choose to say. He may have known that the deepest truth is not truth at all unless it is born through the long travail of the minds which in the end come to recognise it as their own, and that He could never be the Son of God to men, unless their whole experience of Him and of the world drove them to fashion that title for Him of themselves. Surely the more we study the words and acts of Jesus, the more does such an explanation of His reticence commend itself to the understanding. It is implicit in His proverbial sayings, " *Seek* and ye shall find ", " *To him that hath* shall be given ". It is profoundly consonant with His manifest anger, when men refused to use their own reasoning powers in spiritual things. " Ye hypocrites, ye can discern the face of the sky, but can ye not discern the signs of this time ? " " Why do ye not even of yourselves judge that

which is right ? " And, as we should expect, the motive
which we have suggested for Christ's reticence is revealed
most clearly of all, whenever He is directly challenged
to say who or what He claims to be. " Go and tell John
the things which ye do hear and see "—and let him judge
for himself. " The baptism of John, was it from heaven
or from men ? "—which is as much as to say, " You are
perfectly able to recognise a good and God-sent man
when you see him ; and if you refuse to do so, I can
explain nothing." What an amazing faith in human
reason, as well as insight into human failings, lurks behind
such severity ! So once more, from a fresh point of view,
Christ's willingness to take risks, to leave the deepest
truths to man's own fallible and often self-deluded judgment, is seen to be one with His absolute assurance of
the ultimately rational order, even now present in man's
mind and discernible by it. Christ believes in man
more than man has ever believed either in himself or in
Christ. Is there not, precisely in the absence of the claim
to divine authority, the surest hint of the presence of the
divine reason ?

But was Christ wrong ? It may be plausibly said that
He was. After all, did not human nature then, and does
it not still, belie His faith in it ? Did not men reject
the message of the kingdom, and put the messenger to
death ? Yes, and yet—and here perhaps is the most
astonishing fact in the Synoptic record—Christ's assurance
of the rational order controlling all things was in nowise
daunted by the clear foresight of His own apparently
ignominious failure. Rather that foresight, whether
present to His mind from the beginning, or gradually
borne in upon it during the course of His ministry,
only enabled Him to apprehend and to proclaim more
definitely the most mysterious law whereby the highest

good of heaven is realised, the law of the triumph of love through sacrifice. From the time that His disciples hailed Him as Messiah, He began to teach them that the Son of Man *must* suffer to the uttermost and die, and that all true men must be ready to take up the cross themselves in order to follow Him. Men to-day are still debating whether that faith, in which Jesus went to Jerusalem and Calvary, is to be judged as the infatuation of a fanatic or as the deepest insight into the nature of the real which man has ever attained. In this debate it seems that right must rest on one side or the other, and, if it rest on the Christian side, further questioning over the justification for proclaiming Jesus Christ as divine seems to lack reality. The conviction grows that none could so interpret the inmost mysteries of experience, save He who is everywhere at home in the universe, because He is Himself the Eternal Son.

Along the line of such considerations we are able to determine what we mean by affirming that the divine reason itself is incarnate in Jesus Christ. The divinest knowledge, after all, is not the conscious apprehension of an infinite number of facts, but insight into the essential order of reality. And, if the Christian theory of the universe be true at all, this is precisely the knowledge which Jesus Christ displays, both by word and action, in a measure altogether unique. The knowledge proves its divinity not in the multitude of facts which it apprehends, but in the capacity to see, in and through whatever facts are present to it, the order and plan of all. Doubtless in man the knowledge which belongs to reason fulfils itself through the activity of the intellect, the knowledge of order grows through the submissive learning of facts ; and Christ Himself was ever learning the rationality of things in the sternest school of intellectual sincerity.

And yet in Him the reason, which was so humanly educated, appears as divine in what it made of that education. And it is possible that the very clarity with which He saw the universal plan and order of the world, produced those sayings of His which the modern mind finds most difficult to reconcile with mere truth of fact.[1] Certainly His whole method of expression was pictorial, not abstract, and a pedantically literal interpretation will always seem to convict Him of error. And yet, through all the language of parable and paradox and myth, there shines the light of a truth which is ever found to be more fully universal, the more widely it is applied. The intellectual knowledge of the twentieth century is immeasurably different from that of the first ; and yet the difference may only vindicate the universality of the reason which is Christ's.

[1] cf. Baron von Hügel, *Essays and Addresses in the Philosophy of Religion*, pp. 130–143, and E. G. Selwyn, *The Approach to Christianity*, pp. 131–137.

CHAPTER V

CHRIST'S LIFE AS A SACRAMENT

(2) THE ATONEMENT

IF the positive conclusions of our last chapter are accepted, it is more than ever apparent that our account of our Lord's life as the supreme sacrament must remain seriously incomplete, so long as we consider it only as the expressive symbol of God's own nature or of His purpose for the world. Granted that in Christ we see the goodness which the world has been created to fulfil, we are still left wondering by what means the world as we know it is to attain that end. Granted that in Christ we gain some apprehension of what God is, we have still to inquire what He does, how He is working in practice towards the achievement of the revealed aim, and how we may be assured of its ultimate realisation.

To ask such questions brings us once more face to face with the fact that when God, as we believe, revealed Himself to save the world, men rejected Him with scorn, and still continue to reject. And that rejection does not look like a mere isolated accident in the scheme of things : it is all of a piece with a certain fundamental negation of goodness, which in some sense belongs to the whole texture of life in space and time. Whether we examine the life of the sub-human creation or of man himself, either before or after the coming of Christ, there appears still an unescapable element of opaqueness to God's light, or resistance to His will. Indeed, from one point of view the coming of Christ has only made this more apparent than before. The tares among the wheat have become more evidently tares ; but they are not uprooted, nor has their growth been even checked.

And here we are forced to recognise a certain negation in Christ's own revelation of goodness. The more we insist that Christ reveals perfection perfectly, and not least perfectly upon the Cross, the more we find that for that very reason He reveals it in unsuccess. And though He came not into the world to condemn it, the world is the more surely condemned because of His coming. The shadows are blackest when the light shines most brightly ; and there is no real or whole perfection after all.

It is precisely this difficulty which the Christian doctrine of the Atonement is designed to meet and to overcome. It bids us look on the life of Christ no longer as the revelation of God's mind, but rather as the instrument of His power, no longer as His expressive word, but rather as His effective act. And, if we will do so steadily, the doctrine of the Atonement assures us that we shall find in the Cross, which is the symbol of defeat, the most potent weapon of victory which heaven could forge. For it is the instrument of good whereby evil itself is made instrumental to goodness. It is the means of real *conversion*.

As soon as we try to follow out this line of thought, it becomes evident that the Christian doctrine of divine omnipotence is bound up with the universality of the Atonement. It is really impossible to treat either apart from the other ; and, before going further, it may be well to establish this identity by some remarks upon the meaning of omnipotence.

Most discussions of omnipotence suffer from the assump-

tion that the main difficulty resides in the omni-, and
not rather in the -potence. Scholastic theologians are
apt to take it for granted that the word naturally
suggests " capacity to do anything and everything ", and
they then proceed to point out that, as predicated of God,
capacity must be limited in two ways, inasmuch as
God cannot do anything which is either (*a*) contrary to
the perfection of His nature, or (*b*) intrinsically impossible, in the sense that it is self-contradictory. Thus it is
held, e.g. that God cannot (*a*) do any evil, or (*b*) create
free spirits which are compelled to do right. It is
evident that, assuming God's perfection, we can include
both kinds of limitation under the second, since for a
perfect being to do evil would be a contradiction in
terms.

But this whole method of statement, when examined,
is seen to be really irrelevant to the problem. For with
our imperfect knowledge we are unable to say, except
within a very narrow range, what is or what is not intrinsically impossible. Many things that seem to involve complete self-contradiction turn out, in the light
of further knowledge, to involve none ; and the converse
process is not less easy to illustrate. How then can we
know that it is not impossible for the love of God to
triumph in the universe ? Thus, it would not be difficult,
by making much of the element of intrinsic impossibility,
to empty the doctrine of omnipotence of all real value,
while keeping within the letter of the definition of it given.
Orthodox theology of course minimises the element of
intrinsic impossibility : but, so far as its own definition
of omnipotence is concerned, there seems to be no reason
why it should.[1]

---

[1] The above criticism seems to hold good against the kind of statement given, e.g. by St. Thomas in *Summa* I. Q. xxv. Art. 3.   Modern

It is really obvious that the traditional solution is so unsatisfactory, because the problem has been misconceived. Outside the abstractions of metaphysics, omnipotence never meant capacity to do anything and everything, but power to achieve a universal purpose in all things. Its practical meaning is to assure us, not that God can do anything that is not impossible, but that certain things are possible for God, and that His purpose of universal love can really be attained. So long as the element of impossibility remains an unknown quantity, it is ludicrous to answer our questionings on this subject by saying that God can do everything even theoretically possible. The whole mistake arises from trying to consider power apart from the thing, or concrete activity, which is powerful. *Mere* power is mere potentiality, and potentiality by itself is just a long word for nothing.

If, on the other hand, the universe is conceived as fulfilling a single purpose of goodness, it is at once evident that the doctrine of omnipotence and the doctrine of a perfect atonement are really saying the same thing, and must stand or fall together. For the world can only fulfil that purpose, if its sin can be taken away, and the evil element in things redeemed, so as to become in its final result, contributory to the goodness of the whole.

scholastics are, of course, more aware of the difficulties. Fr. Joyce, S.J., defines power as belonging to God's will in its externally directed activity, and it follows that omnipotence must involve the complete fulfilment of a divine purpose of goodness in the whole created world. But Fr. Joyce, I gather, would object to the argument which follows in the text, on the ground that it is tainted with "optimism". According to him, orthodoxy does not allow that God created the best world which it was possible for Him to create. Whatever God does is good; but "He is not held to any particular degree of goodness". Hence, although God is omnipotent, and everything in the world must subserve His purpose for it, the total result apparently need only be positively good, not ideal. (See *Principles of Natural Theology*, pp. 412–421 and 577–582).

G

This is exactly what the doctrine of Atonement seeks
to assert ; and, if the assertion be vindicated, the omnipotence of God is vindicated also.

It is when the metaphysical problem is thus viewed,
that we begin to appreciate the meaning of the Cross of
Christ as the effective sacrament of God's power. All
attempts to deal with the problem of evil, which are not
grounded upon the power of the self-sacrifice of love,
inevitably leave the evil unredeemed in the end. They
may pronounce the evil, and the whole " outward "
world into which it enters, to be illusion—which is only
to leave it more evil and more unaccountable than
before, and in any case makes any real sacramentalism
impossible. Or else they may point us forward to some
far future millennium when our remote descendants may
safely forget the noblest element in human life, the
heroism of self-sacrificing endeavour, which, on this
supposition, will have wasted itself in producing a paradise
certainly " unfit for heroes ". And, again, the evil is
unredeemed, if not, in some measure, finally triumphant.

But the gospel of the Cross speaks better things. It
enables us to see very dimly, as in a mirror, how all this
mixed good and evil world of our space and time may by
its passing away be instrumental to fulfilling the goodness
of an eternal world which is already in some partial sense
expressed and embodied within it.

One fundamental principle of the doctrine of the Cross
may perhaps be stated thus. To submit willingly to the
loss of real goods embodied in what is outward, is the
only means to the perfect embodiment of those goods
in the order of eternity. This is certainly one supreme
principle of Christ's life and teaching which receives
varied expression in both. To cling obstinately to outward existence and to existing goods is the sure way to

perish with them and to lose them for ever. On the other
hand, since the goods embodied in the outward are real,
they are not at all to be recklessly thrown away. They
are to be used, spent, laid out as money which is valuable
in the last resort only as a means to obtaining something
which its expenditure brings. The man whose heart is
wholly wrapped up in the goods of existence is like a miser
who mistakes money for something which has intrinsic
worth as an end. And the same principle is supremely
true of human life itself, in so far as it also exists in space
and time. It, too, must not be grasped and clung to ;
it must be willingly laid out, and in the end laid down, for
the sake of some higher, fuller life, that of the Kingdom of
God, in which ultimately the spender of the earthly self
will find both his eternal being and the ultimate values even
of earth included and restored.

Again, the willing surrender and expenditure of existing
goods, which finds supreme expression in the Cross of
Christ, is the very means whereby that which exists as
evil is overcome, and made in the end contributory to
goodness. It is not merely that the goodness displayed
in the self-sacrifice of love wins the hearts of evil men, and
so, in the ordinary sense, converts them. That, if not a
superficial, is at least a very limited and insufficient interpretation of what Christianity means by the Atonement.
It has often been pointed out that the Cross of Christ
has already in human experience done much not only
to convert sinners but also to convert their sins, i.e. to
make even them, as overcome, actually minister to the
goodness of which it is itself the embodiment. After all,
the blackest crimes of ecclesiastical hypocrisy and selfish-
ness, of official cowardice and callousness, of mob-madness
and legalised brutality, now take their place in the story
which makes what is for Christians the holiest and most

blessed commemoration of all time. Even representations of common dice and instruments of torture have found their way into Christian sanctuaries; and, confronted by such paradoxes, the mind begins dimly to divine the method of a power which can really take away the sins of the world.

Now, philosophically considered, what the Christian calls redemption is just the process by which the relation of instrumentality towards goodness is universalised; and what the Christian calls atonement is that process completed whether in the whole or in part. Wherever, and in so far as, any evil has been overcome and made, in result, instrumental to good, the evil has been redeemed and atonement made. And, when it is asserted that the Atonement wrought by the Cross of Christ is universal and all-sufficient, we desire to understand that the Crucified Saviour is in space and time the one perfect sacrament of the power by which in the end, or in the whole, all evil is redeemed, and the rational perfection of the universe vindicated and fulfilled.[1]

It follows then that the life and death of Christ, thus considered as the instrument of God's power, are again seen as unique among all the events of time; but again they sum up in themselves and interpret the ultimate significance and value of the temporal process as a whole,

---

[1] Fr. Joyce, S.J. (*op. cit.* pp. 604–606), following St. Thomas Aquinas (*De Verit.* Q. v. Art. 7), argues that when any soul is finally lost, it becomes purely instrumental to the good of others, a means to a good end, instead of being an end in itself. "Its fate," he says, "serves as a warning to those whose probation is not yet over. And the stern sanctions of the divine laws to which it is subject reveal to the just certain attributes of God—the rigour of His justice and His indignation against wrong—which otherwise could not have found manifestation in the created order." But I cannot see that such dialectics dispose of the plain truth that, if any soul finally reject God's love, that love has so far *failed* of its aim, and therefore has not made the soul perfectly instrumental to itself.

and also are the visible embodiment of the power by which that process is directed to its end. And we shall confirm and interpret our faith in the Cross of Christ as the sacrament of God's effective operation, if we can illustrate how the essential principle of the Cross penetrates everywhere the life of the temporal world as that which lifts existence on to higher levels, until man finds himself in presence of the truth that *every* outward good must be given up and pass away in the end, if the one pearl of great price is to be possessed. We shall verify our belief that we have dimly divined the principle which explains the temporal world as a whole in relation to eternity, if we are able to find that same principle at work in the stages by which the highest values have been reached in the temporal world itself.

(1) Doubtless it would be an exaggeration to say that we can trace the operation of the principle of the Cross itself in the course of pre-human evolution ; yet even there may be found something strikingly analogous to it. That evolution is a history of pain and struggle, a history of increasing pain, as life rises in the scale. To many that fact has been a potent argument against the goodness of the ultimate power determining the creation. And yet it is at least a clear and noteworthy lesson of nature that elaboration of protective armament has never achieved lasting success. Sensitive and adaptable creatures have always on the whole advanced their species and won control at the expense of those who hedged themselves about with cumbrous safeguards so that they could not feel. The highest and in the end the most biologically successful animals are the most easily hurt. The moral of evolution is written plain : "Take risks, launch out, expose yourself, be ready to suffer for a forward step. Do not cling to what you have, or seek to dig yourself

in where you are. That is the way to stagnate, if not to perish and lose all." This is the law of life which has in the end produced man, whose suffering and sorrow are certainly greater than that of any other of stern nature's offspring. And yet, when we reflect, we can hardly say that we would have it otherwise. It was not the noblest or the profoundest of philosophers who expressed the longing to conspire with fate that he might grasp this sorry scheme of things entire and shatter it to bits. For we feel more deeply than any abstract argument can express that the goods, evolved from an apparently relentless struggle and held on such precarious tenure, are somehow an atonement for all ; they have begun to convert struggle and mortality themselves into instruments of goodness. We cannot watch a mother-bird risking her life to protect her nest from a marauder, without feeling that her instinct is somehow a redemption of that other predatory instinct which called it forth, and without reflecting further that after all one touch of nature makes her behaviour akin to some of the noblest deeds of human heroism. The instincts which bear fruit in human self-sacrifice have their roots deep in that same nature which in moods of superficial cynicism we picture as " red in tooth and claw ".

(2) But, though even on the lowest levels of evolution we may find hints and suggestions of the principle of redemption and atonement fulfilled in the Cross, we shall naturally look to human experience for our main illustrations of its working. And the more deeply we consider that experience, the more universal appears the law that the highest values are never reached but by the surrender and loss of some already existent good which may appear to be itself a goal, but turns out in the end to be but a blind alley for those who have not the courage to treat it

as a thoroughfare. This law indeed finds applications in every aspect and mode of human activity.

(*a*) The most obvious of these applications is found in the life of feeling, in the antithesis between pleasure and true happiness. Pleasure at first may appear as an end to be sought for its own sake. But the world obdurately refuses to grant us the complete and enduring pleasure we demand. The result for the pleasure-seeker is misery, unless he willingly renounces it and fixes his affections on some higher aim. As he does so, he begins to appreciate the nature of a happiness which atones for the loss of pleasure, because it has converted both the pleasure and the loss of it into the instruments of a greater good. It is indeed impossible to regard even happiness as an absolute value in itself, for at its highest it is only the result in feeling of the realisation of some other good. But true happiness may be treated as an inseparable accompaniment of the realisation of the highest ends, and it is achieved only through the renunciation of its own lower forms.

(*b*) Or, again, consider the achievement of beauty in human art. The lower achievements of art are rightly called pretty or delightful ; and these represent the good craftsmanship of artists who have attended only to those aspects of the world which appear to be beautiful at first sight. They see or hear only what pleases ; they record it skilfully, and they have their reward. But their greater brethren launch out on a more arduous quest. They turn away from the obviously beautiful ; they face and contemplate the things which hurt and jar and clash, and they suffer for it. They produce works which the undiscerning find repellent, and even the discerning painful ; yet somehow those works which incorporate so much of what is ugly and terrible, have nevertheless incorporated the ugliness and terror into a whole of beauty, from which those who have once seen it can never turn back again to prettiness. Because the artist has suffered and renounced, he has achieved a redemption and an atonement ; and to redeem the evil even imperfectly is a worthier thing than to rest in what first appears as good. No understanding student can fail to admit that Shakspere's King Lear has atoned for much cruelty and meanness in human nature. And why ? Because here the dramatist has suffered for and with the evil which he records ; the iron has entered into his soul, and, in entering, has somehow strengthened and set it free. And for us human life appears a nobler thing, because he has made us feel the pathos of its pettiness. The difference between the true realism in art, which redeems, and the false realism, which only accentuates the evil, lies precisely in this, that the true realist has suffered intensely for his vision, and the false has not. The artist who delights to shock our sensibilities has his reward as fully as he who is content merely to charm them. But just as the true Saviour came not to call the righteous but sinners, so the true artist comes not to record the beautiful but to convert ugly things into the service of beauty ; and the method of all redemption is one.

(c) The life of the intellect must also form part of the atoning process by which the eternal order of goodness is finally vindicated and established, and it too requires very real sacrifices. The mind is often called upon here to make the extremely difficult surrender of that kind of knowledge which may be named appreciative. It must suspend all judgments of value, it must refrain from taking sides with the prima facie good against the prima facie evil, in order that it may know some realm of facts or events simply as they exist or have happened. The intellect itself perhaps does not judge the value of what it comes to know. But the appreciative faculties of the mind, accepting the decisions of the intellect concerning what exists and the order of outward existence, often find them grievously difficult to reconcile with what they themselves apprehend of the good in existence and its ultimate meaning in the universe. It is this conflict which provokes such cries of despair as that uttered with noble eloquence in Mr. Bertrand Russell's famous essay *The Free Man's Worship*. Yet time after time the loyal recognition of apparently disastrous fact has in the end but purified and strengthened the confidence that the ultimate order is rational and good. Few would deny that, at least in the best minds of the age, religious faith itself has gained very greatly both from the discovery of evolution and from the historical criticism of documents, which religious men met at first with horrified condemnation. We now see that it was their faith itself, quite as much as their sense of history and science, which was at fault when they hurled their anathemas. The conflict between science and religion continues, and tension, at least, there must always be. But whenever faith has refused either to reject the fresh discoveries of science, or to prostrate itself in hasty panic at their feet, but has steadily sought to learn from them and to strengthen and test its own equipment by their help, the result has been a real atonement of fuller understanding. The justification of modernism in the Church is precisely the fact, not that the minds of modernists are habited in the latest fashions of the philosophic and scientific world, but that, where intellectual matters are concerned, they seem to grasp more firmly the essential meaning of that faith in the Atonement, which it is the pride of orthodoxy to keep pure and undefiled.

(*d*) The moral life, considered in itself, also displays a similar law of progress through the surrender of lower values for the sake of higher. What prima facie appears to be morally good or right is " distributive " justice, viz. the apportionment of rewards and punishments according to some more or less arbitrary scale of moral desert. But further experience soon shows that the existing world is only in very small measure ordered according to any justice of this type. The effect of this discovery is sometimes an embittered sense of grievance, sometimes a theory, at best unverifiable, of compensations in another world which shall restore the balance. But the higher and more courageous conscience of mankind is willing to let the ideal of distributive justice go, because it discerns a nobler ideal in the fellowship of love, and perceives that such fellowship can only be consummated through the service which willingly surrenders external reward—a service which in a world of distributive justice would be impossible. Thus both the first ideal of distributive justice and its rejection are made contributory to the self-sacrifice which both embodies a higher ideal and is a means towards its realisation. In this more strictly moral sphere we are evidently but interpreting the Christian doctrine of Atonement as it has been already very generally understood. It is by moral activity at its highest, pre-eminently as seen in Christ Himself, that we are enabled to guess how even the moral conflict between good and evil can itself be brought to an end, and the evil be made to contribute to the victory of the good, precisely through the apparent defeat which good sustains at the hands of evil. But here we are more especially concerned to emphasise the fact that the very conditions on which such atonement is possible involve the surrender of what appears at first as a moral ideal, namely, distributive justice ; and the existing world has to become still more " unjust " than it was before, if the atoning sacrifice is to be complete. Whatever may be truly said concerning the moral defect of some " orthodox " theories of the Atonement, it is inevitable that the central doctrine itself should be attacked as immoral by those who recognise no moral value above " fairness ".

(e) A final and striking illustration of the law, that human life only rises to its highest by willing surrender of the goods it has and even of the goodness of its own exitence, may be drawn from facts emphasised in recent years by therapeutic psychology. Many ills of mind and body, we are told, spring from the vain attempts of the personality to stand still and protect itself at a certain level of development, from a refusal to pass out of a stage of life known and loved into another stage unknown and vaguely terrible. The child may be reluctant to become the adolescent, the adolescent dreads to become the man, the man struggles not to be middle-aged, or not to be old—and all sorts of upsets and break-downs in the psycho-physical organism are the result. Here we have what seems to be indeed a characteristic disease of modern life. A civilisation which knows itself to be middle-aged at least, and dreads its own decay, idolises the so-called spirit of eternal youth ; and the image of Peter Pan, in truth the offspring of our panic, is set up as the fit symbol of a decadent worship. But Peter Pan, the boy who would not grow up, represents precisely for that reason only a morbid and self-centred boyhood. To have the true and normal spirit of the child is to look eagerly for the time when childish things shall have been put away. Thus the modern world, with all its reverence for youth, only succeeds in setting in its shrine the spirit

of middle age in a youthful body ; but the rock on which
the Christian Church was founded is another Peter,
in whom the undaunted spirit of real youthfulness spent
freely, and finally surrendered, a body already old, that
Peter whose last adventure was to stretch out his hands
that another might gird him and carry him into the unknown. Certainly it is true of the individual life that to try
to rest permanently in the good of any stage already reached
brings disaster ; but willingly to surrender that good
and pass on in the knowledge of what it has taught, is
not wholly to lose it, but to include its results, at least in
part, in the different values of the stage which succeeds.
Here again, there is atonement through loss. And so of
the last stage of earthly existence a poet, who had a full
measure of the youthfulness which may indeed be eternal,
has written memorably :

> I shall thereupon
> Take rest, ere I be gone
> Once more on my adventure brave and new :
> Fearless and unperplexed,
> When I wage battle next,
> What weapons to select, what armour to indue.

There will always be some critics who find Browning
incurably childish.

The principle of redemption and atonement through
loss, the working of which we have traced in so many
different contexts, reaches its full embodiment in the
life and death of Jesus. Just as the sacramental meaning
of the Incarnation is to present Christ's life as the full
expression of the divine goodness in the world of space
and time ; so the Atonement on the Cross concentrates
at a point the instrumental operation of the divine power
whereby alone all things can be made to contribute to the
final good. Its effectiveness is, potentially at least,

unlimited and all-inclusive, just because its method is one which turns very loss into gain and very defeat into victory. It is impossible to assign limits to a power which can derive its very means of expansion from that which checks it.

And again we now see more clearly why it is that the Incarnation as the sacrament of God's self-expression, when considered by itself, must be imperfect, and requires for its own completion the Atonement, which is the sacrament of God's power in act. In the mixed world of space and time the most perfect outward embodiment of the divine goodness is necessarily fugitive and transitory. And we can see why this must be so, why the Son of Man must suffer and be put to death. It is because the Cross in completing the revelation of the divine love removes that perfect revelation from earth, and, in removing it from earth, makes its earthly failure the means whereby the evil of earth is redeemed and the eternal atonement brought to pass. Perhaps the most deeply Christian hope of our souls is that in heaven we may be able to say of all the evil in the world what we have already begun to say about the crimes of those who were responsible for our Lord's death, namely, that, evil as they are, we could not now will them to have been otherwise, since even they have been made to bear their part in the triumph of God.

Finally, we notice that the principle of atonement through the Cross, as we have been interpreting it, involves and includes in itself the reality of resurrection. Resurrection stands for the law of gain through loss, of realisation through sacrifice, in its application to life itself. And the resurrection and ascension of Jesus Christ are profoundly sacramental, in that they form both the representative case of the operation of that divine law, and also the means by which it works effectively for the redemption and salvation of the world.

Perhaps our modern theology and philosophy have hardly yet perceived either the width of the gulf which separates a belief in resurrection from a belief in mere immortality, or by what providential guidance the Church was enabled from the first to stand firmly on the side of resurrection. The inherent difference between the two doctrines seems to be this. Resurrection as such implies restoration of life after death and possibly through death : immortality as such implies persistence of life untouched by death.

At the beginning of the Christian era both types of belief had for some time existed side by side in the ancient world, and were apparently quite distinct from one another. Apart from pagan nature-myths of a dying and rising God, where the resurrection was conceived in a most vague and shadowy manner, the resurrection-belief, in so far as it had religious importance at all, was almost wholly confined to Judaism. At the last day, in the great theophany which was to mark the end of the age, the righteous and, according to some, the wicked also were to rise again with their bodies from the tomb, to receive the reward of their righteousness or of their sin. Quite different from such ideas were the doctrines of the immortality of the soul, which were current in the Gentile world and had also influenced the later Wisdom-literature of the Jews. According to these doctrines a certain element in the human personality, namely, the spiritual or, as some said, the divine part of it, would survive the death of the body, and itself not partake of death, but rather be set free for the fuller realisation of its own proper life by casting off the gross material, out of which both the body itself was fashioned, and bodily passions and appetites arose. Compared with the extravagant fantasies of Jewish apocalypse, this seems to be a much more refined, philosophic and spiritual type of belief ; and at first sight it is strange that the whole Christian hope of life beyond the grave should have been raised and developed upon the Jewish, rather than upon the Gentile, foundation. What is the reason ? Is it just that the Church was unable to shake off the encumbrance of primitive materialism with which its Jewish ancestry had burdened it ? Is it that a natural but unfortunate mistake which the apostles made concerning the mode of their Lord's resurrection had seemed to invest the cruder hopes of Judaism with a fresh authority from God ? Or is it, after all, that the belief in resurrection crude and primitive as it was, contained the germ and the potency of a deeper and fuller truth than any to which belief in mere immortality could lead ?

Of course, so long as resurrection is taken to mean simply the restoration of life at some indefinite point *after* death by an arbitrary fiat of God, it remains primitive and fantastic, on a lower level altogether than the nobler doctrines of the immortality of the soul. But the moment we give it the fuller meaning of life *through* death, we begin to see in it possibilities of which no doctrine of mere immortality is capable. Doctrines of immortality are strictly negative in regard to death. Their aim is to prove that the personality, or at least some element within it, does not die. They are therefore constrained either to argue that death is no more than a delusive appearance, or else to divide man's psycho-physical organism very rigidly into two parts, body and soul, the one destined to perish, the other immune from death. The advance of human knowledge has proved unfavourable to both expedients. The notion that death is an illusion may be safely left to Christian Science. And, as to the second alternative, it is not easy to deny that "scientific knowledge of the bodily basis of consciousness is greatly increasing for us the difficulty of accepting survival as a fact ".[1] In truth, death is universal in nature ; everything that is living seems also, for that very reason, to be dying. Life and death almost imply each other. Everything in ourselves which we would claim to be immortal turns out on examination to be wholly bound up with mortality ; and no philosophy or faith, which seeks to escape this fact or find exceptions to this law, can any longer prove convincing to the candid mind.

And it is exactly in these circumstances of modern thought that the old gospel of the resurrection, centred in the sacrament of Christ's person, may be enabled to show its strength. It faces all the facts and puts in no claim for exemptions. It fully acknowledges that all that lives on earth must die. But it also inspires the hope that, when all the values of earth, even to life itself, have been willingly surrendered, the very completeness and reality of that surrender may turn out to be the means of a triumph which is more than restoration.

Earlier in this chapter we were dwelling on the thought that the spiritual progress of man is a history of repeated failures, losses and disappointments issuing in the birth of nobler hopes and faiths which are the earnest of better victories to come. We saw that the highest happiness is achieved only by those who have found out that their first claims to pleasure are such as the world will not suffer to be met. True knowledge of reality is gained only by those who have learned in the stern school of experience that facts will not suffer them to believe what they like. The victory over moral evil, the victory which is the

[1] R. F. A. Hoernlé, *Matter, Life, Mind and God*, p. 205.

highest form of moral good, is won only through the self-sacrifice which has ceased to demand the distributive justice of reward and punishment. Even art derives its greatest beauty from loyal observation of the elements of ugliness which the world presents. The greatest achievements of literature are tragedies, wherein goodness is defeated or defeats itself, and yet by that very defeat seems somehow to be crowned afresh. And so, finally, if a gospel of resurrection is preached, asserting that the highest life is attained only through the negation of life in death, we feel that its message is deeply in accord with the mysterious contradictions, and still more mysterious rationality, of our universe. If I am required to believe that some portion of my present being will go on existing and preserve its consciousness after my body has decayed, then my imagination is distressed and my mind recoils.[1] But if I am led to consider how again and again it is true that the heights of personal life are only scaled through humiliation, the best only realised through the defeat or exhaustion or surrender of the good, and if I am asked what I should infer from this as to the effect and meaning of the law which decrees the giving up of life itself—then indeed I think I see a glimmer of light upon the path ahead. What if all the goodness of this world of our experience, a goodness achieved with such infinite labour, and still so inexplicably mingled with intolerable wrong and bitter disappointment, were a treasure provided by God for sacrifice, so that through the sacrifice it should be recovered pure and glorified and whole ?

And here we touch the very heart of the Christian gospel. According to the oldest tradition, what we may describe as the general law of resurrection formed one main topic

---

[1] See Prof. C. C. J. Webb's remarks on this subject in *Divine Personality and Human Life*, pp 255 *sqq.*

H

of our Lord's teaching, especially towards the end of His life. The lessons of giving or spending all to have all, losing to gain, dying to live were the constant themes of parable and discourse. The idea that the life wholly given or lost is the life wholly kept or restored is in strong contrast with both contemporary and subsequent beliefs in the immortality of the soul. And, almost instinctively, we tend to interpret our Lord's words on this subject as though He had said that he who gives or loses his bodily life shall save or keep his immortal soul. Yet this represents neither His words nor His meaning. To Him there was no immortal part in human nature ; there was only the *psyche* (a word strictly untranslatable into modern English), which, freely and wholly spent up to death, is by that very means more than fully restored.

Thus the fact of the Lord's resurrection became to Christian faith the assurance that He had in His own person perfectly fulfilled and proved the law of life through death which He had preached. His death and resurrection meant something much more than the liberation of His spiritual self from an outworn vesture of flesh and blood. Throughout life His whole manhood, soul and body, had been dedicated and surrendered to the service of God's kingdom. The surrender was fulfilled and completed in agony which terminated on the Cross. And as the surrender had been whole and complete, so also was the restoration and exaltation into glory. Nothing in Him had been, as it were, kept back from death. " My soul," He had said, " is exceeding sorrowful even unto death." And as the death had been more than merely physical, so the risen life was more than merely spiritual. The whole man had died and risen, and risen because He had been content to die.

Nowhere in the New Testament can we escape this idea

of a balance and correlation between complete giving up to death and complete restoration into life. St. Mark and St. Paul both preach with equal clearness the gospel not of a life only but also of a death, a death as completely real as the fulness of the life to which it ministered. Contrast what they believed about the Lord's resurrection with what the author of Wisdom taught about the souls of the righteous. " In the sight of the unwise they seemed to die ; and their departure was taken for misery, and their going from us to be utter destruction ; but they are in peace. For, though they were punished in the sight of men, yet is their hope full of immortality." Such a gospel concerning the immortality of Jesus Christ would certainly have caused no scandal in the Gentile world ; on the contrary it would have been received with much sympathy, not least in philosophic circles. But it is precisely not the gospel of the resurrection found in the New Testament. There the Cross is not less real, not less important for faith, than the rising again of which it is the condition. That which had been humiliated, spat upon, scourged, crucified by men, had therefore been exalted to God's right hand. This was the main folly and scandal of the Christian preaching. But it was also the source of its characteristic power. For it was the guarantee that the Lord of the Christians had not simply withdrawn, as He was before, into the distant heaven from which He had made a brief excursion earthwards, but that He was eternally characterised by the very marks of those sufferings whereby he had opened a way to God's throne for the humblest slave who was willing to suffer with Him.

Thus the law of atonement is completed in the law of resurrection, and Christ's life in its whole action and operation is seen as the perfect sacrament of both. Through it Christians possess as their eternal hope not a gospel of

immortality only, but of life through death, of winning
through spending even life itself. They are to think of
" heaven " in terms not so much of what happens or goes
on *after* death, as of what is achieved through the completed service which death seals. " Behold my hands and
my feet, that it is I myself." Because Christ's manhood
is sacramental, every son of man is completely himself as
soon as his own surrender of himself has been fully made.
And by the self-denying service, in which he realises himself, he makes also his infinitesimal contribution to that
atoning work of Christ by which in the end the world of
space and time, having been made altogether instrumental
to God's purpose, itself enters the eternal whole in which
His goodness is expressed. For that which has been
redeemed by the atonement of the Cross becomes the body
in which Christ Himself is mystically incarnate, and is
thus taken up into that communion of the Trinity which
is the very being of God.

CHAPTER VI

CHRISTIAN SACRAMENTS : THEIR NATURE AND OPERATION

CATHOLICS to-day often speak of the Eucharist as an extension of the Incarnation, and the Schoolmen taught that the sacraments derived their efficacy from the Passion of Christ. The foregoing discussion will have made it evident that we should think it legitimate to speak of all Christian sacraments as extensions both of the Incarnation and of the Atonement. All divine goodness, as it comes into relation with our world, must be conceived either as expressed or as actively operative in it. All this divine self-expression is summed up in the Incarnation, and all this divine operation in the Atonement ; and the same divine Person, Who was perfectly expressed and omnipotently operative at Nazareth and on Calvary, is " in divers manners and portions " expressed and operative also wherever He is and acts. It seems therefore that, in the last resort, wherever any reality of the spatio-temporal world stands in a positive relation to the goodness of God, we have a sacrament of some kind, which may be called an extension of the Incarnation or of the Atonement.

A grave objection felt by the orthodox against such a statement arises from the suspicion that it implicitly destroys the principle of distinction between immanence and incarnation. Theologians would tell us that the Godhead is incarnate in Jesus Christ alone ; in all other good realities of space and time it is immanent, but not incarnate. And many perhaps would on that ground tend to restrict the phrase " extension of the Incarnation " to its application in reference to the Eucharist, where they would acknowledge that Christ is again, not immanent only, but actually embodied. We have therefore to consider carefully the force we are to attach to our terms.

We would suggest that the phrase " the Incarnation of God the Son or the Logos " is properly applicable to two distinct realities: (1) the created manhood, spiritual, mental and bodily, of Jesus ; and (2) the created universe, considered as fulfilled whole and complete, when God's purpose has been perfectly achieved therein. The term incarnation is to be applied to both, because each is in its kind a perfect and inseparably intimate expression of God's nature in created being, and, as we have seen, the affirmation that Jesus Christ is the Incarnate Son is based upon the acknowledgment that His life uniquely represents to us the divine purpose operative in the whole world of our experience.

Doubtless, the orthodox critic will not feel that in saying this we have gone any of the way towards meeting his objection. He will reply that after all we are only suggesting that good men and good things express imperfectly what is perfectly expressed both in the life of Jesus and in the fulfilled communion of saints which is Christ's mystical body : we thus make the difference between immanence and incarnation a difference of degree.

But we have something more to add. We do not separate incarnating expression from atoning act. And the thought of the life and death of Jesus as God's own supreme act in history adds something beyond mere expression to the very nature of the Incarnation itself. If it be really God the Son or the Logos Who acts in all the human life of Jesus, then the orthodox doctrine is justified that His very self, the active and initiating principle of His being, is divine, and that here therefore in concrete and ontological reality is God. And, when we go on to say, as we must, that God also acts in all human lives, in so far as they obey His will, yet we may legitimately draw a distinction between the divine action in Jesus Christ and the divine action in other men, a distinction which is roughly analogous to that between a man's action through his own body and his action through some artificially constructed instrument. Just as man's action through an artificial instrument is rightly described as an extension of his own proper activity through his body, so the divine action throughout the spatio-temporal world is, perhaps in an infinite variety of degrees, an extension of the proper activity of God the Logos in Jesus Christ. And, just as man's action through artificial instruments presupposes and is derived from his activity in his own body, so everywhere God's action in His world either implies or adumbrates or issues from His activity properly embodied in the life of Jesus.[1]

Yet we may continue to apply the term incarnation also to the created universe as a fulfilled whole. For we have already suggested that in this created world of our present experience the divine activity has always atonement, in

[1] After writing the above passage, I became acquainted with the comparison in St. Thomas : " *Sacramentum operatur ad gratiam causandam per modum instrumenti. Est autem duplex instrumentum : unum quidem separatum, ut baculus; aliud autem conjunctum, ut manus. Per instrumentum autem conjunctum movetur instrumentum separatum, sicut baculus per manum. Principalis autem causa efficiens gratiae est ipse Deus, ad quem comparatur humanitas Christi sicut instrumentum conjunctum; sacramentum autem sicut instrumentum separatum. Et ideo oportet quod virtus salutifera a divinitate Christi per ejus humanitatem in ipsa sacramenta derivetur* " (Summa III, Q. 62, Art. 5). It should be noticed, however, that in St. Thomas the analogy has a different application from that given to it above.

the more literal sense, as its aim and motive. It seeks to uplift and to incorporate into its own very life all that in which or on which it operates. And, when we strain almost desperately at the bonds of our finitude in order to conceive the divine purpose as wholly and finally realised, that which inevitably is presented to our minds is just the fulfilled and complete Atonement which is also the mystical Incarnation, namely, that ultimate universe where God is all in all, and all things in the Person of Christ are also within the eternal communion of the Blessed Trinity. These terms therefore, atonement and incarnation, by which we present to ourselves the final state of the whole creation as fulfilling God's purpose for it, we also apply only to the historic life of Jesus Christ as that by which supremely the end is achieved and in which uniquely it is represented. And, just because that life uniquely repre-sents and effects the final whole, the divine Person, Whose life it is, must also in different manners and degrees be mirrored and operative everywhere in His world, until at last His creation is perfect, that is, altogether the embodiment of Himself.

Thus, as the most general definition of the term sacra-ment we might offer the following : a sacrament is any spatio-temporal reality which by its occupation of space or time expresses to us God's will and purpose and enables us the better to co-operate with them. And all such realities may be covered by the phrase " extension of the Incarnation and the Atonement ", if we are willing sufficiently to stretch and attenuate the meaning of the term " extension ". For in all the good realities of space and time the Divine Logos expresses Himself and is active towards us.

But such a definition is evidently too general to be of much practical service. And a distinguishing feature of those realities which we may more properly call sacramental seems to be this ; that in them the outward consists of one member of a class or one part of a whole, which is severed and differentiated from the other members or parts, in order both to represent the true relation of the whole to God and to be means whereby this relation is more effectively realised.

Judged by this canon, the life of Jesus Christ is seen at once as the perfect sacrament. The manhood of Jesus is severed and differentiated from that of all other men, in order both to represent what all manhood truly is and is meant to be, and also to be the means whereby all manhood may realise its end. But this general mark of sacramental nature applies much more widely, and is instructive in many connexions. Sunday, for instance, may be said to be severed and differentiated from all other days of the week, in order both to represent to us the meaning and purpose of all days, and also to be the means whereby the purpose is fulfilled in all. The Church-building is severed and differentiated from other places with an exactly analogous intention. Again, the Church as an organised society is sacramental, inasmuch as its aim is to represent the ultimate meaning and purpose of all human society and to be the living means whereby all human society is incorporated into the fellowship which it represents.

Sacramental rites, inasmuch as they consist of acts rather than of things or persons, demand a slight variation of the definition, which we shall consider presently. But we may say at once, by anticipation, that Baptism both represents and declares a spiritual birth which belongs to all human beings as God's children, and is also the means whereby that spiritual relationship is made effectively real in the baptized. And the Holy Communion, whatever else it may be, is at least an act in which the Godward meaning and purpose of all life are embodied and by which they are realised in the souls of faithful receivers.

Thus we may say that, as Jesus Christ Himself is the perfect sacrament of created being, so in the light of that one sacrament the Church appears as the sacrament of human society, Baptism as the sacrament of man's spiritual birth to God, Holy Communion as the sacrament of human fellowship in Him, holy days as sacraments of time, and holy places as sacraments of space.

Underlying this conception of the nature of sacraments there is everywhere the same principle of separation for the double purpose both of true representation and of effective inclusion. And this principle gives its most characteristic meaning to the Christian idea of holiness, apart from which Christian sacraments are unintelligible. The Jews, as St. Paul so clearly saw, were separated off from all other nations to be the people of God, in order that they might ultimately draw the whole human race into the circle of their holiness. And as soon as the missionary purpose of their election was fully declared through Christ, the old Israel had to be merged in the new Israel of the Catholic Church. The God of Israel was revealed first as jealous and holy in the negative sense, in order that the claim of His jealousy might ultimately be revealed in Christ as the exacting demand of all-inclusive love, which can only be satisfied by the incorporation of all men and of the whole of every life into the fellowship of His family. Thus in Christian thought holiness always contains within itself a double movement, a movement first of separation away from everything that is " common " or " profane ", a movement secondly of inclusion, whereby the separate-holy goes forth again to draw into itself everything from which its separation has removed it. This duplicity of movement is exactly represented in the difference between the holiness of Jehovah in the Old Testament and the holiness of the Father of Jesus Christ in the New. The presence of the One was sought by withdrawal into the dreadful emptiness of the Holy of Holies. The Other has sent forth His Son, consubstantial with Himself, to be partaker of common flesh and blood for common man's redemption. Yet there are not two Gods in the Bible but one, manifested in two Testaments. And the same double movement of holiness goes on endlessly repeating itself in relation to everything to which in Christian thought the term holy is specially applied. The life of Jesus Himself, as the ministry proceeds towards its climax, manifests an ever increasing tension between the completeness of His spiritual isolation and the perfection of His spiritual sympathy. And we can hardly begin to understand the meaning of such Christian titles as Holy Communion and Holy Catholic Church, until we realise that they involve something like a contradiction in terms. For holiness in its original meaning of mysterious separation is precisely the negation of catholicity and communion—the connexion of " communion " with " common ", of κοινωνία with κοινός, is something more than an etymological accident. And indeed the fact that the Christian ideal of holiness points, as it were, in two opposite directions at once, has been one of the commonest sources of controversy in the Christian Church. Should Christians continue to emphasise the awful " otherness " of God by banishing from their worship all material images of the divine ? Or does the Incarnation justify the sensible representation even of Godhead, and perhaps enable us to acknowledge the presence of spiritual truth even in what seems outwardly to be idolatrous ? Is the holiness of a Christian Church more honoured by the stillness which promotes awe, or by the sounds of foot and voice which tell of common people coming and going unafraid ? Is the Christian Sunday best observed by the rigorous foregoing of week-day occupations, or rather by the freedom which may help to redeem what it allows ? Is the true type of Christian saintliness to be found in ascetic withdrawal from the world, or rather in that life of family cares and business worries which yet seems to sanctify all by seeking in them the service of the Kingdom ? Christians have differed and will continue to differ in their answers to such questions. Yet perhaps the truly Christian mind will be willing to acknowledge that everything which it calls holy is separated and set apart, only in order that it may both represent the whole and in the end effectively include it.

And so we may come at last to consider the exact meaning of the term sacrament when it is restricted to its most ordinary use as signifying a certain type of religious rite or liturgy. We will offer at once the following definition of a Christian sacrament. A sacrament is a ritual act, using a certain form and matter, which both represents some universal relation of human life to God through Christ, and also, in thus representing all life, makes life worthy to be thus represented.

Five of the seven Catholic Sacraments may readily be brought under this rubric. Baptism and Confirmation, which were never separated from each other in primitive thought, together represent a reception into membership of God's family, which in spiritual principle belongs to all human beings as represented in Jesus Christ, but which is made effective in the baptized and confirmed through those sacraments, and through the baptized and confirmed in others also whom they convert. The Sacrament of Holy Order analogously represents and effects a universal priesthood of man toward God, wherein every man through Jesus Christ must offer to God both himself and everything over which his authority extends, and wherein also he has committed to him that ministry of reconciliation towards his fellows which is further represented and effected in the Sacrament of Penance. Finally, Holy Communion represents and effects that universal life of self-offering to God and fellowship with God, which is fully realised in Jesus Christ's own sacramental manhood, and must include all men in so far as through Christ they also are made God's priests and children.

Catholic theology is accustomed to distinguish from all other sacraments Baptism, Confirmation and Holy Order, as those which confer indelible *character* and therefore cannot be received twice. In this doctrine also we can see profound truth from our present point of view. The aim of these three rites, we may say, is to confer on the recipient a sacramental status, in which he stands set apart to express before the world a Godward relationship which belongs inherently to every son of man. Every man has the capacity to enter God's family, to offer to God all that is his, to bring his fellows into God's presence, to forgive them in God's name. Special sacraments confer the inalienable characters of sonship and priesthood specially upon some, because in truth they belong to all, and yet cannot effectively belong to all, unless they are first bestowed on some who are commissioned to extend them to others. For in the end they belong to all, because from the first they belong to One only, the Only Begotten Son of God, the High Priest after the order of Melchizedek. The Christian holiness, which belongs to all, nevertheless spreads outwards from the One, through the few, to the many.

It is then the unvarying characteristic of Christian sacraments both to express a universal truth, and to consist of a holy action whereby this truth is realised, whether or not the action confers also a specially sacramental status upon the person who receives the sacrament. And all sacraments are truly extensions, interpretations, applications, of the life of Jesus Christ in Whom the meaning of all is summed up, and from Whom they derive their effective power. We have now to consider how a clear view of the double aspect of Christian sacraments, as representative and effective, may enable us to correct the main aberrations into which sacramental doctrine and practice have strayed, and to meet the objections of opponents which these aberrations have provoked.

Historically speaking, the most common aberration has been to lose sight of the representation of the universal in every sacrament. And in consequence the most common accusation brought against the sacramental doctrine of the Church is the allegation that its source is magic. Let us see how aberration and accusation are connected. If, in thinking of the sacraments as means whereby God brings certain men into certain relation towards Himself, we forget that those sacraments also represent universal relations of all men toward God, then it is but a short step from this to the further thought that the particular sacrament is the *only* means whereby the particular relation to God can be made real. And when it is supposed that the outward sign of the sacrament is the *only* means whereby a spiritual relation can be realised, it is easy to suppose also that, wherever the outward sign is performed, the spiritual relation accompanies it by a sort of mechanical necessity. Now this binding of the divine action to the performance of a certain ritual is the common characteristic of magic all the world over. Catholic orthodoxy has on the whole repudiated it. It has always insisted on the necessity of spiritual preparation on the part of those who receive the sacraments, if they are to receive really the spiritual grace or virtue and not the outward signs alone. And moreover the great scholastic authorities have been generally followed by orthodox theologians in maintaining the principle that God is not bound by the outward signs of His sacraments,[1] and that therefore it is wrong to deny the reception of divine grace apart from them. Nevertheless, in their anxiety to emphasise the necessity of sacraments as means of grace, Catholic teachers are sometimes inclined to suggest that the grace received by those who do not partake of Christian sacraments is of an inferior order to that enjoyed by the loyal Catholic. In practice it is exceedingly difficult for them duly to balance the stern-ness of the dogma, *nulla salus extra ecclesiam*, with the equally authoritative principle, that those who have not the personal guilt of their separation from the Church will not suffer the eternal penalties thereof. Thus, they may use language which implies that Catholics necessarily enjoy some privilege of divine favour from which all others are necessarily debarred. Hence the exclusion of magical notions by Catholic theology has not in practice been complete.

Surely the most thoroughgoing reply to any charge of magic is not in any way to minimise either the solemnity or the efficacy of sacraments, but rather to insist upon their representative character. As a final safeguard against all magical implications it seems that this doctrine of the sacramental representation of the universal may be found both requisite and unassailable.

Its effect is immediately clear in disposing of the notion that God's grace is in any sense confined to the outward

---

[1] Both St. Thomas and St. Bonaventura assert the principle, *Deus non alligatur sacramentis.*

signs of appointed sacraments. Belief in the historical
Incarnation of Him Who is the light that lighteth every
man, should make it easier, not harder, for us to discern
and gladly to acknowledge the tokens of a divine quality
appearing everywhere in human life. And in the same
way the sacraments in which Christ's presence and action
are re-expressed in His Church should help us to discern
and acknowledge tokens of the same spiritual presence
and action operating also outside the Church's organisation. We need more and more to realise that Christian
breadth of mind is no easy-going tolerance of differences,
but rather a penetrating insight, which, because it knows
the one Saviour, can detect His activity issuing from the
Nazareths as well as from the Bethlehems of the world.

The relevance of the doctrine of representation in
rebutting the charge that the sacraments are thought
to work mechanically is more subtle but no less real. The
critic endeavours to maintain that, when the sacraments
are conceived as channels of grace, the divine grace or
gift is thought to be put into a person by the outward sign
as though the grace were a sort of material or tangible thing.
Now, in one sense our doctrine of representation obliges us
to affirm that a sacrament can put nothing into a person
which was not there before, since it must represent a
relation between the recipient and God which was already
real. In another sense it is no less true that the relation
is realised through the sacrament ; yet it could not be so
realised if it were not present before in germ, though not
in fulness. In other words, if we take the doctrine of
representation seriously, the appropriate figure for indicating the instrumental operation of a sacrament is given
not by the term *insert* but by the term *elicit*.

The gospel of the Incarnation is in part derived from the
fact that Christ's life did not change anything in the actual

substance of human nature, nor add anything thereto, but rather elicited from a manhood shared by all men its fullest possibilities. Again, conversion to the Christian faith is possible only because the soul, still unconverted, yet stands in a certain relation to God which the preaching of the gospel enables it to recognise as already existing. No Christian missionary, Catholic or Protestant, would ever dream of speaking to unconverted people as though he were offering them the free choice of entering into a certain relationship towards God, and merely recommending them to exercise that choice in a particular way. Whatever the precise nature of his appeal, he would be sure to urge that his hearers, according to the truth of the Christian religion, already stood in a certain relation toward God, and were on that account under an obligation to accept the Christian faith and to become members of the Church. In other words he would seek to convert them, not by inviting them to accept a wholly new relationship towards God, but rather by eliciting in them a recognition both of a relationship toward God already existing and of certain obligations arising from that relationship. Similarly, the sacraments do not pour spiritual gifts into the soul from without, as one pours water into a jar—and that because nothing spiritual can be simply put into a man at all ; it must be drawn out of him. Nothing can make a mean man generous, if he has no element of generosity in him already.

We have here touched upon a far-reaching truth, of which Plato gave a philosophical interpretation in his doctrine of ἀνάμνησις, Croce in his principle that there is no impression without expression, and to which many Freudians have supplied a psychological commentary by showing how futile for the training of character must be the mere imposition of rules and duties from without.

I

The philosophers in different ways have been concerned
to show that what we claim to know of the world is never
something imprinted wholly from without upon our minds
as upon a blank tablet which merely receives impressions.
Rather what we know is always something to which the
actively perceiving and knowing mind has already made
a contribution. Real knowledge therefore is never
knowledge merely ; it is always also recognition. Its
object is never something simply imposed ; it is always
in part something elicited. For the mind can always
discern by careful analysis some reflexion of itself, or
some mark of kinship with its own nature, in everything
which it can be said to know. In the same way the
psychologist and the moralist would remind us that the
soul can only be positively affected or infected by those
ideals or standards of goodness to which it makes positive
response, because in them its own natural instincts find
expression and develop into fuller life.

It is perhaps not fanciful to assert that our Lord Himself
had the truth of this same principle in mind when He
uttered His paradox that it is not that which goes into
the man that defiles him. The evil suggestions which are
conveyed from without through the senses are simply
cast out by the mind, as the body casts out the waste
part of that which enters it, unless they meet with some
evil response from the man's soul, unless, that is, his soul
is led to express itself by their means—then alone, and
then only by what is elicited from his own inner being,
is the man defiled. And in the same way, as our Lord
surely hints, the man is sanctified by what comes out of
him, not by what goes in. The divinest goodness can
make no impression on a human soul, unless the soul is
able to express that same goodness in response. Man
could not be stirred even to the extreme of self-abasement

before the holiness of God, if there had not been kindled in him that sense of an affinity to God which enables him to condemn his own wretchedness before the divine glory : and then his worship becomes his own proper expression of the holiness which is its object. It is this truth which Otto's description of the divine as the " wholly other " so unfortunately obscures.

The action of a sacrament therefore must be always such as to elicit from man what he has it in him to be. And because man can only become in fulness of growth that same thing which in germ he already is, the sacraments do their work of eliciting partly by representing to man his ideal relation to God as a universal truth already realised, which he only needs faith to apprehend.

This account of the matter enables us to understand the paradox always inherent in the Church's teaching that repentance and faith are necessary conditions for a worthy and beneficial reception of the sacraments. This teaching, when thought out, is paradoxical, because a soul completely penitent and faithful would have no need of sacraments ; and therefore, if lack of penitence and faith prevents reception of sacramental grace, it becomes difficult to see what good in principle the sacraments can do. Thus to minds dominated by a certain type of logic the Church's doctrine seems constantly to halt between two mutually exclusive opinions, first, that the sacraments are meant for sinners, and, second, that they can only be worthily received by saints. The principle of ἅγια τοῖς ἁγίοις conflicts with the principle that only the sick need medicine. Such logic is of course perverse, because its exact dissection ignores the reality of living growth. The soul can grow only by receiving that goodness to which it is capable of responding ; and the capacity for response is already a token of the presence in it of that goodness which it is to receive. But it does not follow that the reception is unnecessary. Rather the prevenient goodness, which is the soul's capacity for response, derives its main value from the fact that it enables the soul to receive more. Thus in the Gospels the principle, that only what comes out of and expresses a man really character-ises him, is balanced by the principle that it is the beggars in spirit, those ever ready to receive, that go first into the Kingdom. It is only to him who hath already, that treasure is to be given ; but what he must have already is the capacity to receive more : and then the receiving, from another point of view is but the eliciting into fuller development of what he already had. All this is again expressed in the Church's teaching that the grace of sacraments can be truly received only by those whose hearts the prevenient grace of the Spirit has prepared.[1]

And so we may proceed to correct the more character-istically modern aberration of sacramental doctrine which we have hitherto ignored. Extreme reaction from magical tendencies, real or fancied, has led many to subordinate altogether the instrumental value of sacraments to their value as symbols or representations. Their function, it is suggested, is to present vividly to the mind what is already true, and only by so doing do they promote the actual

[1] Hence the essential futility of all those controversies, such as that connected with the name of Mr. G. C. Gorham, which turn upon the questions, what exact amount of spiritual life must already have been received in order that a sacrament may confer any more, and what exact amount of lack can be said to exist still after a sacrament has been received ? It is my hope that the above and following paragraphs, taken in conjunction with what is said elsewhere (see chap. vii.) about the symbolic nature of Baptism, makes it unnecessary to discuss in detail the well-known theory of " charitable presumption " put forward by Dean Goode and Dr. J. B. Mozley during the controversy mentioned, and the more difficult doctrine of " visible donation " advocated by Dr. Dimock, and recently by Dr. A. J. Tait (see the latter's *Nature and Function of the Sacraments,* esp. pp. 58 *sqq.*). For " visible donation " in connexion with the Eucharist, cf. p. 216.

realisation or working out of that truth in the faithful recipients. If the word " only " were omitted we could readily accept such a statement, as far as it goes. But, even so, it seems to limit unduly the representative element in the sacraments. The sacraments not only represent a reality which is already true, but also the process whereby an ideal truth is actualised. In one sense, all men are children of God already. In another sense, no man is really a child of God until he has reached the full stature of his spiritual growth in Christ, or at least until he is thoroughly and finally purged from evil. This growth or purification is brought about by a process of divine action and human response, which response is also, in the last analysis, made possible by divine action. And the sacraments from first to last not only represent the ideal truths, which the process actualises, but also the process itself. Now, in representing this process as a whole, the sacraments are themselves part of it. They are in fact the *holiest* part, that part, namely, which has been specially separated from the rest in order both to represent the meaning of the whole and to be the means whereby the purpose of the whole is accomplished. Thus the saving and gracious activity of God, which in truth permeates all life, is naturally found at its fullest and clearest in the sacraments, just in so far as these are always transcending themselves and spreading their illumination and influence over the life which is beyond them.

To separate the sacraments from the rest of life, so as to suggest that here alone God's grace is to be found, tends to magic. But to evacuate the sacraments so completely of direct and proper efficacy that they become no more than pictorial or dramatic presentations of realities, to which they can add nothing except the presentation, has consequences not much more desirable. It leads either to a barren rationalism, which finds God nowhere because it seeks Him everywhere at once, or else to a narrow mysticism which identifies the reality of God's action with the explicit consciousness of it in the soul. The *via media* seems to lie in insisting that the sacraments are both true parts and yet representative parts of that process whereby the divine activity elicits from human souls the heavenward growth, of which they are capable in virtue of their inherent and unchanging relation to God.

Finally, the line of thought which we have been following may indicate the right approach to the historical problems connected with the institution of the sacraments. Much criticism has been recently directed against the traditional belief, explicitly reaffirmed in our Prayer-Book, that our Lord expressly appointed at least the sacraments of Baptism and the Eucharist. It is now generally admitted that the actual command to baptize, contained in Matthew xxviii. 19, does not belong to the most primitive and authentic record of our Lord's sayings ; and, although the direct evidence for His institution of the Eucharist is much stronger, yet the different accounts of what was said and done at the Last Supper vary considerably from one another, and differences of interpretation are still possible, even when the facts have been agreed upon. On the other hand, our documents seem to warrant the assertion that Baptism, the Laying on of Hands, and the Breaking of the Bread were practised from the earliest times in the Christian community ; and it is a natural inference that these ceremonies had had some authority given them in the precept or example of the Master Himself.

To enter upon any detailed investigation of a strictly historical problem would carry us beyond the scope of

the present volume. Moreover, such comments as must be
made upon the origins of particular sacraments are better
reserved for those chapters in which the particular sacraments are severally discussed. It may, however, be well
to state at once, as a general conclusion from the historical
controversies of the last half-century, that we are no
longer justified in resting the whole, or even the main,
weight of the authority for the doctrine and practice
of any sacrament upon the bare fact that the Bible
attributes a particular form of words to Christ Himself.

Nevertheless, in so saying, we need by no means sever
the doctrine and practice of the sacraments from most
intimate connexion with the historic life and work of
Jesus Christ. That life, as we have striven to show, is
itself the supreme sacrament of the Christian religion ; and
the particular sacraments derive their ultimate authority
from the fact that all down the course of the Church's
history they have been found to be the appropriate means
whereby that life, now exalted into the unseen, has continued to declare its eternal meaning and to effect its
saving work. Just as the full truths of the Incarnation
and the Atonement were not formulated once for all by
the lips of the Incarnate Himself, but gradually emerged
in the process of Christian experience and are still capable
of further explication ; so the doctrine and even the form
and matter of the sacraments, which are truly both
instruments and expressions of Christ's incarnate and
atoning life, need not have been laid down in any precise
terms by Jesus Himself, but may have been evolved, and
still be in process of evolution, as the Church under His
Spirit's guidance has learned and learns to fulfil His
mission upon the earth. And, if Gentile as well as Jewish
thought made its contribution to the clearer statement
of the doctrine of Christ's Person, there can be no reason

why it should not have made its contribution equally to the interpretation of the sacraments.

But, having fully and freely acknowledged all this, the Christian is still entitled to assert that some at least of the Christian sacraments did actually appear before Gentile influence within the Church had had time to make itself seriously felt, and these seem to be derived unquestionably from hints, if not from actual directions, conveyed in the words and acts of Jesus.[1] Above all, that sacrament, which all down the centuries has been found to minister the most intimate union of Christians with their Lord and with one another, is also the sacrament which almost indisputably took its origin from that infinitely solemn and tragic scene in the Upper Room, when Jesus in the same night that He was betrayed took bread. It may well be that the more courageously we rest the authority of that sacrament, not on the events of the Last Supper alone, but on the meaning of Christ's sacrifice of Himself interpreted in the faith of Christendom, the more convincingly probable it will appear that the bread was indeed then broken and the wine poured out with a deeper significance than any which even orthodoxy itself has so far succeeded in expressing.

NOTE TO CHAPTER VI

In the Roman Communion it is held as *de fide* that our Lord instituted all the seven Sacraments. According to a well-known text-book, Tanquerey's *Synopsis Theologiae Dogmaticae*, the affirmation that our Lord instituted all

---

[1] After reading Mr. N. P. Williams's admirably clear and " objective " argument in *Essays Catholic and Critical*, I rather think that a more definite assertion would be justified. But, being no expert in such matters, I am anxious not to claim too much.

of them *directly*, and not indirectly through guiding ecclesiastical developments in the Church, is maintained, not indeed as in the strictest definition *de fide*, but as so certain
that the contrary opinion is " inadmissible ". "*Admitti
nequit theoria eorum qui dicunt quaedam sacramenta implicite
tantum fuisse instituta, eo saltem sensu quod Christus
quaedam verba protulit aut actiones perfecit, ex quibus
conscientia catholica paulatim haec sacramenta eduxit, quin
Christus ipse vere ea determinaverit etiam substantialiter.*"
At the same time it is acknowledged as a legitimate
opinion, backed by considerable authority, that the matter
and form of some sacraments (Baptism and the Eucharist
excepted) was not *specifically* determined by Christ Himself, but by the Church with His authority ; in which case
Christ Himself may be said to have instituted them,
directly indeed, but in a more general manner, as by
determining the grace proper to the sacrament, but leaving
discretion as to the nature of the outward sign. Indeed,
that our Lord left some power to the Church of making
outward changes, so long as the *substance* of the sacrament
remained intact, Tanquerey regards as evident from
history. Hence he adds as a note to the passage previously
quoted : "*Si vero admitteretur implicita institutio eo
sensu quod Christus determinaverit gratiam propriam
sacramenti, et modo tantum generico signum sensibile cui
adnecteretur, haec esset hypothesis probabilis.*" (See op.
cit. vol. iii., §§ 270-280.) It may be doubted whether the
Council of Trent would have gone even as far as this in
admitting " implicit institution ". The relevant passage
runs as follows : "*Praeterea declarat (sancta synodus)
hanc potestatem perpetuo in ecclesia fuisse, ut in sacramentorum dispensatione, salva illorum substantia, ea
statueret vel mutaret, quae suscipientium utilitati, seu
ipsorum sacramentorum venerationi, pro rerum temporum*

et locorum varietate, magis expedire judicaret." (*Sess. xxi.
Cap.* 2.) The whole discussion is well worth men-
tioning, because it shows so clearly the complexity
of the issues and the subtlety of the distinctions involved.
It will be seen that I should plead, even in the case of
Baptism and the Eucharist, for the possibility of Christ's
institution having been implicit *in some degree*. On the
whole, evidence is against the tradition that our Lord
explicitly determined the Trinitarian formula in Baptism,
inasmuch as, apart from the question about Matthew
xxviii. 19, the New Testament itself suggests that Baptism
into the name of Jesus Christ only may have been the
original practice of the Church. For the institution of
the Eucharist, the reader is referred to Chapter IX.

CHAPTER VII

THE CHURCH, ORDERS AND UNITY

WE have suggested that the term Incarnation may properly be used in two senses, first of the historical life of Jesus Christ, secondly of the created universe as perfectly expressing or embodying the nature of Him through Whom the worlds were made. The link between the historical and the universal Incarnation of the Divine Logos, so far as our earthly experience is concerned, is the life of the Church militant. And as in the life of Christ, so in the being of the Church, which is the extension and fulfilment of that life through a human society, the aspects of incarnation and atonement are constantly passing into one another. Ideally the Church is in itself the expression of Christ's Person, and is always so actually, in so far as it realises its true nature. And when we regard its fellowship under this aspect, it is seen as founded upon the Incarnation alone. The Cross is in the background. For the proper and positive self-expression of Christ is not in the death even of sacrifice, but in the joy of true life and love which His disciples knew even before Calvary, when their Lord spoke of them as the children of the bride-chamber. But the expression of all heavenly goodness on earth has a purpose beyond itself, and therefore cannot abide unchanging. The Incarnation led up to the Cross. And the life of the Church on earth is not a true extension of the Incarnation, unless the mind of the Church concentrates its main attention not on the joy of its own internal fellowship, but on the sacrifice which is still required to save the world. Yet the Incarnation includes the Cross, not the Cross the Incarnation ; the Resurrection restores the Incarnation perfected through the death of sacrifice for the world, and the sacrifice itself derives its worth from the fact that the life offered was already the perfect expression of goodness. Therefore the Church is bound to bring in the joy of the Kingdom of God among all God's earthly creatures ; she is bound in the spirit of that joy to promote the social happiness of man upon earth, even while she seeks it not as an end in itself but rather as an image of the true end of life, an image which must ultimately be surrendered before the full reality can be won.

Thus the Christian thought of the Church swings constantly to and fro between the image of a family expressing in its own joyful fellowship the heavenly life upon earth, and the image of an army, rigorously training itself for arduous endeavour and the surrender of life itself, in order to conquer the world for God by the power of the Cross. The family is the natural type of an " expressive " fellowship, the army of an " instrumental " fellowship ; and the Church is the sacramental anti-type of both. Affection is the true bond of the one type of fellowship, comradeship of the other ; and members of the Church must find both within the love of Christ.

In studying the New Testament we find that St. John especially emphasises the idea of the Church as a family, and dwells upon that aspect of its nature in which it appears as continuing the Incarnation. In St. John's thought the work of the Paraclete is essentially to continue and interpret the revelation contained in the life of the Incarnate Word. And in his Gospel the main importance of the Cross is to make possible the Paraclete's coming. Christ through the Spirit comes again, and more fully, to His disciples than He came first in the flesh. And the Church evidently presents itself to St. John's mind as the continued expression of Christ's life in the world, rather than as His instrument for winning the world. It is the love of the brethren for one another, not their activity towards outsiders, which is the constant theme of Johannine sermons. And in the great high-priestly prayer the words are attributed to our Lord, "I pray not for the world; but for those which Thou hast given Me out of the world". It is true that St. John also represents our Lord as saying "I, if I be lifted up, will draw all men unto Me". It would therefore be untrue to assert that he ignores the universal mission of the Church or that he does not connect it with the Cross. But he certainly suggests that the missionary work of the Church is to be carried out mainly by the sheer attractiveness of that mutual love of the brethren which manifests the presence of Christ within it. The death of Christ plays its part as enabling the Incarnation of the Logos to have its fruit and continuation in the presence of the Paraclete with the Church.

St. Paul's genius interprets Christian truth in a rather different way. For him the Church was not born until after the Resurrection. It is the crucified and risen Saviour Who is its Head; and the apostolic function is to complete Christ's atoning work of reconciling the world to God. In no sense does he neglect the truth that the Church is the living expression of Christ's activity in the world. We owe to him the great image of the Church as Christ's body. But in him the burning zeal of the missionary inevitably dwells on the activity of Christ's messenger towards the unbelieving world. This constitutes the very essence of apostolate. He is consumed with the effort to become all things to all men, if he may by all means save some. He attributes to his own sufferings in that cause something of the atoning value of Christ's. And we feel sure that, if he had lived to see his own converts pass definitely beyond the stage of infancy in Christ, he would have pictured to himself more distinctly the whole Church as an apostolic body enduring in its own members the sufferings of the Cross, so that by their means it might bring the world into communion with its risen Saviour. The Atonement is ever in the forefront of St. Paul's thought, as the Incarnation is in the forefront of St. John's. And according as we take the characteristic point of view of each in turn, we have presented to us a different aspect of the Church's life and nature.

It is then the mission of the Church to represent God to the world, both as the expression of His incarnate being and as the instrument of His atoning work. We may also affirm, though this thought is only hinted at in the New Testament, that it is its mission to represent the world to God, both as the first-fruit which witnesses to the holiness of the lump, and as the priest through whom the people are sanctified and brought near to God. To the Church therefore essentially belongs that self-transcendent and missionary holiness, the notion of which is one of the most precious contributions of Christianity to human religion. One aspect of the Church's holiness upon earth consists precisely in the fact that it exists primarily for the sake of those who do not as yet belong to it; just as the holy Son of God lived on earth primarily for the sake of those who were as yet outside the fellowship of God's Kingdom. And, just as He for the sake of all men restricted His activity in the flesh to the healing and teaching of the few, so any restrictive conditions, which the Church imposes for membership in her body, can only be justified as necessary means for making her membership all-inclusive.

So far there seems to be no reason in principle why Christians of all denominations should not agree as to the essentially sacramental nature of the Church's being. Even a Quaker may argue that sacraments are to be rejected, partly because they obscure the truth that the Christian fellowship is the one sacrament of Christ's life now upon the earth. And, at the other extreme, Catholics have always regarded the Church, not only as the trustee or steward of certain sacraments, but also as having herself on earth a sacramental being of which the external marks have been definite and manifest from the beginning.

But what are the marks or signs by which the Church on earth is recognised ? The Catholic usually answers this question by enumerating certain marks of organisation, profession of certain creeds, maintenance of the apostolical succession, practice of certain sacraments, communion with the see of Rome, and the like. The Free Churchman usually answers in terms of the manifestation of spiritual life, faith, hope and love. And here the Free Churchman seems at first sight to have an initial advantage. But a little reflection shows that, though both kinds of mark are in a true sense visible, they are not really both on the same plane, and therefore need not necessarily conflict with each other. In fact, the difference in the kind of answer given to the question proposed really reveals a wide divergence between points of view, which must be measured and allowed for, if mutual understanding is to be reached.

It is not yet widely enough recognised how distinctive of Catholic thought is its conception of *validity*. This

notion of validity arises from the belief that we have
sacramental reality not merely when something outward
is the expression and instrument of some inward and
spiritual good, but also, and in a special sense, when some
particular outward thing has been specially appointed by
divine authority to be the expression and instrument of
some inward and spiritual good, so that, when the
appointed sign is performed, the spiritual good is embodied
and conveyed through it.   It is in the appointedness of
its outward element that the official or ritual sacrament
differs from what may perhaps be called a " natural "
sacrament, i.e. the sacramental reality which exists
wherever the Divine Spirit uses either the material world
or human action to be the expression and instrument of
His goodness.   Thus we have a " natural " sacrament in
every beauty of nature and of art and in every act of
human love.   But the external element in such sacraments
is not in any special sense appointed or authorised or
fixed.   We do not admire a sunset or a landscape, because
we think that Providence has decreed that this one
particular combination of form and colour should be
beautiful ; nor do we reverence the heroism of a man who
plunges into a dangerous current to save another from
drowning, because we believe that the same authority
has attached a special value to the act of jumping into
deep and rapidly moving water.   These things are
undoubtedly true sacraments, since in them the divine
goodness uses outward means of expression and action
towards man ; but, inasmuch as their outward element
is not fixed by appointment, the question of validity does
not arise in regard to them.   In the same way no question
of validity can be asked in regard to the supreme and
single sacrament of the life of Jesus.   We may ask per-
tinently whether He is in fact and in power the Incarnate

God, but to ask whether He is so validly would be to talk nonsense.

But when we believe that our Lord, whether by His own lips in the flesh or through the operation of the Holy Spirit in the Church, has appointed a certain use of water and bread and wine to be the means of His gracious action and self-expression toward man, then immediately the question of validity becomes real and relevant. " Is the sacrament valid ? " we ask : and that is the equivalent of asking, "Has the appointed outward sign been duly performed ? " If so, the sacrament must, because of the divine authority appointing it, be a real sacrament. If not, either the sacrament has not been celebrated at all, or else it has been performed in a manner so gravely defective as to render its reality doubtful.[1] " Valid ", therefore, is a term applied to a sacrament of which the divinely appointed sign has been duly performed, and to which therefore is necessarily attached the divinely promised gift.

Now, evidently at this point the Catholic doctrine approaches the border-line of magic, if the attachment of the spiritual gift to the outward sign is at all mechanically conceived. But, as we noticed in the last chapter, Catholic theologians safeguard themselves from magic by teaching (1) that the gift, though really present in the outward sign, yet can only be effective for salvation in those who are spiritually fitted to receive it, and (2) that those who by no fault of their own fail to receive the outward sign

---

[1] It may indeed be questioned whether the notion of " a doubtfully valid sacrament " does not involve a contradiction in terms. For the purpose of appointing a fixed outward sign is to give assurance of the grace bestowed ; and a valid sacrament seems therefore to be the equivalent of an assured or guaranteed sacrament. In practice, however, it may be uncertain whether a particular guarantee is or is not present ; and in that sense a sacrament may be doubtfully assured.

K

may nevertheless, if spiritually fitted, enjoy to their salvation the spiritual gift apart from the outward sign altogether.[1]

Thus the whole Catholic theory of sacraments must depend upon the distinction between validity and efficacy. The spiritual gift is necessarily inherent in every valid sacrament, but the valid sacrament is not efficacious for good in the recipient, if he receive the sacrament unworthily. Conversely, the same gift which is inherent in the valid sacrament may in certain conditions be efficaciously received apart from it. The outward sign, then, of the valid sacrament is appointed as a visible pledge or guarantee of the spiritual gift which accompanies it, and not in order that the gift may be otherwise unobtainable.

We are now in a position to answer the question, why it is that the Free Churchman and the Catholic have apparently such different conceptions of the marks whereby the sacramental Church is to be recognised. The

---

[1] While the doctrine of validity is being considered in connexion with possible implications of magic, it should be added that the assurance of the outward would be rendered nugatory, if the reality of the sacrament were thought to be dependent upon the faith or spiritual condition of the minister who performs it. According to Catholic doctrine, therefore, the sacraments confer grace *ex opere operato*, i.e. by reason of the thing done (according to Christ's ordinance), and not *ex opere operantis*, i.e. as though the sacrament were the personal work of the minister. On the other hand, it would evidently be absurd, if the reality of the sacrament were to depend so entirely on the bare performance of the outward sign that it might be done altogether unintentionally or by accident. According to Catholic doctrine, therefore, it is necessary to the validity of a sacrament that the minister should have the intention " to do what the Church does ", i.e. he must perform the sacramental act wittingly. Both these mutually complementary doctrines of the minister's intention and of grace *ex opere operato* have been made the target of much ill-directed criticism. I have here avoided the subtler intricacies of the doctrine of intention. In its main significance it is simply a matter of religious decency and common sense. For a somewhat fuller discussion, see the appended Note at the end of the chapter

Free Churchman, not recognising the notion of validity as applicable to the Church, is inclined to think of the Church as having the character of what we have called a "natural" sacrament, and therefore the marks of the Church are to him marks of spiritual efficacy alone. There is a true sacrament, an outward expression of God's nature and instrument of His operation, wherever the fruits of the Spirit are manifest. And wherever the Spirit unites human souls in faith, hope and love, there the true Church appears and works in power upon the world. The Catholic may be as eager to affirm all this as the Free Churchman. But he has much to add, or perhaps to say in preface, to it. For to him the Church is not only a "natural" sacrament, the outward signs of which are recognisable only as the manifold and ever-varying expression of the Spirit's inward energy ; it partakes also of the nature of a ritual sacrament, for which a certain outward uniformity has been appointed by God to be a mark of validity. Just as there may be the efficacious reality of spiritual communion apart from the Sacrament of the Eucharist, and yet the validity of the Sacrament depends upon the due use of fixed and appointed signs, so the Church may exist in spiritual efficacy apart from any one system of organisation, and yet a certain system of organisation may be necessary to its existence as a valid embodiment of the fellowship which Christ came to establish upon earth. And, on the other hand, just as a valid Eucharist is entirely without benefit to those who receive it unworthily, so there may be some embraced within the order of the valid Church, who yet by reason of their spiritual unworthiness never partake of the spiritual fellowship which by divine gift is still inherent in the Church's appointed order.

Thus, just as the Catholic theory of the sacraments

necessitates a distinction between validity and efficacy, so the Catholic theory of the sacramental Church necessitates a distinction between the Church " visible " and the Church " invisible ", if we allow ourselves to use the generally current but very misleading terms.[1] The Church " invisible " is the Church as efficaciously present in spiritual fellowship and recognisable in the spiritual fruits of goodness. The Church " visible " is the Church as preserving its divinely appointed uniformity of outward order. Undoubtedly the Catholic will assume that on the whole the spiritual fruits of the " invisible " Church will appear within the borders of the Church " visible "; and he will point to the evidence that this is so as proof that what he regards as the " visible " Church is indeed the one true Church upon earth. But there is no need for him to allege that on earth the " visible " Church and the " invisible " are exactly conterminous. Indeed he could not allege this without contradicting his own principle that the operation of the Spirit is not bound.

Moreover the Catholic has ready answers to certain general objections which are sometimes urged against his doctrine. " Why," it is asked, " is there any need to suppose that there is only one external form authorised and appointed for the visible Church on earth ? " On rational grounds the answer may well be given that, apart from some unity of organisation recognised as authoritative, the Church militant can hardly conduct a victorious warfare for the conversion and salvation of the world. On the one hand, those within the Church, being people of very various race, class, education, taste and tempera-

---

[1] The same distinction is more accurately made by using an obvious analogy and speaking of the *soul* as contrasted with the *body* of the Church. This is preferred by Catholics, because it cannot be taken to imply the existence of *two* churches. I use the other expressions only for convenience of language.

ment, can never grow into the fulness of Christian fellowship unless they are at first held together by strong bonds of authoritative order and custom, which will prevent them from splitting up into groups or sects, each made up of those whose natural preferences and views are more or less the same. On the other hand, those who are as yet unconverted need for their conversion the evidently united witness and the coherent activity of a body which has some common organisation as well as a common spirit. It is not for nothing that the call for reunion comes most insistently from the mission-field.[1]

Or again, if the critic press the further question, "Why then are not the marks of the one validly accredited Church more clearly indicated in the New Testament?" the Catholic may at least retort that the writers of the New Testament never contemplated the possibility that the Church of Christ could be outwardly divided, and that, had they done so, it can hardly be suggested that they would have viewed the prospect with any feeling but horror. Where no division is dreamed of, there is no motive to define marks of unity with precision.

So far then it would seem that the Catholic has at least a strong case for his doctrine of the sacramental Church. His real difficulties arise when he is confronted with the fact of schism. It would seem at first sight self-evident that, if the one "visible" Church is to be recognised at all by any appointed marks of outward order, one of those marks must be the maintenance of one undivided communion and the acknowledgment of a common allegiance to some single organisation. If this were so, it would of

---

[1] This is only an expansion of the old observation quoted by St. Thomas from St. Augustine: "*In nullum nomen religionis, seu verum, seu falsum, coadunari homines possunt, nisi aliquo signaculorum seu sacramentorum visibilium consortio colligentur*" (Summa III, Q. 61, Art. 1, from *Contra Faustum*, XIX, 11).

necessity follow that there could be no such thing as
schism *within* the Church. If then it happens that there
are two separate bodies both professing Christianity,
we must conclude that only one of them can be the
" visible " Church and that the other must be outside it.
But in fact since the time of St. Augustine hardly any
Christian theologian, at any rate in the West, if we
except certain fanatical Protestants, has held this view
with all its logical implications. All the main tradition
of Catholic theology has now come to admit in some
sense and in some degree the possibility of schism in
the Church, i.e. that as a fact, contrary to the divine
intention though it be, two Christian societies may
be divided in communion and acknowledge no common
allegiance to any one body upon earth at all, and yet
neither of them be altogether excluded from the life of
the one " visible " Church. Thus there may be degrees
of defection or separation from the " visible " Church ;
and the mere severance of outward communion only
marks one such degree. The possibility is recognised
of a state of schism which is less than complete outward
alienation from the one Church. And, in proportion as
this possibility is recognised, it is of necessity presupposed
that the outward marks of the " visible " Church are not
wholly bound up with any actual union of organisation,
but may in varying degrees really persist, when " schismatic " bodies, severed from the outward communion
and jurisdiction of the one Church, nevertheless retain in
themselves elements of outward order of which the one
Church was historically the source. Thus the logically
difficult conclusion emerges, that the reality even of the
" visible " Church may in some degree be found outside
the one communion of any one body.

How has this form of the Catholic doctrine of the

Church been reached, and how can it be justified ? Again it is to be noticed that the theory of the " visible " Church is closely bound up with a certain theory of the validity of sacraments.

Two doctrines concerning the conditions of validity were current in the early Church.[1] According to the one, which was apparently more primitive, and may be called Cyprianic, after the name of its leading exponent in the West, the validity of every sacrament was essentially derived from its authorisation by the one " visible " Church. The sacraments were the sacraments of the Church, and therefore not only were right form and matter necessary for their validity ; it was a further condition that they must be performed within the Church by a person accredited to act in the Church's behalf for this purpose. It followed according to the logic of this view that sacraments performed outside the " visible " Church were as regards validity simply null and void.

Augustine, however, successfully combated this doctrine in maintaining against Cyprian the validity of heretical baptisms. In order to do so he found himself obliged to argue that the only conditions necessary for valid baptism were due form and matter, combined, as later theologians would have added, with some intention " to do what the Church does " in baptizing. On the strength of the Augustinian argument it is even held that an unbaptized person can validly baptize another. And evidently this separation of the validity from its authorisation by the Church must

[1] The facts in the history of the early Church referred to are here stated very roughly and in outline. For an exact statement of the points at issue between St. Cyprian and St. Augustine and the relation of the controversy to earlier doctrines of the Church and the Sacraments, the reader is referred to Professor Turner's and Dr. Bernard's Essays in *The Early History of the Church and the Ministry,* and to Lecture IV in Dr. Headlam's *Doctrine of the Church and Christian Reunion.*

in any case have very far-reaching consequences. It is true that Catholic theologians have never extended the possible validity of the Eucharist or of Orders nearly as far as they have extended that of Baptism. Nevertheless it has become the recognised and prevalent view among Catholics that any ordained minister of the Church retains in perpetuity the power to perform validly all those sacraments which belong to his ministry, even when he ceases to hold any office in the Church or has perhaps seceded from its body. A priest who has lapsed into schism can still celebrate valid Eucharists, and a bishop who has lapsed into schism still perform valid ordinations.

This second and less primitive theory of the validity of sacraments inevitably reacts upon the theory of the Church itself. Suppose that a body, comprising validly ordained bishops and still professing the essentials of Christian faith, separates itself from the main body of the Church ; it can hardly be maintained any longer that it has separated itself from the " visible " Church altogether. For, granted the sufficiency of its faith and the validity of its sacraments, it must follow that it admits men into all the essential privileges of Christian life according to the external signs guaranteed by divine authority.[1] It is therefore in some sense part of the " visible " Church still, though a schismatic part, i.e. one separated from the main body in a manner contrary to the divine will. Thus the condition of what may be called " schism in the strict sense " is made intelligible. It depends, as we have seen, on a theory which divorces the validity of sacraments from their authorisation by the Church. But it is

---

[1] Theoretically it is still possible to maintain that, though the formal confession of faith be sufficient and the sacraments valid, those who minister and receive them are guilty of such sin in so doing that their efficacy is lost. Obviously, however, to apply such an argument soon becomes intolerable.

almost impossible not to think that valid sacraments
confer upon the body which ministers them some claim
to belong to the " visible " Church. Hence, pushed to its
logical extremes, the theory in question would lead us to
derive the validity of the Church from the validity of its
sacraments,[1] and would come to be the exact opposite of
the Cyprianic theory which derives the validity of the
sacraments from the valid and validating authority of the
Church.

Now in order to understand the present situation in
relation to problems of reunion, it is necessary to remember that force of circumstances has driven Anglo-Catholic
theologians especially to emphasise the argument which
would prove the Catholicity of their Church from the
validity of its sacraments. For their desire for reunion
with Rome and with the East leads them to seek to con-
vince Roman and Eastern theologians that the Church of
England, almost alone among the bodies which separated
themselves at or after the time of the Reformation, remains a true part of the one " visible " Church, and that
the schism between her and the main body of Western
Catholicism differs from that between Protestants and
Catholics for exactly that reason. But most Catholic
theologians have hitherto rejected this claim and declared
the Church of England to be in a state of total separation
from the one Church. Clearly therefore Anglo-Catholics
must seek to over-persuade them by showing that there

[1] The Bishop of Gloucester (Dr. Headlam) writes : " The theory he
[St. Augustine] established altered the whole basis of the theology of
orders. Orders in the ancient Church depended upon the Church.
Orders in the medieval Church depended upon the bishop. In the
early Church episcopal ordination was necessary because the bishop
was the person appointed by the Church to perform its functions. In
the medieval and modern Church the idea has grown up that the Church
depends upon the due ordination of bishops " (*The Doctrine of the
Church and Reunion,* p 162).

is no reason to question the validity of Anglican sacraments, or the sufficiency of Anglican confessions of faith. But if it is assumed that the validity of a Church's sacraments is dependent upon her position as part of the " visible " Church, it is clearly impossible for the Anglo-Catholic to bring forward a case which does not beg the question from the start. Thus it comes about that the Anglo-Catholic theologian adheres strictly to the theory that the possession of valid sacraments is in such wise a credential of the " visible " Church, that the validity of sacraments cannot be derived from their authorisation by that Church, but is rather what gives to the Church its visible character.

This doctrine determines the attitude of Anglo-Catholics to Protestant bodies whenever proposals for reunion are brought forward. Free Churchmen, they hold, are competent to perform valid baptism, and baptized Free Churchmen are members of the " visible " Catholic Church to that extent to which baptism by itself secures admission thereto. But those sacraments which require a validly ordained minister for their validity are lacking in the Free Churches ; and therefore, if the Free Churches are to be recognised as parts of the " visible " Church and so to enter into communion with the Church of England, the first necessity is that their Orders should be validated through the historic episcopacy.

Free Churchmen, on their side, as a rule scarcely yet recognise or appreciate the Catholic conception of validity at all. To them the notion of validity, as distinct from spiritual efficacy, seems to be a barren and formal abstraction to which none but a pedant could attach very serious importance. This makes it harder for them to understand that the validity of their Orders may be called in question in an important sense, without any doubt being necessarily cast on the reality of the divine grace received by and through their ministers ; and they find it proportionately difficult to support the validity of their Orders and sacraments on grounds which appear to the Catholic to be relevant. Moreover the very fact that the sacramental Church on earth is, in the view of most Free Churchmen, to be recognised by the manifestation of spiritual fruits alone, and not by any formal unity of order, leads them to attach very much less importance than the Catholic to organic reunion of any kind. Small wonder, therefore, that the conditions of reunion put forward by Anglo-Catholics seem to Free Churchmen wholly unacceptable.

Rome, on the other hand, is so completely assured in her possession of everything that historical and outward catholicity can give, that she does not need to defend her claims in this regard by any one line of argument alone. It is indeed doubtful whether an acceptance on her part of Anglo-Catholic contentions in the realm of historical fact would make any substantial difference in her attitude to the Church of England. There are so many questions of belief and authority upon which the Roman and the Anglican minds radically differ, that Rome can scarcely be expected to recognise at present the Catholic position of the Church of England in any matter of importance. But this security of Rome in her leadership of the Catholic world has two very different consequences. On the one hand it prevents her from feeling any need to make concessions to the claims of those who are outside her communion. On the other hand it gives her great freedom of action, if at any time more liberal counsels should prevail at the Vatican. Rome after all is the only Catholic authority which need not be deterred from following any course by fear of the judgment which Rome may pass upon it.

Meanwhile those outside the Roman communion, who still long for a genuinely Catholic plan of reunion and refuse to let go the ancient belief that Christ's will for His Church was and is that it should be organically one in faith and order down the ages, may be excused if in the present impasse they turn their thoughts to exploring the possibilities of more ancient theories of the Catholic Church than that which has prevailed in modern Catholicism.

Evidently, if the Church was from the first intended to be outwardly one organisation throughout its history, the cardinal point of its outward unity lies in the appointment and recognition of its official authorities. In fact, from the second century onwards the duly appointed bishops of sees were looked upon as the organs and guardians of the outward unity of the Church. Thus the unity depended upon the universal recognition of a validly constituted hierarchy. Recognised validity of Orders in bishops and priests was the link whereby the body of the Church was held together. But so far it is not clear whether the validity of the Orders was derived from the unity of the Church, or the unity of the Church from the validity of its Orders. If the former, then either " schism in the Church " is an impossibility, or else the validity of all orders would be impaired, if schism were admitted. If the latter, the full validity of all Orders might remain in a Church rent by schism ; but then the paradox seems to follow that two bodies severed from one another can both still belong to the outward or " visible " Church whose very *esse* is to be one.

The former of these alternatives is the Cyprianic. And those who in antiquity adopted it denied the possibility of schism in the Church, and thus avoided the paradox of supposing that schism might impair the validity of all the Church's Orders and sacraments. According to them, if there were schism at all, the schismatic body was simply outside the Church, and therefore destitute of any valid sacrament. But in the West from the time of Augustine the harshness of this doctrine was modified, at some cost of logic, by the adoption of the Augustinian view of validity in sacraments, which, as we have seen, points in the end towards a different theory of the ground of catholicity in the Church. The validity of Orders was made to consist in the use of due form and matter by any validly ordained bishop, whether or not he was still in communion with, and still authorised by, the whole Church. Thus, although communion with the Pope was still required as a necessary condition for membership in the " visible " Church, the door was to some extent opened for schism within the Church itself, inasmuch as those schismatic bodies which possessed valid sacraments could not be *completely* excluded.

But in fact the Augustinian doctrine of validity is open to such grave objection that it may well be doubted whether the signs of the times do not call for a return towards older theories and a restatement of their implications in a more liberal sense.

The question can only be decided by a re-examination of the essential meaning of the Sacrament of Holy Order. It seems that every ordination either to the priesthood or to the episcopate must have a double intention and purpose. On the one hand a divine gift of power for spiritual work is to be bestowed by God, as it were directly. On the other hand a certain solemn authorisation to act in the Church's behalf is to be conferred, also indeed from God as its ultimate source, but by God as working through the body of the Church which is Christ's Body.[1] This

[1] See note, p. 145.

double aspect of the ordained minister's office arises from the fact that he is, as we argued in our last chapter, a sacramental man. On the one hand he is a man of God ministering gifts of spiritual life to his fellows ; on the other hand he is *persona ecclesiae*, and the true representative of those to whom he ministers, and of whom the ecclesia is composed.

Having thus distinguished two elements in the essence of priesthood, we may perhaps be allowed for convenience to denote them respectively by the two single words " power " and "authority ". The two realities denoted are clearly distinct in thought and even, to a certain very limited extent, separate in fact. Thus the " power " characteristic of priesthood may up to a point be found in persons unordained ; and the signs of its presence may often be taken as constituting a call to the priesthood, and so lead to ordination. On the other hand an ordained priest, though he possesses authority to act in Christ's and the Church's behalf, may yet appear to have "mistaken his vocation ", because he does not manifest in life and conduct the " power " with which his " authority " should be accompanied. " Power " and "authority" then are not the same thing; Nevertheless each after a certain point tends to pass into the other, and in their fulness they are inseparable. On the one hand a priest who is manifestly a man of God must for that reason be felt to act with more real authority in the Church's behalf, except in such matters as are purely ritual and formal. On the other hand, a faithful priest cannot but receive incalculable increase of " power " from the very fact that he has been solemnly authorised to act in Christ's name. Moreover, both elements are necessary. A man destitute of formal authority, however real his power, cannot be validly a priest. And a man, who possesses the formal authority of priesthood alone, is a living self-contradiction.

Now it is the element of authority in Holy Orders which the Augustinian theory seems either to undervalue or to misconceive. It teaches that any man, once consecrated bishop, can continue, even after he has ceased to hold office in the Church's body and has even been outwardly severed from its one communion, to perform ordinations and consecrations which are fully valid. But this really stultifies the authority of Orders altogether. For we are required to accept the intolerable paradox that a man, who has received ordination in some hole-and-corner fashion from a wandering bishop deprived of all office and jurisdiction, is fully and validly ordained, whereas one who has received the solemn authorisation of one, say, of the great Presbyterian communions, is not ordained at all. This seems contrary to reason, if authority is really of the essence of Orders. Capacity to exercise authority, and a fortiori capacity to transmit it, must reside in the office held rather than in the person of him who holds it. And without disputing that there is a sense in which a bishop can never cease to be a bishop, we may surely maintain that his capacity to transmit his authority to others is dependent upon the condition that his status as the holder of some definite episcopal office in the one body is still recognised by the body itself.

If then the body is divided, it follows that, since the whole body no longer concurs in and takes responsibility for the appointment of any of its officers, all officers lack fulness of authority, and therefore that the validity of all Orders in the Church is in some degree impaired. No doubt this suggestion may seem at first sight to be a worse paradox than those which we have condemned ; and yet we venture tentatively to submit that after all it may be found to indicate the true path of Christian charity and reason.

The main difficulty is to see how in any circumstances, even those of a kind which ought never to have arisen, validity can become a matter of degree. The whole conception of validity in sacraments implies that a certain plain outward sign has been defined and appointed as a pledge, guarantee or means of assurance. Where the outward sign is, there the inward and spiritual gift of the sacrament is assured. But if, it may be said, we start talking about degrees of validity, everything is made uncertain and indefinite, and the whole point and meaning of the term vanishes in a mist of doubt and confusion. Such a situation would be intolerable.

Now we do not at all seek to deny, rather we are eager to insist, that in a certain sense the situation is intolerable indeed. A condition in which the validity of all Orders in the Church is in some degree impaired must injure the healthy activity of the whole body, and is not for a moment to be acquiesced in. Hence the urgency of the call to reunion. Nevertheless it need not at all follow from what has been said about Orders, that no fully real or valid sacraments are at present celebrated in the Church. Our contention is that the Sacrament of Holy Order holds a unique position among the sacraments of the Church, inasmuch as the conferring of authority enters into its spiritual essence and meaning. It is not part of the immediate aim or intention of the Sacrament, say, of Baptism or of the Eucharist, to authorise any particular person to act in behalf of the whole Church. But, if this is not part of the immediate aim and intention of the Sacrament of Holy Order, the whole sacrament becomes unintelligible. And no rite or ceremony, in so far as its purpose is to confer authority, can be valid or real apart from the implicit concurrence and recognition of the authorising body.

Of course it is not disputed that in the case we are discussing the sole fount of authority, as of power, is Christ Himself. Nevertheless, if it be true at all that according to Christ's will there is an appointed unity of order for His Church upon earth, it must follow that it is His will also to confer authority upon the Church's officers through, or at least not apart from, the co-operation of the whole body of the Church, which, as represented at least in every congregation, takes its part in presenting the candidates, in solemn prayer for the divine gifts to be bestowed upon them, and in recognition of those gifts as bestowed. When the communion of the whole Church is divided, the representation of the whole Church in each congregation for these purposes is no longer a reality; the will of Christ is hindered; and something essential to the very thing signified in ordination is no longer fully present. Once admit that part of the essence of Orders consists in an authority conferred in such a manner as to implicate the whole body of the Church as one, and in a divided Church the validity of Orders becomes inevitably a matter of degree.[1]

[1] The sum of the argument is stated in these vague and general terms in order to cover as far as possible divergent views concerning the manner in which the whole body of the Church takes its essential part in ordination. To the modern mind, no doubt, it appears natural to suppose that, where the thing conferred is authority to act in the whole Church's behalf, the authorisation must be given *through* the whole body of the Church as represented both by the ordaining bishop and by the presenting and praying congregation. In that case the force of the conclusion reached above is most immediately obvious; and, inasmuch as all ordination implies a commission to act in the Church's behalf, it seems very hard to deny that the ordaining bishop must act as the representative of the whole body. But even if it be held that the authority of Orders is bestowed by Christ, not through the whole body of the Church, but only through the ordaining bishop in answer to the Church's presentation of candidates and prayer, we

L

If this position then be frankly accepted, it surely becomes natural, though perhaps not inevitable, to affirm further that even in those Christian bodies which have not retained the apostolical succession through bishops, ordinations are still not null or void of validity altogether. It need not be questioned that for fully valid Orders the episcopal succession is a necessity ; and a reunion which should restore the full validity of Orders throughout the Church may well be held to require the validation of existing ministries by the episcopal laying on of hands, where that has not already been received. But, on the other hand, if authority to act in the whole Church's behalf is of the essence of Orders, and if the authorisation is everywhere through schism incomplete, it seems reasonable to hold that, wherever a separated Christian body solemnly sets men apart to be ministers of the word and sacraments, not in this or that sect, but in the Catholic Church so far as it understands its nature, there something essential to the nature of valid ordination has been performed, that Christ through that part of His disunited Church has bestowed a certain authority to minister in His Church upon the men so set apart, and that they are really, however defectively, ordained men, who celebrate, however imperfectly, the real sacraments of Christ's appointment.

According to this plea we should regard practically all the divisions of Christendom as being in principle schisms

may still maintain that the part played by the congregation is really essential to the sacrament, and that the whole authorisation is impaired in validity, if schism prevents the whole body of the Church from being properly represented in each congregation. Moreover, whether or not the ordaining bishop is held to be a representative of the whole body of the Church, it seems that he must at least act as a representative of the whole episcopal order, commissioned according to Catholic tradition through the apostles, and therefore schism within that order might still be thought to impair the full validity of the authorisation given.

within the Church. And by frankly stating this conclusion we avoid the difficulties inherent in two rival doctrines, both that which declares all schism within the Church to be impossible, and that which, relying on the Augustinian theory of validity, separates schisms into two classes, and maintains that the schism between Rome and Eastern Orthodoxy, or the schisms between Rome, Eastern Orthodoxy and Anglicanism are of a quite different kind from others. The first doctrine, in its strictness, is morally intolerable. The second is logically bound in the end to propose validity of Orders as a criterion to determine whether a body can be said in some sense to belong to the " visible " Church or not. But we reject this criterion, on the ground that it is impossible to pronounce upon the validity of Orders, until it has already been decided whether or not the body in which they are bestowed belongs to the " visible " Church. We conclude then that, the " visible " Church being manifestly divided, all bodies professing Christianity belong to it imperfectly and in varying degrees. The one " visible " Catholic Church still exists upon earth, but it does not exist completely or exclusively in any one of its divided fragments. Perhaps God has concluded all under the sin of schism that He may in the end have mercy upon all through the grace of union.

Finally, it may be well that we should briefly indicate the practical implications of our argument in regard to such concrete proposals for reunion as are now under discussion. Reunion itself, according to the basic principles laid down in the great Lambeth Appeal of 1920, means nothing more and nothing less than full intercommunion between the Christian bodies now divided. The conditions of such intercommunion are (1) the profession of a common faith recognised by all as sufficient, and (2) a commonly agreed answer to the questions, what persons are qualified to receive, and what persons authorised to administer, the Church's sacraments, what sacraments are essential to the order of the Church, and what minimum form and matter are necessary for their administration. No further uniformity is required for union.

With reference to the relations of Anglicanism and Eastern Orthodoxy it is perhaps enough to say that considerable steps towards union have already been taken, and, though grave difficulties remain to be overcome, the prospect is not unhopeful. At least doors are gradually opening, and none seem to have been decisively shut and barred.

Between Rome and the Church of England, on the other hand, though discussions have taken place in the friendliest spirit, no tangible progress whatever has been made. And here it has to be observed that at present a definite impasse seems to exist in matters of belief, and will have to be overcome before questions of order can enter the range of practical discussion. If Rome and Canterbury were to agree on the necessary content of Christian faith, it is hard to believe that any questions about Orders and sacraments would create an insuperable barrier. In all such matters Anglicans would go to almost any lengths of concession, short of denying what they are confident they have already received, in order to satisfy any demands which Rome might feel bound to make. Moreover, Anglicans would doubtless be willing to acknowledge the Pope as primate among all bishops, and, therefore, as in a real sense the head of the visible Church, so long as his claim to jurisdiction were not put forward in such a way as to interfere with what they regard as the legitimate autonomy of the Catholic diocese or province. But, even if we leave on one side the vexed question of papal infallibility, what is inconceivable is this, that any Anglican bishop or priest who at all appreciates the main methods and results of scientific and historical enquiry, could put himself under the authority of a Church which still insists that the whole Bible must be taught as historically inerrant, still requires a quite uncritical attitude to evidence, and still proposes to deal with its ordained ministers as Rome has dealt with some whose scholarship led them to inconvenient conclusions. Let Rome take her yoke of repression off the intellect, and give it freedom to take up its cross of sacrifice ; and the dawn of a really œcumenical Catholicism may be within sight.

Meanwhile the difficulties which hinder the reunion of the Church of England with Free Churches are of a different kind. Some no doubt are concerned with the profession of a common faith embodied in creeds ; and these must not be minimised. Nevertheless the representative theologians of the Free Churches and of the Church of England, who recently held a series of conversations at Lambeth, did not find any insuperable obstacle to re-union in matters of faith.[1] The gulf which they had no success in bridging was that between the claim of the Free Churchmen that their ministries should be recognised as fully valid ministries of the word and sacraments in the universal Church, and the requirement of the Anglicans that Free Church ministers should receive the laying on of hands from a bishop as a condition of inter-communion being established.

It is just here that our previous argument might conceivably indicate a reconciling point of view. For if

---

[1] See *The Church of England and the Free Churches*, ed. by G. K. A. Bell and W. L. Robertson, which embodies the proceedings of the Conferences held at Lambeth Palace, 1921–1925

it is once admitted that no separate Christian body can claim to possess in all its fulness the whole valid and validating authority of the one " visible " Church, the way is open to accept all lesser claims to validity sincerely put forward by all Christian bodies, without that acceptance being understood to imply that any Christian body has no need of the further validation which others can confer. It seems that the impasse reached at Lambeth must continue, so long as either side persists in assuming that, if any ministry is recognised as a real ministry of the word and sacraments in the universal Church, then its validity is recognised as full and complete and not, perhaps very gravely, defective. To put the same point crudely and bluntly, the impasse results from the assumption that, if a man has been really ordained at all, he must have been ordained completely. The assumption is natural and has a show of self-evident logic. And yet we have been venturing to suggest that, once it is granted that " authority " is of the spiritual essence of Orders, the assumption is not justified either by reason or facts. If the authority and the validity of Orders is derived from the unity of the " visible " Church, in a divided Church all Orders are more or less defective, and their validity is a matter of degree.

What then is required, if two or more divided fragments of the one Church desire to come together again in union ? Surely one condition must be that suggested by the Lambeth Appeal, that each should further validate and authorise the other's official ministry, as much as it lies in its power to do so. Such a method of procedure requires no one even to appear to deny or to doubt the reality of anything which he believes himself to have already received, while at the same time it is a most effective witness to the importance of that principle of validity which all who believe in organic union must desire to uphold.

How should this further authorisation take place, as between the Church of England and one of the Evangelical Free Churches ? As to the authorisation of Anglican ministers, no concrete proposals have so far been made by Free Churchmen, largely because, owing to what we think is a fundamental misconception, the whole idea seems to them, as to many Anglicans, to lack reality. As to what is to be given by the Anglican Church, a good deal, of course, must depend on what the particular Free Church in question claims to possess ; for this is not always clear. But, granted that the Free Church does claim to perform ordinations to a ministry of the word and sacraments in the universal Church, Anglicans may still reasonably desire that its ministers should receive a solemn imposition of hands from the diocesan bishops of their Church who are in the historical succession of the Catholic episcopate ; for this is the element of outward validation which those ministers at present lack.

Two forms in which this rite might be per- formed have recently been suggested by the Anglican participants in the Lambeth Conversations.[1] The first consists in a form of conditional ordination ; the second proposes that the bishop should use different words from those appointed at normal ordinations. The first alterna- tive, it should be said at once, seems on general gounds objectionable as well as inconsistent with the line of argument we have been following. The conditional form of a sacrament is only justifiable in reason, where there is real lack of evidence to determine what has already taken place, as, for instance, when it is impossible to ascertain

[1] See Bell and Robertson, *op. cit.*, pp. 67–74.

whether a person has been baptised or not.[1] But to use a conditional form, when ample evidence is available to show exactly what has been done and with what intention, is nothing but a most unedifying confession of divided counsels or moral timidity. In such a case as we are contemplating, it seems right to hold that an ordination has really been performed already, but that, owing to the lamentable schisms of the Church, it was performed defectively and therefore needs completion. The use of a special form of words by the bishop would therefore obviously be appropriate.

This kind of proposal, which has already on many occasions been made, has so far failed to receive consideration on its full merits, because of the rigid distinction accepted on all sides between " ordination " and " mere authorisation ". If the suggested ceremony, it is argued, be regarded as an ordination, the Free Churchman must reject it ; if it be regarded as a mere authorisation, the Anglo-Catholic will not accept it ; and, if the point be left open to various interpretations, the ambiguity will be fatal to that mutual good faith and open-mindedness, without which the whole proceeding would be almost a sacrilege. The reply to this logic is to point out that, if " authority " is really of the essence of Orders, to talk of " mere authorisation " as though it were something wholly apart from ordination is to make an entirely false antithesis. No one doubts that ordination is much more than authorisation, but that authorisation is part of the essence of ordination seems almost equally unquestionable ; and talk about " mere authorisation " as something quite unspiritual certainly sounds strangely on the lips of those who in other contexts are wont to

[1] For further discussion on this point, see appended Note at the end of the chapter.

equate faith and order as the twin pillars of Catholicism. After all, who shall say that the solemn confirmation and authorisation of a Free Church minister's Orders by the hands of an apostolic bishop adds nothing to them, or who shall fix the precise limits of what it adds ? And who, again, shall say that the acceptance by an Anglican bishop or priest of solemn authorisation to exercise his ministry in a Christian body now reuniting with his own does nothing in a similar way to complete the meaning and reality of his own ordination ?

Our present purpose, however, is not to discuss in detail any particular proposals for reunion which have been put forward ; rather it is to indicate a general doctrine of the sacramental Church and its ministry which may possibly to some minds at least make our present differences and divisions seem less impossible of reconciliation. At present the Church of England in particular is hindered by divided counsels from making full use of her unique opportunities in the cause of union. On the one hand Evangelicals and Modernists appreciate so little the Catholic notion of validity that they often seem willing for the sake of reunion to give up exactly that which to the Catholic makes reunion both obligatory and expedient. And it seems quite justifiable to point out both to them and to our brothers of the Free Churches that it is really useless to press for reunion in outward order by methods which, when examined, seem to imply that matters of outward order are spiritually unimportant. On the other hand the difficulties and confusions which beset the position of Anglo-Catholicism as usually held have become more and more apparent. One small, yet not insignificant, indication of this has been the attempt of some Anglo-Catholics to dismiss the results of the Lambeth Conversations with the remark that reunion with the Free Churches is wholly impracticable while Free Churchmen obviously entertain a conception of the ministry altogether different from their own.   In fact nothing is more evident from the Lambeth Conversations than that the main difficulty in regard to Orders arose from the claim of the Free Church representatives that their Churches possessed a fully ordained ministry in the Catholic sense of the words. If Free Churchmen really held a conception of the ministry radically different from the Anglo-Catholic, there would be comparatively little obstacle there to reunion, since Free Church ministers could hardly then be claiming to possess already that which the bishops would desire to bestow upon them.   It is precisely because and in so far as Free Churchmen do attach the same meaning to ordination as Anglo-Catholics, that reunion in order appears at present to be impossible.

The intolerable paradox of such a situation does seem to call for some re-examination and restatement of the fundamental doctrine of the Church and the ministry, which belongs to the Catholic heritage of the Church of England.   It is as a very tentative contribution to this task that the foregoing discussion is offered to the judgment of all who have the cause of reunion at heart.

NOTE TO CHAPTER VII

A. THE THEORY OF VALIDITY

The main objection to the Augustinian theory of validity, at present accepted in the Church of Rome, may be roughly stated thus.   It makes the essence of a valid sacrament consist in a divine action performed in response to the utterance of a particular form by a person who has

a *ministerial power inherent in himself*, rather than by
a person who has a *ministerial authority in virtue of an
office held*. Thus, Roman Catholic theologians teach in
effect, that every human being who can form an adequate
intention has the power of baptizing, every ordained
priest has the power of consecrating the Eucharist, and
so forth. And it is evident that this *power* is conceived
as being in principle quite independent of any *authorisation* through the Church. For any pagan can baptize,
and any excommunicated or heretical priest can consecrate the elements. By this teaching then the notion
of validity in a sacrament is completely removed from
the notion of *authorisedness*, to use a barbarous but
exact term ; and it follows further that the Church, considered as an organised unity, has no real control over the
administration of valid sacraments, since these can be
propagated without limit by schismatic bodies and individuals.

This doctrine certainly has a tendency to approximate
the forms of sacraments to magical formulæ. For however carefully the tendency is corrected in other ways,
the impression is given that, when a particular person
utters a particular form of words, then, and for that
reason alone, something spiritual happens. If in any
given case subsequent doubt arises as to " validity ",
the main thing to be determined, apart from what concerns the matter, is the question whether the form was
exactly uttered ; and, if either form or matter is found
to have been slightly different from what is held to be
exactly right, it is usual, in the case of such sacraments
as Baptism and Ordination, to go through the rite again
sub conditione. According to this view, therefore, so
little does the authority of the Church count in the validation of sacraments, that there is a wide range of varieties

in form and matter, upon which the Church cannot pronounce. The validity of a sacrament entirely consists, as it were, in the use of a certain form and a certain matter which elicits a certain response from God. And, where the appointed sign has not been quite exactly performed, the Church often cannot say whether the response has or has not been elicited.

We have argued that this whole theory is unsatisfactory, because it divorces validity from authorisation. Canon Bate has lately reminded us[1] that the Greek equivalent of the Latin *validus* is βέβαιος, which means " firm " or " assured ", and that " when St. Ignatius, in the second century, speaks of a Eucharist celebrated by a bishop of his deputy as βεβαία, he means that it is one in which the faithful can partake without any misgiving as to the conditions under which it is celebrated ". Clearly the implication is that a Eucharist, to be in this sense valid, must be celebrated by a properly authorised person. And if we may bring back into our conception of validity this old notion of βεβαιότης, it would seem that valid sacraments ought to be defined as those performed in the appointed way by persons holding due authorisation in the Church for that purpose. Here precisely lies the reason for deprecating the performance of a sacramental rite *sub conditione*, except where genuine doubt exists as to what actually took place on the previous occasion when the sacrament may have been performed. If the outward facts are fully known, then the Church should be able to decide whether or not they constituted a valid sacrament, or wherein the validity was deficient. Of course it is agreed that the Church has no power over the sacramental action of God, and, so far, no control over

[1] In the chapter he contributes to *The Future of the Church of England*, edited by Sir James Marchant, K.B.E. (p. 193).

the sacraments. But the Church can and must settle questions of validity, in so far as validity turns upon ecclesiastical authorisation. Validity does depend upon such authorisation, in so far as it rests upon the authority of the minister ; and surely the validity of " doubtful " variations in form and matter should be determined in the same way by the authority of the Church. At the same time it must always be borne in mind that a negative decision as to authorisation prejudges nothing as to the grace actually received through an " invalid " ceremony on any given occasion. It is strange that Roman Catholicism should, in reference to the sacraments, seem to belittle unduly the authority of the Church.

The difficulties of Catholic theologians about the doctrine of intention seem to be derived in part from the same source. *Some* doctrine of intention there must be, if the Christian sacraments are to be saved from the absurdities, and worse than absurdities, of magic. But the Augustinian theory of validity seems to make the sacrament, on its human side, depend upon the *personal*, rather than upon the *official*, action of the minister, and therefore to require a *private* intention in the minister's own mind to perform the sacrament, and not merely a *publicly expressed* intention, for which the apparent fact that a man is acting in an official capacity is sufficient evidence. In this antithesis we have roughly indicated the point at issue between those theologians who require " interior intention " in the minister of a sacrament, and those who hold that " exterior intention " is enough. In the Roman Communion the necessity of interior intention is now generally accepted, in spite of the weighty arguments of Salmeron and Catharinus, which have been revived and restated by Dr. Langford James in his recent monograph, *The Doctrine of Intention*. At first sight this is strange ; for the difficulties of the now prevalent doctrine are obvious. It necessitates the almost intolerable conclusion that in the last resort the minister can render the sacrament invalid simply by forming and adhering in his own mind to a contrary intention, while he outwardly performs the sacramental acts. But the acceptance, reluctant as it is, of this disquieting paradox seems to be ultimately due to the same theory of validity which we have been criticising. Once it is made clear that a valid sacrament must, from one point of view, have the nature of an official and authorised act, the private or interior intention of the minister can in principle make no more difference to its validity than a judge's private thoughts can make to the validity of a sentence which he delivers.

B. THE VALIDATION OF ORDERS IN REUNION

The general method advocated in the preceding chapter for dealing with the problem of Orders in reunion differs in some important respects from the suggestions made by the Bishop of Gloucester in his Bampton Lectures on *The Doctrine of the Church and Christian Reunion*. The Bishop proposes that validity of Orders should be recognised in all those bodies who ordain with laying on of hands and prayer. In the case of ministers of such bodies reuniting with the Church of England, there should be no further laying on of hands or any ritual of ordination, but only a public commissioning for ministry in the Church of England.[1] This method of procedure seems to be less satisfactory for several reasons.

(1) Surely, once the strict theory of Apostolic Succes-

[1] p. 306.

sion has been relaxed, it is arbitrary to confine validity to those ordinations in which the solemn laying on of hands is practised, especially seeing that the essential matter of this sacrament has been notoriously a subject of uncertainty and various opinion even within the main stream of the Catholic tradition, and cannot with any sort of plausibility be said to have been defined by Christ Himself. To suggest that to extend still further any recognition of validity would be to " recognise slovenliness and indifference " seems to lead to harsh judgments which in particular cases it might well be impossible to justify.

(2) If from one point of view the Bishop's proposals appear to be too strict, from another they certainly seem to err on the side of laxity. They underestimate that element in the validity of Orders on which we have been specially insisting, viz. *authorisation*. The Bishop does not say whether he would regard an ordination performed with prayer and imposition of hands by two or three entirely independent and unauthorised persons as equally valid with any other ordination in the Catholic Church. Probably he would not. But in that case he has not really defined all the conditions he would require for validity, or all the significance he attaches to the term.

(3) There is also a moral factor to be considered. The method of recognising existing ministries, and merely adding an enlarged commission apart from any sacramental rite, seems too slight a way of healing the wounds which schism has inflicted. If the outward order of the Church is not to be regarded as a sacred thing, reunion must be a mockery. If outward order is regarded as sacred, something more than a merely legal commission or licence is needed to mark its restoration. Moreover, the spirit of charity and humility seems to indicate that each reuniting body should seek to receive from others

what it lacks, and to supply to others what they lack, rather than to insist upon the recognition by others of its own sufficiency, beyond what is necessary in the cause of truth.

(4) Finally, in the present confusion of Churches, the only practicable method of expressing our genuine desire to make a fresh start, as well as of setting at rest all the various scruples and hesitations of the many consciences involved, seems to lie in agreeing that we will all in outward things mutually give and receive as much, rather than as little, as truth, reason and charity may allow. I do not at all suggest that the proposals, for which the Bishop of Gloucester has made out so strong a case, are or ought to be intolerable to the genuinely Catholic mind. But it may well be that other proposals, nearer in form to those put forward in the Lambeth *Appeal*, will appear on examination to be both sounder in logic and more appropriate to our needs.

CHAPTER VIII

HOLY BAPTISM

BAPTISM is essentially the sacrament of the divine Fatherhood, or of man's filial relation to the God of whom all fatherhood in heaven and earth is named. It has indeed other meanings. The New Testament in various passages represents it as a sacrament also both of ablution and of resurrection. But ablution and resurrection after all are in the end only parts or aspects of the process whereby man's filial relation to God through Christ is finally and completely effected. As aspects of baptism, then, they are subordinate to the essential notion of regeneration as the act whereby a human soul is taken into the heavenly family of God. In a very real sense, therefore, baptism may be called an extension and effect of the Incarnation and the Atonement. For it is only as represented in the life of the Incarnate Son and as sharing the fruits of what He has done for man, that any human person can take upon his lips the word of Christ's address to God, Abba, Father. And it is for the same reason that, according to Catholic order, no unbaptized person may receive Holy Communion. In the sacramental scheme of spiritual life, as in the reality of that life itself, a soul must be born into God's family, before it can take its place at the family board.

The whole of our baptismal teaching, therefore, must necessarily depend upon the idea of God's Fatherhood which we have received through Jesus Christ. And it is here that we must look for the solution of those problems which are the occasion of so much scruple and questioning in the modern mind as regards the real meaning and effect of the sacrament.

Clearly there is no sacrament in which the symbolic and instrumental aspects are more liable to come into conflict. It is fatally easy to emphasise either at the expense of the other. We may on the one hand insist that God is Father of all, and all without distinction are His children, until baptism becomes for us purely a declaratory rite, in which nothing is effected beyond the vivid presentation of a universal truth. We may on the other hand asseverate that in baptism a real gift of new life is bestowed, until we are forced by logic into the conclusion that the Fatherhood of God towards men is not really universal at all, but is a relation which exists only towards the regenerate : God, then, in effect, is the King of all and the Father of some.

Unquestionably the last sentence roughly represents a view which may seem to be suggested by much of the traditional orthodoxy both of the Catholic and of the Protestant type, and is not without support even in the language of the New Testament itself. It therefore deserves careful examination.

Catholic tradition has certainly done much to encourage the idea that only those persons who have been received into the Church by baptism can properly be regarded as children of God. Doubtless God created and rules over all, and wills to make all men His children through incorporation into His Church. But the unbaptized are not yet His children. The consequence of the Fall and the fact of original sin mean just the deprivation of those gifts and capacities characteristic of God's children, which do not belong to human nature as such,

but which, forfeited by Adam, are restored by free
grace to all his descendants who enter Christ's Church
by the Sacrament of Baptism. Until those gifts and
capacities of sonship are restored, men are under the
sway of God's regal authority, but not within the circle
of His Fatherly love.[1]

It should be noted in passing that the historical identification of the Catholic Church with God's *Kingdom* upon
earth has not, in the developed theology of Catholicism,
been held to conflict with this distinction, so as to push
the unbaptized outside even the law of God's kingly
justice and mercy, or to make them merely enemies of
His rule. That kingly rule is held to be universal, and
the natural religion which is common to all men shows
God as Creator and Sovereign of all. The " Kingdom of
God ", on the other hand, which is the subject of Christian
revelation, continues and perfects the special relation of
God to His chosen people, and, through its embodiment
in the Christian Church, becomes identical with what we
speak of as God's family. Thus the distinction of status
between God's human subjects and those who are in the
full sense His children is made to correspond to the distinction between " natural " and " revealed " theology.

Protestant theology has, of course, been far less completely unified in any single system. But it too has not

[1] Doubtless modern Catholic theologians prefer a language which
does not exclude the unbaptized altogether from sonship toward God,
but distinguishes two grades of sonship. Dr. Darwell Stone defines
their position with his usual lucidity when he writes that Catholic
Christians look on the unbaptized " as beings who are capable of
receiving the great gifts of regeneration and life in God ; they recognise
in them the elemental sonship to God which is theirs because they are
His creation and share the nature taken by the Son of God in the
Incarnation, an elemental sonship which pleads for the higher sonship
of the baptized " (*Holy Baptism*, p. 209). In practice, however, it
seems true to say that in Catholic tradition the sonship of the unbaptized is treated as a potentiality, rather than an actuality, of sonship.
Their *actual* condition is better described by the term subject.

infrequently suggested that the true Fatherhood of God is confined to a certain circle of converted persons ; and at times it has gone beyond the more modern orthodoxy of Catholicism in maintaining that His universal rule spells nothing but eternal wrath for all who are outside the family of the converted.   Traditional Protestantism here differs from traditional Catholicism chiefly in making the actual transition from the status of subject to that of child to consist in an inward experience unconnected with a sacramental rite.

The exact force of the teaching of the New Testament upon the universality of God's Fatherhood is somewhat difficult to estimate.

It is clear that our Lord did insist upon the truth of God's Fatherhood so strongly and in such a special sense that this teaching may legitimately be said to form a fundamental principle of His message as well as a mark of its originality.   It has often been pointed out that our Lord, according to the evidence of our evangelists, never spoke of God by any other title than that of heavenly Father.   This is in itself an enormously significant fact. But scholars have shown that a still more profound impression is to be derived from a comparison of Mark xiv. 36, Rom. viii. 15 and Gal. iv. 6.   There are very few Aramaic words preserved in the text of the New Testament.   Abba is the only one which occurs more than once. It occurs three times in all, twice in letters of St. Paul addressed to Gentile converts.   In each of the three passages the Greek translation of the word is added, while the Aramaic original is retained as well.   The inference is irresistible that the word Abba as an address to God was peculiarly characteristic of Jesus, that He taught His disciples to use it as He used it Himself, and that the relation to God which the word denoted was the great legacy which He had bequeathed to all His followers.

But is this right to address God as Father a privilege restricted to those who had definitely accepted Christ's gospel and the Christian faith ? Does the Fatherhood denote a relation which holds between God and some men only ? There is no passage in the Gospels where our Lord directly speaks of God as the Father of all. And the Pauline texts seem almost inevitably to imply a Father-hood restricted to believers. It is into the hearts of Christians only that God has sent the Spirit of His Son crying Abba. That is the mark which differentiates them from the rest of the world. And Bishop Gore has pointed out[1] that, so far as the explicit assertions of the New Testament go, the work of the Holy Spirit is almost con-fined to His operation within the society of God's chosen people, whether the old Israel or the new. Only one phrase in the New Testament seems to be quite explicit about universal Fatherhood; that is the εἷς θεὸς καὶ πατὴρ πάντων of Ephesians iv.

There is therefore a genuine foundation in the Bible for the traditional theology which virtually limits to the Christian circle the filial relation of man to God. And, inasmuch as baptism in the New Testament at least marks the entry into that circle, there is good ground for saying in a general sense that according to apostolic teaching baptism *makes* men children of God in answer to their profession of faith in Christ.[2]

Nevertheless there are at least two considerations,

---

[1] *The Holy Spirit and the Church*, pp. 9 *sqq.*

[2] It is a singularly perverse, though not uncommon, exegesis, which takes St. Paul's words, " I thank God that I baptized none of you ", etc. (1 Cor. I. 14), as a belittling of the importance of Baptism. St. Paul's point is that the fact that he did not baptize prevents anyone from saying that he was baptized into the name of Paul. Baptism is

drawn directly from our Lord's teaching, which should make us beware of thinking that anything like a restriction of God's universal fatherhood towards men could be in accordance with the mind of Jesus.

(*a*) It is remarkable that in the only recorded saying which definitely states the condition under which sonship towards God is to be realised (Matt. v. 45 ; Luke vi. 35), our Lord makes that condition consist in a certain behaviour of love towards those who have no apparent claim to be God's children at all. The disciples are expressly told that they will display their family likeness to the heavenly Father chiefly in showing an invincible kindliness to those who seem to deserve it least. There is a clear implication that the special and full sonship received through the gospel itself consists in the recognition that God is the loving Father of sinners also, and that His behaviour, in point of fatherliness, is the same to all.

(*b*) It is instructive to contrast our Lord's image of God as the Father, uniquely emphasised as it was, with the Old Testament image of God as the Husband of His people. The relation of father to children differs from that of husband to wife in two respects, each of which is significant.

(i) Under a law of monogamy, which the prophets took for granted, the relation of husband and wife is an exclusive relation of one person to one other. The relation of father to children is an inclusive relation of one person to a plurality of others, which directly involves a further relation between the children themselves. The suggestion here is that the old exclusiveness of Jehovah's relation to Israel is being broken down.

the mark of Christian unity in Christ ; and, in view of the Corinthian divisions, it is on its supreme importance in this sense that St. Paul desires to insist. Even if it were said that the preaching was Paul's, at least the baptism clearly was not Paul's, but Christ's.

(ii) The relation of husband to wife is a contractual relation ; that of father to children is a natural relation. Does not our Lord's emphasis on fatherhood suggest that the new covenant of which He was the herald was something more even than a covenant, and that the proper analogue of God's relation to His people is not a mere contract of any kind, but rather that relation of father to children which can have no beginning or end except the beginning or end of the child's existence ? If so, it would seem to follow that a human being already brought into existence cannot in the strictest reality *begin* to be a child of its heavenly, any more than of its earthly, Father ; it can only begin to realise the meaning, powers and obligations, of that filial relation in which it already is. It is exactly here that St. Paul's legal metaphor of sonship by adoption may perhaps be inadequate to the full depth of the gospel. For no one can in full reality be made the son of another by adoption ; there is an element of legal fiction in the proceeding just in so far as it must be legal only.

On the whole then we may say that New Testament teaching displays a real ambiguity as to what may be called the extent of God's Fatherhood, and therefore as to the meaning of Baptism as the sacrament of that Fatherhood. On the one hand the acceptance of the gospel, together with the sacrament which completed it, undoubtedly meant a really new life to the first Christians. They knew themselves to be born again in the realisation of God's Fatherhood towards them through Jesus Christ. The new was as different from the old as life from death. But this was the language of devotion, not of metaphysical logic, and the very truth of it depended on the fact that it was not the whole truth. For the very newness of the new life was characterised in part by its apprehension of a relation of God toward all men, which, because it was universal, could not be newly brought into existence, though it was newly revealed. Indeed the new birth of an already existing soul is always, as the logic of Nicodemus indicated, a self-contradiction. And it is a self-contradiction which Christian theology has never completely overcome.

We certainly cannot profess to overcome it. But by viewing it in relation to the Christian theory of life as a whole, we can see in it a mystery, and not a mere negation of meaning. According to this theory the separateness of the child of God from other men is always to be measured by his capacity to represent in himself something which is true of them also, and in so doing to elicit it effectively from them. He who was born of Mary represents in Himself all manhood, and by so doing elicits from all men their heavenly capacities. And as men are separated from the world to share Christ's Sonship, so they are endued with the office and power of His manhood. They are born again through Him, that they may declare all men born as His and therefore to be called to follow Him. There is a sense in which all Christians are baptized, if not " for the dead ", still for the not yet reborn. Even the silence of the New Testament about the operation of the Spirit outside the Church ceases to cause difficulty, if we may interpret it in the light of the doctrine that the Church represents the world and brings it before God no less truly than it represents God and brings Him before the world.

We thus reach a point of view from which modern difficulties as to the nature of the sacrament can be seen in their true perspective. And it seems that most of them have arisen because neither the orthodox nor their critics have sufficiently realised that the change from adult-baptism to infant-baptism as the normal practice of the Church should have involved a shifting of emphasis from the instrumental to the symbolic aspect of the sacrament.

In primitive times, when heathen or Jewish converts were baptized, the main emphasis was naturally laid on the instrumental aspect, that is, on the actual change which the sacrament wrought. In concrete fact an old life was left behind, a new life entered upon. The defilements of the old life were washed away ; the old self was dead ; the man was a new being in Christ's service. Thus ablution, resurrection, new birth were spiritual fact actually accomplished in Baptism. St. Paul, however, by his teaching of baptismal resurrection, makes it perfectly clear that Baptism must symbolise a reality deeper and fuller than anything which at the moment of its performance it effects. His converts are bidden to walk in newness of life because in Baptism they have been raised ; but clearly that resurrection symbolised in Baptism is not in all senses actually complete —otherwise there would be no need of his admonitions. Strictly speaking, no one is fully risen or fully a child of God while he is still liable to fall into the sins which contradict his new life and sonship. In a true sense, therefore, Baptism only effects the beginning of a process of which it symbolises the end and the whole. And yet the baptized person must be adjured to lead the truly Christian life on the ground that he is already risen and already God's child. Here we come in sight of the unescapable contradiction which St. Paul's doctrine of justification by faith was intended to overcome. The faith in Christ, which the convert professed in being baptized, was an earnest of his will and desire to rise to the life of sonship ; and God through Christ was, as it were, enabled to accept this earnest as a fulfilment, so as to treat the baptized person as already risen to sonship, and thereby to elicit from him through His fatherly care that actuality of sonship which in present fact was very imperfectly his. Thus Baptism to St. Paul symbolised more than it effected, and yet what it left to be effected afterwards was only the consequence of a reality which it had effectively symbolised already.

This teaching, as subtle as it was profound, exceeded the mental grasp of the early Church as a whole. Most Christians interpreted Baptism much more simply as an instrumental rite. One consequence of this was seen in the morbid fear of post-baptismal sin which led many to defer Baptism till the approach of death. And even the complete reversal of policy, which presently established a universal custom of approximating Baptism as nearly as possible to birth instead of death, did not bring any return to Pauline symbolism as a means of restating baptismal theology.

Clearly the apparent formalism of the orthodox theology of Baptism, which is apt to give genuine distress to the modern mind, is the result of an attempt to regard the Baptism of infants as an instrumental rite in exactly the same manner as it had first seemed natural to regard the Baptism of converted adults. What in the case of new-born infants is the old life which is to be left behind, the defilement of which is to be washed away, and from which regeneration is to be sought ? The answer was found in the doctrine of original sin. All human beings naturally born into the world are born in a fallen state, which has been diversely interpreted as meaning either a positive defilement or perversion of human nature, or else a deprivation of that supernatural life which God had bestowed upon the unfallen Adam in addition to his human nature

strictly so called. It is from this fallen state, the effect
of original sin, that Baptism raises or purifies the infant-
soul, and in so doing restores to it, in virtue of Christ's
atonement, the supernatural gifts of heavenly life which
Adam had enjoyed before the fall.[1] But Baptism does
not remove from the soul the possibility of actual sin, of
falling from grace, nor the experience of those tempta-
tions whereby the powers of evil seek to drag it back
from salvation. Against these dangers and the falls
which they occasion, the sacramental remedy is not in
Baptism, but in Penance and the Eucharist. Meanwhile
the function of the sponsors in Baptism is retained as a
witness that not even the effect of original sin can be
removed in any magical or mechanical way without
demand made on the soul thus raised to new life; Baptism
can only be effective in answer to that soul's profession
of faith in Christ, even though that profession has to
be vicariously made through god-parents,[2] and must

[1] No doubt the tendency to reduce the meaning of original sin from
depravation to deprivation is itself due to the introduction of infant
baptism as a practically universal rule. The resulting difficulties for
traditionalism are well illustrated by the following very carefully
balanced statement which I quote from a modern Roman Catholic
writer, Mr. E. J. Watkin : " If dirt has been aptly defined as matter
in the wrong place, original sin, being essentially nature in the wrong
place (that is, exclusive of supernature), is truly termed an uncleanness,
and baptism a cleansing from stain. No physical defilement, nor uncleanness of nature as such, does the Church intend by such language,
but simply and solely birth into a nature-self deprived of the supernature which should have completed it. Thus is the personal innocence
of the new-born babe, its innocence in the natural order, compatible
with a guilt of its nature in relation to the supernatural order. Thus
also is it dear to God because substantially united to Him as its natural
ground and end, yet " a child of wrath " in its separation from Him
and aversion from Him as its supernatural end " (*God and the Supernatural*, ed. by Fr. Cuthbert, o.s.f.c., p. 150). Dr. E. J. Bicknell's
contribution to *Essays Catholic and Critical* provides a more liberal-
orthodox statement on Sin and the Fall, with which I find myself in
complete agreement.

[2] St. Thomas, quoting St. Augustine, writes (Summa III, Q. 68,
Art. 9, ad. 2) : " *In Ecclesia Salvatoris parvuli per alios credunt, sicut*

anticipate the process of instruction which will afterwards enable the baptized person to make it actually his own.

But this whole account of the matter is open to grave objection. It is not that the doctrines of the Fall and of original sin are in themselves incredible. However mythical the story of Adam may be when considered as history, it is a truth, verifiable in history and present experience, that mankind is born into a fallen or gravely defective condition of moral and spiritual being, from which it needs to be raised, and can be raised, into newness of life through the gospel. What cannot at all be verified in experience is the supposition that Baptism in itself makes any such change in the spiritual condition of an infant as is implied by asserting that it removes from it once for all original sin and its hold on the soul. So far as experience can show, the sinful tendencies or spiritual defects of a baptized and of an unbaptized child are very much the same. And, while no doubt it is always formally possible to allege that apparently similar sins in the baptized and the unbaptized are not really the effects of the same inward causes, " actual " sin in the one operating for " original " sin in the other, the whole distinction remains unverifiable, and therefore must appear purely formal and unreal.[1]

ex aliis, quae in baptismo remittuntur peccata traxerunt. . . . Fides autem unius, immo totius Ecclesiae, parvulo prodest per operationem Spiritus Sancti, qui unit Ecclesiam, et bona unius alteri communicat."

[1] Roman Catholic orthodoxy at this point is extremely subtle. It asserts categorically that Baptism removes all stain (*macula*) and guilt (*reatus*) of sin, and therefore also the punishment due to it (*poena debita*). Nevertheless facts compel the admission that the penal conditions of this present life (*poenalitates praesentis vitae*), which are consequences of man's fall, are not taken away in this world from the baptized. Moreover, among these *poenalitates* it is found necessary to reckon not only pain, death and the like, but also concupiscence, the unruly or " deordinated " desire which still shows itself in the baptized as in others. But, if concupiscence persists, how is it really intelligible to say that original sin has been removed ? It is said that the hold

Moreover, it seems that such scholastic subtleties are not really necessary to enable the Church to maintain her rule of infant-baptism and to justify her faith in its value. Let us follow out St. Paul's hint that Baptism symbolises much more than what at the moment it effects. Let us first consider its symbolised meaning with reference to the future. A perfect washing from sin, a perfect resurrection to new life, a perfect membership in God's family through Christ, these are identical with the final salvation of the soul. Baptism, therefore, in symbolising the ultimate end of salvation, symbolises also by anticipation all those many purifications from sin and gifts of new life, of which the progress towards final salvation is made up.[1] The end is identical with the completed achievement of the process, and both end and process are appropriately symbolised at the beginning. They are, moreover, *expressively* symbolised, for the process is only possible to the soul in virtue of the fact that the relation to God as Father which is perfected at the end has also been real from the beginning ; and this reality constitutes the very nature of Baptism itself. And, with this thought in our minds, we may consider the symbolism of the Sacrament

of concupiscence has been weakened in the baptized, so that it need no longer be feared. But in what sense is this verified ? (See St. Thomas, Summa III, Q. 66, Art. 7, ad. 3 ; Q. 69, Arts. 1–3. Council of Trent, Sess V, Tanquerey, Synopsis III, §§ 412–417.)

[1] Dom Anscar Vonier, o.s.b., writes : "Much confusion of thought in the doctrine of the sacraments . . . would be spared us if we never let go of that elemental definition of the sacrament, that it is a relationship of signification. Whatever reality there is in a sacrament is deeply modified by this rule of signification. Baptism, to quote only one sacrament, is not any kind of cleansing of the soul, but it is a cleansing of the soul which is a burial with Christ and which is a resurrection with Christ. Baptism is not only the present, but also the past and the future." He proceeds to quote Rom. vi. 3–5 (*A Key to the Doctrine of the Eucharist*, p. 22). J. B. Mozley (*Review of the Baptismal Controversy*, p. 322) quotes the following from Peter Lombard (L. IV. dist. 4): *Nec mireris rem aliquando praecedere sacramentum, cum aliquando etiam longe post sequatur.*

retrospectively also. Even Baptism is not an absolute beginning. The soul, born naturally into the world, needs the powers and graces of a new and higher life. But those powers and graces themselves are but the more perfect appropriation and enjoyment of what God has always been, and what He has always willed, towards it and towards all.

It is evident that, if we are permitted thus to emphasise the symbolic aspect of the Sacrament, we can justify the baptism of infants without being obliged to separate the effect of Baptism upon original and pre-baptismal sin from its relation to sin as a whole. But in thus insisting upon symbolism, are we reducing the effectiveness of Baptism to vanishing point altogether, or simply making it consist in the clearer knowledge gained through symbolic presentation ? This question brings us face to face with a real difficulty ; and we must make clear wherein precisely the difficulty consists.

So long as we confine our attention strictly to baptized persons, it need not give us much trouble. We have already argued that Baptism is an " extension " of the Incarnation and the Atonement, in the sense that Baptism symbolises in a single act for each individual the whole process and end of that new human life which the life of Jesus Christ has brought into the world. Baptism itself must in any case be regarded as one event in that process ; and, since it is that event which is in a special sense appointed to symbolise the whole, it is only natural to hold that it is also in its actual effect specially important and decisive. We need not at all be disturbed by the impossibility of defining its effect if we isolate it from the process of Christian life which follows it. For its proper and characteristic effect is exactly to initiate that process. And, if in any particular case through human sin or neglect

the subsequent stages of the process are hindered, we
need not hesitate to say that the particular baptism has
so far been made ineffective ; it will not at all follow that
the process was not really initiated or may not even now
be resumed. Moreover, we may readily admit that to an
indeterminate and varying degree the process, which
Baptism is properly meant to initiate, has already been
going on in the soul as yet unbaptized. The Sacrament
of Baptism still stands for the fact that man needs a
double birth, spiritual as well as natural, and membership
in two families, a heavenly as well as an earthly. And,
however truly the double birth and membership may
have been real before the sacrament was conferred, he
would surely be a narrow-minded theologian who would
contend that the solemn action of the baptismal rite
does not itself mark a really critical step in the process
which it symbolises.

But the real difficulty which the modern mind feels
concerning the efficacy of Baptism arises from a comparison of the lives of baptized persons with those of
unbaptized, and that especially in countries where the
influence of Christianity has spread far beyond the acknowledged members of any Christian Church. When the
spiritual and moral health of so many of the unbaptized
is apparently so superior to that of so many of the
baptized, that it has become difficult to allege that even
on the whole Baptism makes a conspicuous difference,
how can the obligation of Baptism be any longer rationally maintained ?

The answers to this question usually accepted as
orthodox can hardly be considered satisfactory. Historical
uncertainties render precarious the reliance on the mere
fact of Christ's appointment. The appeal to the unbroken
practice of the Church is rationally insufficient, unless

some good reason can be given why the universality of the practice should be maintained. And to assert that, while God may doubtless receive into His spiritual family some souls apart from Baptism, nevertheless Baptism gives the only assurance of that membership, is a plea which is open to still graver objections. If an infant has died unbaptized or if an unbaptized person manifestly shows the fruits of the Spirit in his life, can we seriously contend that God's acceptance of the soul in question is any real sense rendered doubtful by the lack of Baptism ? To affirm such a doubt is really to doubt the very love of God itself.[1] And if God's love be doubtful, of what can Christianity assure us ? Let God be found righteous, even if every orthodox theologian be made a liar.[2] We must, if necessary, alter our ecclesiastical rules to fit the Christian idea of God, not alter the Christian idea of God to justify an ecclesiastical rule. And perhaps the most pernicious of all defences of orthodoxy is that suggested in the retort attributed by *Punch* to an Irish priest, who was assailed by a critic with the remark, " I've never been able to see the difference be-

---

[1] For this reason I cannot accept Dr. Darwell Stone's assertions that " we are simply in ignorance to what extent or under what circumstances God may Himself relax His own law " (of Baptism), and that, as to the salvation of unbaptized infants, " it can only be said again that such a matter is outside the limits of our present knowledge " (*Holy Baptism*, pp. 112, 115).

[2] The orthodox Catholicism of the West is in certain respects much more liberal on this subject than some suppose. The authority of St. Augustine, St. Ambrose and the Schoolmen is accepted for the belief that a spiritual repentance (*actus perfectae contritionis*), which includes, at least implicitly, a desire for Baptism, is sufficient to obtain the grace of the Sacrament. The implicit desire, says Tanquerey, " *Certo sufficit in eo qui legem baptismi invincibiliter ignorat, et valde probabiliter etiam in eo qui eam novit sed de ea actu non cogitat* ". But this extension cannot include unbaptized infants who are incapable of the spiritual act required. These, it is held, are deprived of supernatural blessedness, but suffer no positive penalty (Tanquerey, Synopsis III, §§ 434–438).

tween a good Catholic and a good Protestant ; and I've lived sixty years in this world ". " Faith ", said the priest, " you wouldn't live sixty seconds in the next, before you'd see the difference." The wit of that ready answer but thinly conceals everything that has made the doctrine of divine judgment in the hereafter abhorrent to the reason and conscience of mankind.

Nevertheless the Church's rule of baptism is quite capable of rational defence if we will frankly abandon the claim that the baptized individual must necessarily possess some spiritual privilege or power which the unbaptized individual necessarily lacks. The rational justification for Baptism ultimately rests not on the explicit appointment of Jesus, probable though it be that He did appoint it, nor upon the mistaken idea that Baptism bestows anything—even a guarantee—which for the individual is otherwise unobtainable, but rather upon a whole conception of that plan for the salvation of mankind which God revealed through Jesus Christ and carries on in the life of His Church. We have already indicated in what sense and for what reason we believe that plan to be thoroughly and radically sacramental. The question with which we are at present occupied is seen in quite a new light, once it is understood that the Christian religion is designed not to save just a few specially gifted individuals, but to save the world. Suppose there were no sacramental ordinances in Christianity at all. Assuredly saintliness would not vanish from the earth. God would not be without witness. Individuals would continue to receive by inward and spiritual means His sanctifying grace, and to manifest its fruit in their lives. But on the whole they would be far less able to co-operate effectively for the salvation of the multitudes, and perhaps even their own saintliness would lack that

N

peculiarly Catholic quality which is the mark of those whom a common discipline in spiritual things has placed on a level with others very different from themselves in respect of natural gifts and social environment. Consider the needs and capacities of the general ruck of mankind, and you begin to see both the necessity of providing a sacramental system for a spiritual religion, and also the wisdom and the love which have provided it.[1] The general value of such a system, as we have already indicated, is to join together into a visible fellowship and common obedience in spiritual things people of quite different types, while it affords to the outsider the clear apprehension of something definite and specific into which he is asked to come and to which his loyalty is required. These arguments apply with perhaps especial force to Baptism. It is to it as the great symbol of the unity and level standing of all Christians in Christ that St. Paul thrice appeals.[2] And thus we may say that, although individuals can be, and most undoubtedly are, saved without Baptism, yet the world as a whole, so far as experience seems to show, could not. For that reason, we may well believe, God has established His sacramental Church, and for that reason He wills that all men should enter it by the same sacramental door. But, if what we believe to be in this respect His general will for all men has not in particular cases been fulfilled, we need not profess to doubt what is God's mind toward those un-

[1] It is worth remarking that the Society of Friends, though in many ways it can put in a better claim than any other Christian body to display the purity and zeal of the gospel, nevertheless has never succeeded in incorporating into its membership any large number of the poorer classes of society. It is also very significant that so profound a theologian as Dr. Inge, who apparently does not believe that Christianity can ever be, or should attempt to be, the religion of more than the select few, should be almost consistently contemptuous of the Catholic doctrine and practice of the sacraments.

[2] See 1 Cor. i. 13–15; xii. 13; Eph. iv. 5.

baptized persons, or to question whether or not they are really partakers of His grace, when the fruits of it appear in their characters and lives.

The main sum of the foregoing argument is the plea that a sound theology of Baptism requires us to-day to emphasise the symbolic rather than the instrumental aspect of the sacrament, while at the same time we must not allow the instrumental to be wholly absorbed into the symbolic. The Fatherhood of God, of which it is the sacrament, is a truly universal reality ; and the washing, regeneration and resurrection, which the sacramental action signifies, constitute in fact a process which only ends in heaven and cannot therefore be intelligibly thought of as wholly complete in the moment when the Sacrament is performed. Nevertheless Baptism is itself a critical and decisive moment in the process of which it is the symbol. It marks and characterises the soul as God's child and member of His family, so that all its subsequent growth in God's grace is but an eliciting or bringing to light of what its baptism implied.

The main difficulty in this method of interpretation is the fact that in some measure it changes the emphasis of New Testament theology. There, undoubtedly, the central thought is that of the actual change brought about by the initiation of Christian life with which the Sacrament of Baptism is connected. But this difference, we may urge, is largely due to the peculiar and necessarily transient conditions under which the New Testament was composed. The thought of a newly born religion, winning its own self-consciousness through opposition to its surroundings, naturally lends itself to sharp distinctions, to a habit of seeing contrasts in black and white. The gifts of the Spirit in the New Testament, for instance, are much more sudden in their coming and more definitely marked in their character than we expect them to be to-day ; but it does not follow that to-day they are less real.   Even to-day, wherever the Christian Church is a definitely missionary body in a pagan land, the conditions of the New Testament and the emphasis of its theology tend naturally to reassert themselves.

The point of the Church's transition out of its missionary youth into the status and responsibilities of an established institution was marked by the substitution of infant-baptism for adult-baptism as the normal form of admission to full membership.   This change, as we have tried to argue, if it is justified at all, must in the end involve the change of emphasis in baptismal theology of which we have been speaking.   And, though we have admitted that the change is real, we have also endeavoured to show that the new emphasis upon the symbolic aspect of the Sacrament is fundamentally consistent with the teaching both of our Lord Himself and of St. Paul. The Johannine saying, which has always supplied the proof-text for the necessity of Baptism, " except a man be born of water and of the Spirit " may be harder to reconcile with the doctrines which have here been advocated.   But, without going into critical problems connected with the Fourth Gospel or into the difficulty of determining what exactly the words were originally meant to imply, it may fairly be pointed out that from the days of St. Ambrose and St. Augustine onwards the Church has never been content to interpret them in what might seem to be the most strictly literal sense.   There has been general agreement that not only martyrdom for Christ, but also sincere repentance combined with the desire for Baptism, are accepted by God in place of the baptism of water.   Thus the apparent harshness of the

words, " Except a man be born of water . . . he cannot
enter ", has by common consent been mitigated ; and
to-day there is hardly perhaps a sane Christian who would
have it otherwise. In any case, therefore, there is no
serious question of taking this text literally.

NOTE TO CHAPTER VIII—CONFIRMATION

Some apology is certainly needed for the absence of
any special treatment of the Sacrament of Confirmation,
which we have affirmed to be inseparable from Baptism
in primitive thought. Baptism, Confirmation and the
Eucharist are indeed always so closely linked both in
theory and practice that the omission seems really an
anomaly. But the truth is that it is impossible to discuss
the theology of Confirmation without raising a host of
historical and pastoral problems which—even if I were in
any way competent to deal with them—would take us
quite outside the scope of this volume. For the justification of this plea I would refer the reader to the excellent
and comprehensive volume on *Confirmation* recently
published by the Society for Promoting Christian
Knowledge. The facts there collected, however, especially
those dealt with by Mr. K. D. MacKenzie, who writes
on the relation of Confirmation to Baptism, seem to
suggest one or two general considerations which it may
be worth while to set down in this place.

The fundamental question is this. Is it the purpose of
Confirmation to symbolise and effect a radically new indwelling of the Holy Ghost in the soul ? Hence arises
a dilemma. For if we answer Yes, an interval of years
between Baptism and Confirmation cannot be justified.

If we answer No, inevitably Confirmation becomes a sacrament of secondary importance.

The Roman Church has followed St. Thomas Aquinas and other scholastic authorities in frankly accepting this latter alternative.[1] According to its teaching Confirmation is not a necessary sacrament in at all the same sense as Baptism ; it confers further graces of the Spirit, especially for growth and stability in the Christian life, and for boldness to confess Christ and " fight manfully under His banner ", but nothing other in kind or in essential principle from what Baptism has already given.

Anglican theologians and historians, however, especially in recent years, have strongly criticised this doctrine on the ground that it does not give to the Sacrament the due honour and importance which belonged to it in the primitive Church. Fr. Puller and Dr. Mason[2] have maintained the primitive and true doctrine to be that the gifts of Baptism are strictly preparatory to that of Confirmation, and that, while Baptism forgives sin, regenerates and joins us to the Body of Christ, it is left for Confirmation to bestow the actual indwelling of the Spirit. More lately still, Professor Turner[3] has argued strongly that both in the New Testament and in the primitive Church Baptism and Confirmation stand together as parts of one Sacrament ordained by Christ. As regards the practice and doctrine of the early Church these Anglican writers are undoubtedly able to make out a strong case. For in early times Baptism and Confirmation were normally joined ; and it seems not unreasonable to hold that, when patristic writers speak as though the gift of the Spirit were received

[1] See Mr. T. J. Hardy's essay in *Confirmation*, vol. i.

[2] Puller, *What is the Distinctive Grace of Confirmation ?* Mason, *The Relation of Confirmation to Baptism*. Both cited by K. D. MacKenzie in *Confirmation*, vol. i (S.P.C.K.).

[3] In a review which appeared in the *Church Quarterly* for July, 1920.

in Baptism, it was Baptism *plus* Confirmation that they had in mind. But if this is so, and if the primitive doctrine ought to be restored, the logical consequence seems to be that we should again join together in time the two rites of Baptism and Confirmation. This consequence Fr. Puller would accept, and Dr. Darwell Stone[1] would follow him in practice, though in his opinion tradition favours the belief that the soul of the baptized, even before Confirmation, possesses the indwelling of the Holy Ghost. Both writers apparently advocate the administration of Confirmation to infants according to the practice of the East.

There is much to be said on theoretical and historical grounds for Dr. Stone's and Fr. Puller's view. After all, the theological objections to confirming infants seem to be equally valid against baptizing them. But for practical and pastoral reasons, which at least are always entitled to consideration in the Church of Christ,[2] it is most unlikely that the Church of England will consent to forgo an established custom which may be, and often is, of such incalculable value as a means of giving strength to the young life about to face, or perhaps already facing, the trials of adolescence, or of " going out to work ". If, then, we do not mean to change our practice, we shall do well to beware of being carried away either by a merely deductive logic or by a more human zeal to teach our Roman Catholic brethren a lesson in Catholic theology. Confirmation, if it be separated from Baptism, must in some degree be modified in meaning, just as we have already argued that the emphasis in baptismal theology must be changed, where baptism of infants, not adults,

[1] See *The Faith of an English Catholic*, pp. 32, 33, and *Holy Baptism*, chap. xiii.
[2] Though Dr. Stone would apparently call them " subjective ", " utilitarian " and similar hard names (*Holy Baptism*, p. 186)

has become the rule. A theory which declares that Confirmation marks the first gift of the indwelling Spirit, and a practice which places Confirmation a dozen years or more after Baptism, point, when taken together, to conclusions which are intolerable.

The argument of the foregoing chapter, while it does not prejudge any historical question about primitive belief, must be taken as assuming that Baptism confers the gift of the indwelling Spirit. We have been speaking of Baptism, therefore, as including what some authorities believe to be the distinctive gift of Confirmation. Granted, then, that Baptism and Confirmation are to remain separated in time, it seems to follow that we must understand the gift of Confirmation more or less in accordance with the general teaching of Western theology since the Middle Ages. Thus interpreted Confirmation cannot be called a primary necessity of the Christian's sacramental life ; nor does it so imperatively require separate consideration in such a general theory of Christian sacraments as that which concerns us in this volume.

CHAPTER IX

THE EUCHARIST

THE Eucharist to the Christian is the culminating point of all sacramental rites. For that reason every presentation of its meaning in philosophical terms is more or less one-sided. In its case even more than in the case of other sacraments it is necessary that different statements should be balanced and combined. In the last chapter we were endeavouring to sketch a philosophical interpretation of Baptism which laid special stress upon its symbolical aspect. To many no doubt that interpretation will seem to do less than justice to the mysterious reality of the divine act which takes place in Baptism itself. But the inadequacy of our interpretation, which we willingly admit even in the case of Baptism, would be far more evident and serious if we were to proceed as though the theology of the Eucharist and of Baptism must follow exactly parallel lines. Baptism is more readily expounded in terms of symbolism, just because it is a sacrament administered to each recipient once for all. For that reason its meaning is naturally felt to go far beyond anything which can be thought to take place at the moment of its performance. There is apparently a certain disproportion between the significance of the Sacrament, which covers the whole journey and goal of Christian life, and the immediate effect, which is but the starting of the soul upon its course. To overcome that disproportion we had recourse to the principle of symbolism which enables us to maintain intelligibly that not all that Baptism truly is in respect of its meaning can actually occur when the soul is first received into the family of God. But in respect of the Eucharist the problem is more complex. The acts of offering and of communion which constitute its essence are indeed in the deepest sense symbolical. For all human life in so far as it realises its own ideal is made up of an act of self-offering to God and an act of communion with Him and in Him through Jesus Christ its Lord. The meaning, therefore, of the Eucharistic Sacrament assuredly must exceed that which is effected on any particular occasions when the Eucharistic elements are received. Yet we dare not here subordinate the instrumental aspect of the Sacrament. For this Sacrament is the constantly repeated act from which the soul draws its spiritual food. Its virtue resides in its repetition ; it is repeated again and again, just because it is constantly needed to effect that contact with divine life and power which, in its aspect of communion, is all its meaning. Here the Christian believes that he takes into himself the very life which makes him one with God. We do not deny—nay, we are eager to affirm—that he does indeed receive that same life in Baptism also. But not according to the same manner of divine operation ; else he would have to be baptized as often as he made his communion, unless one of the sacraments were to be made altogether superfluous. But Christian experience seems to show that what the Christian actually receives in Baptism, beyond the symbolical seal of membership in Christ, is but the initial impulse of the divine power to start him upon his heavenward way. The habitual and ever more profound renewal of that contact with God which he requires, takes place, so far as sacramental media are concerned, in the communion of the Eucharist. Here, then, is the empirical basis of the Church's constant belief that the presence of Christ in the Eucharist is to be accounted something different from His presence in Baptism, something more intimately close, more vitally apprehensible, than even His coming to accept and endow a new member of the Father's family. The spiritual " marking " conferred at Baptism, even when we regard it as perfectly achieving its purpose, remains essentially symbolic,[1] and has its full effect not as the direct result of Baptism but in all that is fore-shadowed by the unrepeated act. But the act of Eucharistic communion only achieves its purpose in so far as the perfection of Christian life is directly effected by it, as well as beyond it, in daily life. For that reason it is constantly repeated until the things of earth have passed away. The more fully grown is the life of the soul, the fuller of heavenly realisation its acts of sacramental communion should become. In the Eucharist, therefore, symbolic meaning and actual effect are more and more joined and fused together without any predominance of one or subordination of the other. In it, therefore, there must be a real presence of the Lord different from that which is found in any other sacrament.

So far we seem to be moving towards a traditional conclusion by what is certainly not a traditional route. And before we come to closer grips with the central problems of Eucharistic theology it may be well that we should compare our method of approach with those other

---

[1] Thus St. Thomas declares the *character* to be itself *sacramentum.* " *Res autem et sacramentum est character baptismalis, qui est res significata per exteriorem ablutionem ; et est signum sacramentale interioris justifica-tionis quae est res tantum hujus sacramenti, scilicet significata, et non significans* " (Summa III, Q. 66, Art. 1 ; cf. Dom Vonier, *A Key to the Doctrine of the Eucharist,* p. 74).

methods which the history of Christian doctrine has made familiar.

Both in ancient and modern times controversies concerning the Eucharistic offering and the doctrine of the Real Presence have often turned upon the precise exegesis of the words attributed to our Lord at the Last Supper. Even modernist writers are not seldom concerned simply to take us back to the Upper Room in order to determine all that we should believe about the Sacrament which issued from it. We do not question the critical importance of what our Lord said and did in the night of His betrayal. Nevertheless to see nothing in Eucharistic theology but a problem of higher criticism and exegesis is to make a very dangerous mistake. It is true that all we need for sound doctrine is to draw out the full implications of our Lord's words and acts. But these implications cannot be drawn out or appreciated if we refuse the help which the subsequent reflection and experience of Christians alone can provide. Narrow pedantry and unimaginative literalism in exegesis have ever been chief obstacles to the understanding of the mind of Jesus. It is only when we consider what He was, has been and is in the history of human life and thought, that we can hope in some degree to enter into His mind, and so to give a true exposition of His meaning and intention in particular words and acts.

Our documents leave us in some uncertainty as to the exact words and acts which have caused Christians to look back to the Last Supper as the institution of a sacrament. This fact is a salutary warning that the construction of Eucharistic doctrine demands something other than a meticulous adherence to the letter of our Lord's speech. There seems indeed to be no good ground for doubting that He said and did substantially what He

is reported to have said and done by the agreement of
St. Paul and St. Mark, even though St. Luke's witness
shows a remarkable variation. But, granted that St.
Paul's and St. Mark's account is substantially correct,
we still have no materials for determining what was the
full reality of our Lord's meaning, if we are to insist upon
limiting our vision, as it were, by the four walls of the
Upper Room. We may attribute to our Lord's consciousness, as He uttered the words of institution, an altogether
supernatural knowledge of future events. If we do, it
is evident that the consideration of those events, as we
now know them, can alone give us the key to the meaning
of the words. But if on the other hand we suppose that
our Lord's conscious knowledge in the days of His flesh
was limited by a psychological mechanism similar to
that of which we have become aware in ourselves, the
impossibility of determining His full meaning by reference
to His immediate consciousness is really no less indis-
putable. It is an elementary fact in psychology, that the
field of attention can never hold more than a fraction of
the content of the mind. All a man's sayings are the
products of a mental content immensely larger than that
which is explicitly within his consciousness as he utters
them. Yet their meaning can only be fully defined by
reference to the whole mental content as it is gradually,
by subsequent reflexion and through the course of subsequent events, brought into the light of conscious knowledge. A man never knows exactly " what he meant
when he said " a thing, until he has afterwards pondered
over the circumstances and conditions of his original
utterance. And when he has thus in subsequent reflexion
defined his meaning with full sincerity and truth, his
account of it must always contain far more than what
was actually occupying his attention at the moment

when he spoke the words. In the case of trivial sayings
the overplus of meaning beyond what was present to the
conscious attention is itself trivial and often negligible.
But the more profound the real meaning of what is said,
the more it necessarily exceeds the narrow boundaries
which mark the mind's field of attention at the moment
of utterance. Our deepest thoughts and sayings are
constantly turning out to be "truer than we knew";
and often, when fresh events reveal fresh implications or
applications of their truth, we may hesitate for a time
whether to say Yes or No to the question, Did we really
mean this originally? The truth is that the total mental
content which produced the original thought or saying is
expressed also in the new application suggested. Yet
this application was not originally present in our consciousness, and the conscious apprehension of it is therefore
felt to add something new to the original thought; it
elicits something fresh from what was originally implicit
in our meaning. In the same way arises the notorious
difficulty of defining with precision what great thinkers
and writers actually meant by their greatest utterances.
Did Plato or Shakspere actually mean all that their best
commentators have elicited from their writings? The
question itself is ambiguous. If we are asking whether
the interpretations of commentators were in substance
present to the consciousness of Plato or Shakspere, the
answer is almost certainly No. But if we are asking
whether the interpretations are true to Plato's or Shakspere's mind, that is, whether they are fresh expressions
of that same mental content or system of thought which
expressed itself in Plato's or Shakspere's writings, the
answer is probably Yes. The work of the true com-
mentator is often to unfold more of the real content
of Platonic or Shaksperian wisdom than was already

unfolded in Plato's or Shakspere's consciousness as he wrote.

All this has a considerable bearing upon the true interpretation of our Lord's words and acts at the Last Supper. It leads us to expect that we shall find the truth by regarding them in a broad context as the product of a mind and life, the unique value of which the history of Christian thinking and living has enabled us to recognise. And if we thus find in them a meaning which goes beyond what many conceive to have been the limitations of our Lord's conscious knowledge before His Crucifixion, we can still maintain that this meaning nevertheless was in a true sense in the Lord's mind, and that one great purpose of the sending of the Holy Spirit was to enable us to exhibit ever freshly the riches of meaning which were latent in what our Lord said and did upon earth.

Suppose the main thought which occupied our Lord's attention was the anticipation of the great Messianic banquet to be held in the coming Kingdom of God.[1] It may safely be affirmed that He did not interpret the notion of " eating bread in the Kingdom of God " in any materialistic manner. The banquet itself was to Him in essence a spiritual communion to be realised through the bearing of the Cross. He Himself, the Messiah, was to be host at the banquet, and He would drink no more of the fruit of the vine until that day when He should drink it new. But the disciples must follow Him first in bearing the Cross, if they were ever to take their places at that table. And when they attained to it, that of which they would partake would be nothing other than the

---

[1] My interpretation is partly based on the conclusions reached by Sir E. C. Hoskyns (*Essays Catholic and Critical*, pp. 174–176), Dr. N. P. Williams (*ibidem*, pp. 402–407) and by Dr. A. E. J. Rawlinson in his Commentary on St. Mark (Westminster Series). Dr. Williams, however, does not seem to be convincing when he refers the saying, " I will no more ", etc., primarily to the Eucharistic Sacrament of the Church.

fulness of the life which had triumphed over evil through
the Cross, namely the life of Himself who would then
receive them into His open presence. But, again, in the
bearing of the Cross, His own life, which had passed that
way before them, must be their sustenance and support ;
so that the strength in which they would persevere was
even now fittingly appropriated by an anticipation of the
heavenly feast, an anticipation wherein broken bread and
wine outpoured were symbols of Himself as sacrificed.
Thus the Sacrament of the Church is indicated as in one
sense a more perfect realisation of the heavenly feast
than the Last Supper could be. For in that Sacrament
the Head of the Church has already attained His triumph
and has become the Host distributing the heavenly life
to those who follow Him on earth. Yet in another sense
the Sacrament of the Church is even more than the Last
Supper an incomplete anticipation and foreshadowing.
For in the Sacrament the Lord and the disciples no longer
meet, as it were, on the same plane, whether of earth or
heaven. The heavenly Christ is hidden from those who
have still the more part of their upward course to travel,
the more part of their self-offering still to make. Truly
the food and drink partaken are the Christ's own life ;
but He does not take His place at the table in the un-
veiled fellowship of glory. The Sacrament therefore marks
an intermediate stage of experience. It hangs between
earth and heaven. It is for a period of transition, and
affords no abiding rest for mind or spirit. In it the Lord
Himself, truly present, sustains His followers with His
own life given to them and for them. But He does not
meet them in the unhindered converse of open vision.
There is, therefore, an element in the Last Supper which
can never be repeated until all foreshadowings have
passed into realisation.

If what has just been written indicates at all the right method of fitting together and making intelligible to the present age those scattered fragments of our Lord's converse at the Last Supper which have been handed down to us as the institution of our Sacrament, who shall mark the precise point at which the interpretation has travelled outside that which was explicitly present in the Saviour's conscious knowledge when His words were uttered ? And is the question really of vital importance ? If we believe that such an interpretation is not false to our Lord's mind and intention, we believe it largely on the ground that that mind and intention have been continuously revealed in the Christian experience in which the Eucharist has played so important a part. But we need not be concerned to maintain that the whole significance and application of His own words must in every detail have been explicit in the consciousness of Jesus at the time when they were uttered. Thus, just because the existence of the Eucharistic tradition in the Church, and the interpretation of the mind of Jesus to which it witnesses, constitute one main reason for our acceptance of a Eucharistic doctrine which is broadly traditional, we shall be more willing than many traditionalists to admit a certain possible uncertainty as to what exactly was the thought present in the consciousness of Jesus as He distributed the bread and the wine to His apostles. That he desired above all things to bring home the truth that participation in the Messianic life sacrificed was the one way to full communion with the Messianic life exalted, seems to be certain, if only because the thought is so profoundly in accord with the whole spirit of His other words and acts. And this is the meaning of the Sacrament which ultimately matters ; this is the eternal truth. How far the vision of an organised Church on

o

earth, enduring through countless centuries and creating the ecclesiastical machinery for the continuous administration of the Sacrament, was present to His conscious knowledge, we cannot pretend to determine. But even if it were not so present, it does not at all follow that the sacramental organisation of the Church, which multifarious influences have doubtless helped to shape, is necessarily alien from His mind or can in no sense claim His authority.

In the sphere of doctrine, therefore, we are obliged to conclude that the appeal to our Lord's words must leave many questions open concerning the exact relation of our Lord's presence to the consecrated elements, and of the sacrifice of Calvary to the Eucharistic offering. If the immediate intention of what our Lord said and did at the Last Supper is such as we have ventured to suppose, the truest doctrine must always be that which enables faithful Christians to hold most surely that in the Eucharist, as in a rite symbolising the deepest meaning of all Christian living, they are made partakers of the life offered for them on Calvary, in order that in the end their communion with that life may be fulfilled in the open and glorious vision of their Saviour before the throne of God. But we cannot determine which of many various doctrines is nearest to that truth, simply by going back to the Last Supper itself and excluding subsequent developments and interpretations of the Sacrament, as though they were necessarily so many extraneous accretions upon a faith which had been originally declared and accepted whole and complete in every detail. We may admit the possibility that the mystery-religions of the heathen world influenced the ideas of the earliest Gentile-Christians as to the manner in which the Saviour's life was made one with theirs in the eating of a sacrificial

meal. What then ? The fact—if fact it be—that Eucharistic doctrines were in some part derived from the mysteries
does not by itself make them either true or false. The
central meaning of the Christian Sacrament was the
sharing, not just of some divine life, but of the life of
Christ in all its unique character of God's perfect love.
In so far as pagan mysteries helped Christians to realise
their communion in *that* life, their influence made for
truth ; in so far as it hindered them, it made for falsehood·
Again, the fact that the doctrine of Transubstantiation,
as finally formulated, is the product of scholastic Aris-
totelianism does not by itself entitle us to accept or to
reject it. The central meaning of the Christian Sacrament is not to affirm any nice distinction between substance and accident, but to assure us that the substance
of the life of Christ, being divine and eternal love and
therefore distinct from all outward and perishable things,
is nevertheless through outward things communicated
to us. In so far as the doctrine of Transubstantiation was
or is the best available means of making clear that truth,
it is itself to be accounted true. In so far as it tends to
make men venerate some material object as embodying
deity, apart from the realisation of the demand made by
the one living God upon man's being, it is certainly to be
repudiated. Again, in modern times it has been held
that our Lord's death is but the supreme example of moral
self-sacrifice, and that the Sacrament is the symbolic
communication of this moral perfection to His followers.
Few Christians would deny that on their positive side
such modernist doctrines do really interpret to us one
aspect of the mind of Jesus. But the notion that the life
of God's Christ is nothing but the embodiment of a moral
ideal seems to do little justice to the gospel-story, and
may obscure, not less than superstition itself, that sense

of other-worldly reality which is often the very food of moral heroism.

We are now in a position to examine more closely the vexed problems of Eucharistic theology. These are usually divided into two, the problem of the sacrifice offered, and the problem of the presence communicated. But it is apparent that the two are really one, if we begin by considering the sacrificial aspect of the Sacrament. The true and ideal doctrine of sacrifice is everywhere that sacrifice is representative, not vicarious. The true prophecy of the sacrifice of Christ lies not in those primitive ceremonies where the victim offered was regarded as a substitute, perhaps an inferior substitute, for the life of a man ; but rather in those where the victim was looked upon as unblemished and uncontaminated by man's sin, and its blood, or life, was shed so that through some sprinkling or similar act of ritual its purity might be communicated to the offerers whose representative it was. Looking at sacrifice from this angle we may assuredly assert, with the writer to the Hebrews, that the blood of bulls or goats or the ashes of an heifer sprinkling the unclean could never take away sins. For the life of the animals remains inevitably on a lower level than man's ; their sinlessness is but the sinlessness of an innocence which has never risen to the level of temptation. But the life of the truly perfect man, being sacrificed once for all, is sufficient to cleanse and to perfect all those to whom it is really communicated. Thus the man-ward purpose of the sacrifice is the communication of the presence. Christ died for us so that He might live in us. And His life in us manifests itself in that same activity of self-sacrifice which He in His own Person perfectly fulfilled.

In saying this we do not at all mean to deny that all sacrifice has essentially a purpose toward God as well as a purpose toward man. Unquestionably Catholic theologians are right in contending that the chief end of sacrifice is to make an offering to God, and its effects upon man must be regarded as secondary or derivative. In the order of importance or value the glory of God must always be placed before the edification, or even the redemption, of man. For the whole purpose of man's redemption is that he may fulfil the end for which he was created, that is, to glorify God with the most perfect worship of which he is capable. But must it not be true that that perfection of worship consists in nothing other than man's free oblation of himself, and of all he controls, to God in the power of divine love which God has given him ?

If this be so, two consequences follow. (1) It is not of the essence of perfect sacrifice that man should offer to God something outward, or other than himself. Rather, if man offers to God anything *apart* from himself, it is a sign of imperfection in his worship. He may make such an offering either with the hope that the oblation will serve as a substitute for himself, or else as a token of his will to offer himself in some measure, or else in order that what he offers apart from himself may impart its purity to him. In the two latter cases it is evidently seen that the fulfilment of sacrifice is in self-offering. (2) Again, if this be so, the religious idea of sacrifice, raised to its highest plane, includes of necessity the ethical heroism which the term self-sacrifice denotes in common use. The self-sacrifice of religion does but reveal a deeper, God-ward meaning in the self-sacrifice of ethics. No human life can be truly fit to be an oblation to God save that which is spent also in the service of men. And no human life serves men truly which does not lead them to offer themselves in worship to God.

Here, then, we find the one satisfactory reconciliation of all those popular oppositions between the moral and the mystical interpretation of the Atonement, and between the sacrifice of the altar and the communion of the holy table, which needlessly vex the conscience and the intellect of Christendom. The offering of the self is the one and only sacrifice which God's love can and does require of every human soul. Most certainly that is true. " Let us proclaim it to the four winds of heaven." But how then shall each soul offer itself ? Only by the communication to it of the perfect life self-offered once for all, not simply as an example to others, but so that, as the Head, it may incorporate ever more truly into itself every member of its mystical body in the fellowship of the Spirit.

Again, the life of the Son of God is an eternal self-offering to the Father. It was through the Eternal Spirit of His deity that the Lord offered up Himself in the flesh of His manhood upon the Cross. But, if so, the activity of His heavenly life is ever one with that offering. And, inasmuch as the offering of the Son includes our manhood, the communication of His life to us joins us with Him in His sacrifice, so that in us and through us, as we receive power to follow in His steps, He is ever afresh, yet ever as in one act, offering up manhood before the throne. The Eucharist then is truly a sacrifice. For it is the perpetual externalisation in human ritual of the self-offering of Christ, which was once for all in fact externalised on Calvary, but is ever real in the inward and heavenly sphere. But the Eucharist, just in so far as it is an effective sacrifice, is also a communion ; for the only way in which Christ's sacrifice can avail for us is by making us one with itself. At the risk of repetition we would insist that Christ's human life is altogether a self-offering, which in contact with the evil of the world becomes strictly a *sacrifice* of self. And under the general description of union with that offering and sacrifice all " the benefits of Christ's passion " are included. Even forgiveness itself is no true forgiveness, unless in some real sense it makes the sinner one with Christ ; the union, therefore, is at least the necessary effect of the forgiveness.

Looking at the Eucharistic sacrifice from this point of view we may eagerly welcome the main principle of the traditional doctrine of Catholicism, that in the Eucharist Christ's people are enabled to offer Christ Himself as their sacrifice. But we should be obliged to make certain reservations. Christian people may rightly offer Christ as an oblation apart from themselves, only in so far as they honestly intend that through their action the Christ, Whom they offer, may draw them into His own self-offering. In so far then as their offering of Christ is a thing apart from their offering of themselves, it is the sign of an imperfect worship ; and an imperfect worship can only be right, in so far as there are found in it the means of removing its own imperfection. Again, the imperative power of Eucharistic intercessions must not be divorced from the self-offering of those who make them. Our prayers at the Eucharist are of special avail, if and because through the Eucharistic action the power of Christ's self-offering reproduces itself in us.

How precisely is the death of Christ related to the Eucharistic offering ? Death is not strictly essential to the idea of sacrifice, if we use that term to cover the offering made in heaven as well as that made upon earth. Christ died once in time, but He offers Himself eternally. In the Eucharist we make a memorial of Christ's death ;

but we make before God an offering which is one with Christ's present and eternal offering of Himself. The death of Christ, therefore, from the point of view of the Eucharist is strictly past, not present. Nevertheless earthly lives cannot complete their own sacrifice apart from death, and the perfect life which incorporates them into its sacrifice is the life of Him who died and bears for ever the marks of the Cross. Thus the life of Christ, which truly offers itself by human and earthly hands in the Eucharist, always includes, not excludes, His death on Calvary, and, in so far as it is communicated to souls still in earthly bodies, it is not merely the heavenly offering of life, but the earthly offering through death, of which these must be made partakers. Thus it is fitting and necessary that part of the Eucharistic action should be held to represent the dying of the Lord on earth ; for although, when we speak strictly in terms of space and time, that which takes place in the Eucharist is only a memorial in relation to the death of Christ, its purpose is to renew in us now by means of His life the spirit and power in which He died.

The doctrine which the Council of Trent has established in the Roman Communion, declares that, though there can be no actual death in the sacrifice of the Eucharist, nevertheless in it there must be some real *immolation* of Christ, lest otherwise its reality as a sacrifice should be impaired. It insists that the sacrifice of the Cross and the sacrifice of the Mass are not two sacrifices but one and the same, and that the purpose of the Mass is to *represent* the sacrifice of the Cross by means of a mystically accomplished immolation without shedding of blood. Immolation is defined to mean properly some destruction or change in the outward thing offered in sacrifice ; and different opinions are still held by Roman

Catholic theologians as to the manner in which the concept of immolation can be applied to the Mass, so as to safeguard the reality of the sacrifice, without in any way implying that the death of Christ is repeated.

Without attempting to follow the intricacies of the discussions which have taken place on this subject, we may well emphasise the important truth expressed by asserting that immolation is an essential element in all sacrifice upon earth. No earthly thing, no earthly being, can be fit to enter heaven and appear before God, without undergoing first some radical change or transformation. So we are taught by an ancient and deep-seated instinct of the soul ; and no modern knowledge invalidates the lesson. Even the earthly manhood of Christ had to be immolated in order to rise itself, and to raise mankind, to the throne of God. And the necessity of immolation both for exaltation and for redemption is one of the plainest truths of Christian experience. That it should receive its due expression in the Eucharistic symbolism is altogether fitting. But what seems an altogether needless complication is to suppose that Christ is immolated in the Eucharist in any other manner than by the representation of His death. St. Thomas Aquinas can hardly have thought any such doctrine legitimate when he wrote : " The celebration of this sacrament is called an immolation for two reasons. First, because, as Augustine says, the images of things are called by the names of the things whereof they are the images ; as when we look upon a picture or a fresco, we say, ' This is Cicero and that is Sallust '. But, as was said above, the celebration of this sacrament is an image representing Christ's Passion, which is His true immolation. Accordingly the celebration of this sacrament is called Christ's immolation. . . . Secondly, it is called an immolation, in respect of the

effect of His Passion : because, to wit, by this sacrament, we are made partakers of the fruit of our Lord's
Passion.   Hence in one of the Sunday *Secrets* we say :
' Whenever the commemoration of this sacrifice is
celebrated, the work of our redemption is enacted '."[1]
Even after Trent Cardinal Vasquez also taught on similar
lines. He distinguishes between the " absolute sacrifice "
on the Cross and the " commemorative sacrifice " of the
Mass.   In the " absolute sacrifice " *destructio* was a
necessary element ; but in the commemorative sacrifice
it is enough that the victim of the " absolute sacrifice " be
presented, and that there be some mark or sign of the
destructio which then took place.[2]

No doubt the theory of Vasquez has been rejected by
the great majority of Roman theologians, on the ground
that Tridentine orthodoxy requires that the Mass should
have its own proper immolation, not merely the representation of another.   But, considering the matter from
the point of view of the philosophical position outlined
in previous chapters, we seem to do justice to the essential
truth for which Catholic theology has here been contending
if we say that the Eucharistic action must *expressively*
symbolise the reality of Christ's death and self-immola-
tion upon the Cross. The symbolisation of a past fact,
if it be truly expressive, must always in some sense bridge
the gulf of time, make the past present, and actually

---

[1] Summa III, Q. 83, Art. 1.   I follow the authorised Dominican
translation except that I translate *immolatio* by the word " immolation ", not " sacrifice ".

[2] My authorities for this account of Vasquez's teaching are Darwell
Stone, *History of the Doctrine of the Holy Eucharist*, vol. ii, p. 362, and
Tanquerey, *Synopsis Theologicae Dogmaticae*, vol. iii, § 689. The latter
makes the criticism of Vasquez which I have mentioned above : " *Sacri-
ficium Missae non solum mortem Christi repraesentare debet, sed etiam
aliquam immolationem in se habere.*"   But Dom Vonier is content to
repeat St. Thomas : " The Cross is Christ's true immolation. Mass is
its perfect image ; therefore it is an immolation " (op. cit., p. 149).

convey the reality of that which it commemorates. And we may well believe that in the Eucharistic action, proceeding from the living Christ Who was dead, this power of the expressive symbol is raised to its highest point.[1]

On the whole, then, it may be concluded that traditional doctrines of the sacrifice of the Mass only run counter to what we take to be our Lord's will and intention, in so far as they are rightly understood to interpret sacrifice as, in the strict and narrow sense of the term, vicarious, not representative. The notion of vicarious sacrifice is associated with an unworthy chain of ideas. According to it, the victim is a substitute which God is supposed to accept instead of man. The victim is offered so that man need not offer himself. Man fears to offer himself, because he thinks his life is forfeit to God's wrath. Thus it is the death of the victim substituted for man, that is the main point and purpose of vicarious sacrifice. This whole rationale of sacrifice, when applied to the Cross and the Eucharist, makes much worse than nonsense of both. In the theory of representative sacrifice, on the other hand, the offerers seek to identify themselves with the victim ; and the victim is slain, not so as to make its death the main purpose of the rite, but so that its purity may be communicated to the offerers, when God has accepted its life. It is this conception of sacrifice which Christ fulfils by the sacrifice of Himself. It leaves room for the idea of the offering perpetuated, when the death has been accomplished once for all. And it unifies completely sacrifice with communion, so that, once it is established that the perfect sacrifice is the life of perfect love, every moral demand is more than satisfied, when *this* is the sacrifice wherewith we must identify ourselves

---

[1] See Appendix A.

as we offer it. We may still, if we so desire, affirm that
Christ's offering is in a sense vicarious, inasmuch as He
did and does for us what we could never do for ourselves.
We must assuredly affirm that Christ's sacrifice is infinitely more than an example, inasmuch as His life is
not just a pattern in the past, but an eternal activity
which gives us power to follow an example by joining
us to itself. There is room for transcendent mystery
here, but no loophole for superstition.

We have already given some grounds for accepting
the traditional belief of Catholicism that the presence of
Christ in the Eucharist is fuller and more intimate than
His presence in Baptism. Our Lord's intention at the
Last Supper was to impress upon His apostles, and to
help them to live up to the truth, that the Messianic
sacrifice must be shared by those who would win to the
Messianic kingdom. And though this truth is also
expressed in the symbolised resurrection of Baptism,
yet it is in the Eucharist that the Church has found it
to be made effective day by day in the lives of its members.
Thus it is in the repeated acts of the Eucharist that the
presence of Christ is found to be fullest and closest.
And how could it be otherwise, if the Eucharist is the
perpetual externalisation in ritual of that offering of
Himself which Christ made and makes for us ? It is
indeed true in an important sense that that offering is in
some degree externalised in every unselfish act of Christian
living ; for the life of the Christian soul on earth, being in
time if not strictly in space, is in regard to the eternal life
of Christ relatively " outward ", and up to that point
may be itself the outward means of His self-expression
and activity. But in the Eucharist the self-offering of
Christ reaches the utmost limit of externality through the

presentation of material symbols, in order that souls in material bodies may have that sensible assurance of Christ's coming to them from without, which their earthly condition craves, even while they cannot see Him come.

It is in close connexion with this doctrine of the Eucharistic offering that we desire to view the still more complex problem which concerns the relation of the Lord's presence to the consecrated elements in the Eucharist. The traditional theories on this subject, Transubstantiation, Consubstantiation, Virtualism and Receptionism, are well-trodden and somewhat dusty ground to theological feet. Traversing them, there is a broad division to be recognised between those who connect the presence in some special way with the consecrated elements themselves, affirming that consecration really changes them, and those who affirm the special presence only in the hearts and souls of faithful worshippers, denying any change in the material elements to be wrought by consecration. The former are said to accept, the latter to reject, the doctrine of the Real Presence. But, in view of the ambiguity of this unfortunate term, it is important to observe that neither do those who affirm the doctrine doubt the necessity for spiritual faith as a condition of receiving the benefit of the Sacrament, nor do those who deny the doctrine question the full objective reality of Christ's presence in a spiritual mode. There is as little ground for an accusation of magic in the one case, as there is for an accusation of " subjectivism " in the other.

Transubstantiation and Consubstantiation both explicitly affirm the Real Presence, the former asserting that the change wrought in consecration converts the substance of the material bread and wine into that of our Lord's Body and Blood, the latter that the change adds the one substance to the other. Receptionism explicitly denies the Real Presence, maintaining that there is no change whatever in the material elements. Virtualism endeavours to mediate between the two extremes. It acknowledges that the consecrated elements, though not changed in themselves, are nevertheless set apart by consecration for a new and most holy use, and are therefore not in all respects the same as they were before ; and as used in the Sacrament they have the " virtue " of Christ's Body and Blood, inasmuch as they are vehicles of Christ's gifts to the soul, though they cannot be ontologically identified with what they convey. Finally, there have been always those who have sought to assert the fact of the Real Presence without committing themselves to any theory of its manner.

Before, however, we attempt to estimate the value of these traditional doctrines, it is important to remember that up to a date, which is not clearly defined but may be placed somewhere near the beginning of the last century, two assumptions were commonly made on both sides, which no modern theologians can take for granted, and but few would accept. It was assumed as a basis of Eucharistic discussion that material objects possess a substantial reality distinguishable alike from their accidents or sensible properties and from their value or use. It was assumed again that heaven is a place wherein the body with which our Lord ascended is extended in spatial dimensions. Thus in mediæval and post-mediæval times one main problem of Christ's presence in the elements took the form of the question, How can the Lord's Body be in two places at once ? Receptionists and Virtualists denied the possibility, and preferred to believe that the Body was not literally received at all. Luther and his followers, adopting Consubstantiation, argued for the omnipresence of Christ's Body, an apparent effort to regard the Body as non-spatial which has perhaps been too little appreciated. Transubstantiation, as defined by philosophers, supposed the substance of a thing to be not only distinguishable, but also in this case separable, from all its perceived appearances, and affirmed that, while everything in the bread and wine which was perceptible to bodily senses really remained after consecration, nevertheless their substance was wholly converted by consecration into the substances of the Body and Blood of Christ, which were present in them not as occupying space, but in somewhat the same way as normally the substance of bread or wine is present complete in every particle of bread or wine. According to this view, the whole perceptible nature of bread and wine was really in the consecrated elements ; it was only in respect of what could never by any possibility be perceived by any bodily sense, that they were truly the Body and Blood of Christ. And inasmuch as the Body and Blood of Christ were in the Sacrament only in this entirely non-spatial way, the law was preserved that even Christ's body could not be *in two places* at once. Thus a heroic attempt was made to refine the crude materialism of popular devotion to the elements, without rejecting the popular demand for some outward object towards which the worship of the Saviour might be directed.

But the intellectual earthquakes of the last century have shifted all the old landmarks. The dividing-lines between the old doctrines are becoming more and more difficult to trace in the new situation. Modern arguments proceed from different premises. To-day it is commonly, though not universally, held that the substance of material objects is nothing other than what they are perceived to be[1] ; and many argue that this substance is in part con-

---

[1] So much is common both to the " realists " who maintain that the real object is given in perception, and to the " idealists " who maintain that it is in some way constituted through perception.

stituted either by the activity of the perceiving mind, or
by the use to which the objects are put, or by the values
which they embody. Again, the notion of a local heaven
has, by tacit consent, been given up. We no longer
think of our Lord's Body in heaven as a locally situate
or spatially extended organism. To us it is really nothing
other than the perfectly responsive organ of His spiritual
activity—at least he would be a bold man who would
attempt a radically different definition. If, then, on the
one hand, we adopt a philosophical theory according
to which the value or use of the elements in the Eucharist
makes a difference to what in themselves they really are,
we can conceive a substantial change made in them by
consecration which yet does not affect their physical
composition. And if, on the other hand, we cease to
regard the Body of Christ as in its proper nature occupying
space of any kind, we can the more readily regard it as
being united with any physical object which Christ uses
for the imparting of His own presence and gifts. Thus the
doctrine of Virtualism may easily become indistinguishable from a theory of Real Presence ; and the main
difficulty which the doctrine of Transubstantiation was
elaborated to overcome simply disappears. Moreover,
it becomes really meaningless either to affirm or to deny
the traditional tenet of Catholicism that the Body of
Christ offered and received in the Eucharist is identically
the same as that which He took of the Virgin. For the
substantial identity of the body is not constituted by
the relation of the body at one time to the body at another
time, but by the constant relation of the body at all
times to him whose body it is.[1] In other words, whatever

---

[1] If the question is rigorously pressed in the old language whether
the Body of Christ is present in the sacrament *in veritate* or *in figura*
or *in virtute*, we must answer, " *In veritate*, provided it be understood
that to us the *veritas* of body consists in a certain relationship

is the organ of Christ's activity is, so far, His Body. We have already suggested that ultimately, when God's purpose in creation has been finally fulfilled, the Body of Christ is the sum of created things.

The field, then, would seem to be open for a radical re-examination of the doctrine of Real Presence in the Eucharistic species. What is the main reason for the strenuous opposition which it still meets among large numbers of those who believe firmly in the Sacrament ? The mere fact of its historical association with Romanism constitutes of course not a reason but a prejudice; and prejudices no doubt are always influential. But, prejudice apart, it is seriously urged that the doctrine of Real Presence bids men look for the presence of Christ in a material object rather than in a spiritual activity, and that thus it weakens the sense of Christ's immanent operation both in individual hearts and in the fellowship of the faithful people who are His mystical Body.

This criticism has considerable weight against the mediæval Catholicism of the West. It has often been noticed that in patristic times, although there was without doubt a strong belief in some Real Presence in the elements, and the Reserved Sacrament was not seldom used practically as a charm, there is comparatively little trace of any adoration of Jesus as personally present in the Eucharistic species. Bishop Gore and others have explained this fact by suggesting that Christians then had such a strong grasp of the truth that Christ from the beginning of the rite was already present as Head of His Church and as the real Doer of what was done in the Eucharist, that it did not seem natural to them to look for His presence

of spiritual life to an outward thing ". It is worth noticing that St. Thomas writes : " *Per hoc quod dicimus ipsum sub hoc sacramento significatur quaedam habitudo ejus ad hoc sacramentum* " (Summa III, Q. 76, Art. 6).

P

exclusively after the consecration or in that which was consecrated. Christ was present to consecrate the elements, and, when consecrated, they were identified with His Body and Blood as His gifts. Moreover, in these times our Lord was not commonly thought of, either in theory or in devotion, as a human person, nor was worship paid to His humanity. This fact may also be connected with a habit of regarding the consecrated elements, even when identified with the Lord's Body and Blood and therefore with His manhood, as still being impersonal things rather than as Christ Himself in His divine person to be adored.[1]

But with the revival of religion after the Dark Ages, the devotional and theological attitude is observed to have undergone a striking change. In the doctrine of the Atonement propitiation-theories take the place of ransom-theories, and this development involves the concentration of devotion upon the manhood rather than upon the Godhead of our Lord. At the same time God, the receiver of propitiation, is conceived of more and more as a remote and awful sovereign, while Jesus or His Mother practically takes the place of the heavenly Father as the Friend of man to whom human needs are to be brought in prayer. Again, as the Middle Ages advance, the multiplication of private and specially endowed Masses begins to impair the character of the Mass as the great corporate act of the Church's worship, and converts it rather into an instrument of individual piety.[2]

To go to the theological root of the matter, we find that in the Middle Ages the thought of divine immanence is comparatively neglected, and with it the magnificent

---

[1] Cf. Bishop Gore, *The Body of Christ*, 4th edition, pp. 99–109.

[2] The fact of this change, and its importance, are strikingly indicated by Chanoine Ch. Cordonnier in his book, *Le Culte du Saint-Sacrement*, p. 99

old Platonistic doctrine of Christ as divine Logos, omni-present Agent in the world, Head of the Church, and active in all that His members do upon earth. As a result, or cause, of this neglect the chiefly prized values of the Eucharist come to be two. (1) It is a propitiatory offer-ing for sin, wherein the sacrificed manhood of Christ averts the wrath of a far-off sovereign Deity. (2) It affords in the consecrated elements a point of personal and objective contact between Christ and His individual followers. The awful remoteness of God is compensated by the nearness of Jesus on the altar and in the taber-nacle. The special Eucharistic presence is interpreted to mean that He is by a miracle personally and actually within the sacred elements, so as to accept man-wise the adoration of men, and with human ears and senses, veiled by a form of lifeless matter, to receive and answer the petitions framed by human lips.[1] It is the passionate demand for a point of personal contact between the individual Christian and his Saviour Jesus, which pro-bably underlies most of the thaumaturgical extravagance

---

[1] St. Bonaventura asserts that in the Sacrament the Body of Christ, or Christ Himself, sees and hears (Sentences, IV, x, 1, 2, 4, quoted by Darwell Stone, *History of the Doctrine of the Eucharist*, I, p. 338). St. Thomas teaches that all that belongs to Christ as He is in Himself can be attributed to Him as He exists in the Sacrament, such as to live, to die, to grieve, to be animate or inanimate, and the like ; and that Christ's bodily eye is under the Sacrament (Summa III, Q. 76, Art. 7, and Q. 81, Art. 4). Cordonnier in *Le Culte du Saint-Sacrement* emphasises strongly the fact of the change mentioned above, though he attributes it entirely to the doctrinal theories of St. Bonaventura and St. Thomas, and does not consider how far those theories were themselves determined by a devotional demand which had for some time been making itself felt. A *result* of these theories, he says, is to make it apparent that " il sera toujours loisible à l'humanité de re-trouver son Dieu ; il suffira qu'elle s'approche de l'hostie " (p. 91). St. Thomas, on the other hand, gives it as a *reason* for Transubstantia-tion, that " it would be opposed to the veneration of this sacrament, if any substance were there, which could not be adored with adoration of *latria* " (Summa III, Q. 75, Art. 2).

associated with mediæval belief about the Sacrament. It was in order in some measure to satisfy this demand, while refining its grossness, that the exact theory of Transubstantiation was elaborated by the Schoolmen.

In modern times, it is small wonder if the same demand is again making itself felt. The discoveries of modern science may seem to have removed God further off from the touch of human need than ever did theologies influenced by feudalism. But the love of Jesus, concrete and personal, still shines from the Gospel-pages into the human heart, and the faith of many is ready to turn its back on the dark riddles of metaphysical theology, if its devotion can but be offered an outward and definite point of contact with Him Whose presence it seeks.

All this the modern opponent of the doctrine of Real Presence may readily acknowledge. But he will urge that man's true need, even in religion, cannot always be satisfied by an attempt to grant his immediate wishes. The only real remedy for modern doubts and perplexities is to reassociate in men's minds the love of Jesus with the omnipresent activity of the Divine Logos. And to this, our objector will say, the doctrine of the Real Presence is an obstacle. The argument is a strong one ; and, if it is to be rejected, it must be fairly met.

On the other hand, modern theories of Receptionism seem to suffer from a serious defect of a different kind. For the Receptionist everything that is outwardly done in the Eucharist is on the level of an acted parable ; that is to say, its whole importance resides in its meaning, not in its effect—just as when a Hebrew prophet acted dramatically a truth which he wished to impress upon his hearers. It is true that the Receptionist may argue that the inward communion of the soul with its Lord takes place at the same time as the elements are outwardly received. But it would appear that for him there is no causal connexion between the outward and the inward series of events. The two series run on parallel but separate lines, and are only interconnected by the relation of meaning, which differs from instrumentality precisely in not being a spatio-temporal relation. Now this outward signifying of a spiritual reality may become in the secondary sense instrumental to its realisation, in so far as a mind grasps the significance of the outward acts as they are performed, and is thus changed in its inward disposition by the meaning which at a given time it apprehends. But in this way the Sacrament can only become effective through its consciously apprehended meaning, and its effect is therefore limited by that which a given mind at a given time can consciously apprehend.[1] This may seem to be a satisfactory theory of the Sacrament to those whose consciousness of spiritual realities is normally strong and definite, and responds readily to outward suggestion. But to those whose spiritual consciousness is weak and faltering the theory brings nothing but disappointment. If accepted, it would take from them the very consciousness which in sacramental worship they value most, namely the assurance that here there happens and is done to them infinitely more than the purblind vision of their straining faith can be aware of. There are some, perhaps many, to whom the doctrine of grace *ex opere operato* is not a superstition but a gospel. It does not do away with the necessity for faith ; it does but assure them that, if they endeavour in their will to receive Christ in the Sacrament, they do indeed receive

---

[1] This does not really conflict with what was asserted above, that the meaning of a saying often goes beyond the consciousness of the speaker. For " my meaning " in what I say is not the same as " its meaning to me ". The latter is comprehended in my consciousness; the former need not be.

Him through the thing done in the outward reception of the elements, not only through the externally stimulated consciousness of His presence, which is to them " the staff of a bruised reed ".

We must now consider a mediating theory, which has recently been put forward by some of the more liberal theologians of the Anglo-Catholic school. It is of special importance to us, because it springs from an attempt to use the opportunity, which we have seen that modern philosophy affords, of developing old-fashioned Virtualism to a point at which it becomes indistinguishable from a doctrine of Real Presence. We shall criticise it the more closely, because it contains so much which we value and cordially accept. According to Mr. Spens's statement of the theory,[1] the reality of physical objects is so thoroughly constituted by their value and meaning for minds, that a physical object is validly definable as " a persisting complex of opportunities of experience ". Now Eucharistic consecration sets apart certain objects, bread and wine, to be specially guaranteed and intimate means for the apprehension and reception of Christ's presence and gifts. Consecration, therefore, really changes the substance of the elements, inasmuch as from consecration new opportunities of spiritual experience are found in them.

According to Mr. Spens, this doctrine on its intellectual side demands no more than an extension of the principle of efficacious symbolism with which ordinary life has already made us familiar. He takes as instances of effectual symbols the accolade and the " token-coinage to which an authoritative decision of the State gives

---

[1] " The Eucharist," by W. Spens, in *Essays Catholic and Critical.* Cf. also a pamphlet entitled *A Cross-Bench View of the Reservation Controversy* (Faith Press), by the same author and Hakluyt Egerton, and Mr. E. G. Selwyn's paper in the Report of the Farnham Conference on *Reservation.* (S.P.C.K.)

certain purchasing value, defined in terms of the sovereign, but quite independent of the coin's intrinsic worth. . . . Those who recognise the authority which appoints the token do not, in fact, use or think of their florins as though they were counters ". So the Eucharistic elements have been as it were marked or stamped by God's word through consecration to be the symbols of a heavenly value, and are rightly treated as really possessing that value which they represent. "The bread and wine are given by Christ's ordinance new properties, which, while they do not annihilate the natural properties of giving sustenance and refreshment, yet so supersede these that we can rightly speak of the objects themselves as wholly changed and transfigured."[1]

Now, whatever be the merits of this theory, it must be said at once that the analogies of the accolade and of token-money seem to fail altogether as illustrations of anything that is rightly meant by the term Real Presence. For these symbols are almost wholly conventional or arbitrary, and do not genuinely at all convey the reality which they signify. St. Thomas takes them as pointing to Receptionism, and his comment is worth quoting. "Some, however, say that the sacraments are the cause of grace not by their own operation, but in so far as God causes grace in the soul when the sacraments are employed. And they give as an example a man who, on presenting a leaden coin, receives, by the King's command, a hundred pounds : not as though the leaden coin, by any operation of its own, caused him to be given that sum of money ; this being the effect of the mere will of the King. Hence Bernard says in a sermon on the Lord's Supper : 'Just as a canon is invested by means of a book, an abbot by means of a crozier, a bishop by means

---

[1] *Essays Catholic and Critical*, p. 429.

of a ring, so by the various sacraments various kinds of grace are conferred'. But if we examine the question properly, we shall see that according to the above mode the sacraments are mere signs. For the leaden coin is nothing but a sign of the King's command that this man should receive money. In like manner the book is a sign of the conferring of a canonry. Hence, according to this opinion, the sacraments of the New Law would be mere signs of grace ; whereas we have it on the authority of many saints that the sacraments of the New Law not only signify, but also cause grace."[1]

In this matter St. Thomas seems clearly to have reason on his side. And his criticism would apply also to another analogy made famous by Waterland when he wrote that in and through the Sacrament " we do receive the very body and blood as properly as a man receives an estate and becomes possessed of an inheritance by any deeds or conveyances ".[2] In fact, if the deeds or conveyances may be said in themselves to confer anything, what they confer is not the possession of the estate itself, but rather a valid claim or title to the possession of it, just as money of itself brings no real wealth, but only a claim to wealth which the community will honour. And this limitation belongs to the very nature of the conventional symbols which we are discussing. Consider Browning's well-known lines :

> " Just for a handful of silver he left us,
> Just for a ribbon to stick in his coat."

Clearly this is a rhetorical figure. No one would suppose that what attracted " the lost leader " was really the

---

[1] Summa III, Q. 62, Art. 1. St. Thomas is, of course, criticising, not Receptionism itself, but the scholastic theory known as Occasionalism, which taught that the outward signs of sacraments were occasions, rather than true causes, of the reception of grace.

[2] *Works* (Ed. 1856), IV, p. 608. Cf. *ibid.*, p. 572.

silver or the ribbon in themselves ; at worst, he desired the goods or the honour to which these outward things would entitle him. But imagine a Quaker becoming a convert to Catholicism. The Friends might well say of him "Just to receive the bread and wine of the Sacrament he left us " ; and we should not understand the words to be a rhetorical way of asserting that the convert had desired not the Sacrament in itself, but something to which the Sacrament would entitle him. The outward act of receiving the Eucharistic elements does not entitle us, or give us a valid claim, to receive our Lord. God forbid. It may well be doubted if any devout communicant has ever really thought of his communion in that way.[1]

If we seek in ordinary experience any principle of symbolism to help us in sacramental doctrine, it must be to expressive, not conventional, symbols that we must look. A work of literary art uses words as expressive symbols. But in that case the words taken one by one are conventional symbols ; it is only in their combination that they become expressive. The words casement, foam and perilous are purely conventional symbols for the various things which they may mean ; and yet the mere mention of them in immediate succession has already brought to the reader's mind certain lines of poetry in which they become the very embodiment of an inspired

---

[1] True, there is even among Catholics a recognised theory of sacramental grace which teaches that what the outward sign confers on the recipient is not, strictly speaking, grace itself, but a disposition which is " exigent " of grace, so that God immediately bestows grace in response to it. This theory is interestingly discussed by Archdeacon Lilley in a paper contributed to the Modern Churchmen's Conference, 1926, and published in *The Modern Churchman* for October of that year. But the whole point of this theory is destroyed if the receiving of the sacrament and the receiving of the grace are not strictly simultaneous. There is no hint of a title or claim to be honoured subsequently. And, even so, the theory seems, from the point of view of sacramental experience, very artificial and unsatisfactory.

fancy. And, according to this analogy, it may at least be plausibly argued that the consecrated elements have their heavenly reality only in a certain context, viz. as part of the matter of the Eucharistic rite.

Finally, we must carry one step further the criticism of the theory which is now under discussion. The interpretation of the Eucharistic presence in terms of mere symbolism, however expressive the symbolism may be, is not completely satisfying. The fact is that the familiar and traditional definition of sacraments as effectual signs or symbols may in these modern times be used so as to mask an important ambiguity. If it means that sacraments are at once expressive symbols and effective instruments of spiritual realities and operations, it can be accepted whole-heartedly. But it may be taken to imply that the efficacy of sacraments is wholly the result of their symbolic expressiveness, and that their power as instruments is limited by their meaning as symbols. This seems to be unsatisfactory, when we consider the relation of the sacrament to those who receive it. So long as we confine ourselves to thinking of the sacrament as it is in itself, or as it is in relation to Christ or God, the notion of expressive symbolism gives us all we need. For in proportion as any sign or symbol is truly expressive of the reality which it means, it may be said really to embody it, at least when the reality meant is something spiritual. But, taken strictly as an expressive symbol, it can only *convey* its meaning effectually to men's minds, in so far as these are capable of understanding and appreciating the meaning in their consciousness. *King Lear* may be a completely expressive symbol of Shakspere's genius. But it can only convey to me an impression of that genius, in so far as I appreciate in my consciousness the worth of the play. Now, the Catholic is bound to claim something more, and something different, for the sacraments, that something, namely, which is denoted by the term grace *ex opere operato*. He believes that, in so far as he receives the sacraments with a pure faith and a right intention, God will use them to bestow upon him infinitely more than at present he can feel or know. And this is his comfort when sensible devotion fails.

It follows then that the whole nature of a sacrament can never be illustrated either by the conventional symbol, the meaning of which is fixed by some more or less arbitrary fiat or custom, or by the expressive symbol which may be said really to embody what it means. Nor can any combination of the two analogies, or alternation between them, serve to remedy the defect of both. From the beginning a sacrament is in principle something more than a sign of any kind, more even than an effectual sign, if by that term we denote something which can only be effectual as a sign, or which is wholly dependent upon its significance for its effect.[1] A sacrament is actually an instrument whereby God's power operates upon us, not solely through the medium of a meaning apprehended by our minds. In the case of the Eucharist, therefore,

---

[1] J. B. Mozley (*Review of the Baptismal Controversy*, p. 303) quotes from Chamier (*De Sacram. in Gen.* c. 12) a few sentences which show how well some of the Reformers appreciated this point. "Inasmuch," writes Chamier, " as some pledges do nothing but affect the mind of the giver and receiver, we add that the sacraments are instruments by which that which is signified is effected, as when Christ breathed on the apostles and that breath both signified the Spirit and gave Him." More recently, the great Free Church theologian, R. W. Dale, was also eager to affirm that " the Service [of Holy Communion] is felt to be an act, not simply a picture-lesson "; but he does not fully tell us how he conceives the relation of the act to the material elements. " There ought ", he asserts rather questionably, " to be no difficulty in understanding that, though the material elements are symbols, the act of Christ when he places these elements in our hands is a spiritual reality." (See his important essay, *The Doctrine of the Real Presence*, in *Essays and Addresses*, esp. pp. 391–393).

we must maintain that the consecrated elements may be called as rightly " significant instruments " as " effectual signs ". Both instrumentality and significance or expressiveness are fundamental constituents of sacramental being, and neither must be made simply adjectival to the other. None of the theories of the Eucharistic presence so far mentioned seem to do justice to the complexity of this truth.

Before we proceed to such constructive suggestions as we have to offer, some remarks seem to be required upon the doctrinal implications of " Devotions " offered before the Reserved Sacrament. Evangelical theologians often regard this whole practice as the fruit of the theory of Transubstantiation, and condemn it on that ground. Undoubtedly the theory has encouraged the practice. But if by the term Transubstantiation we denote the exactly formulated doctrine of the Schoolmen, it seems much more probable that the theory was constructed in order to satisfy, and so far as possible to spiritualise and refine, the popular demand for the practice which already existed.[1] Indeed it appears that the mediæval theory of the Eucharistic presence, just in so far as it is made to justify Devotions, takes us into a circle of ideas quite remote from that to which properly belongs the theology of the Mass. The theory of the Mass, whatever its abuses, has always associated Christ's presence with a definite action. Indeed so strictly have Catholic theologians insisted on the reality of the act that they have sometimes seemed almost to teach that every Mass repeats the Sacrifice of the Cross. " What thou doest do quickly " is a text which has been used (no doubt figuratively) in order to justify speed in performing the rite. But in

[1] *Vide supra*, pp. 210–212.

the theology of the Reserved Sacrament we seem to be moving on a different plane of thought. Here the presence of Christ is found not in an act but in a thing which is thought to be its shrine, as long as the accidents or sensible properties of the material object hold together. It is difficult to resist the conclusion that here the demand of a popular and growing cult has deflected philosophical theology into a course it would not otherwise have taken. Whether this strengthens or weakens the grounds on which both the theory and the practice rest, is no doubt a matter of opinion.

Few, if any, Anglo-Catholic theologians would defend Devotions by means of the Roman theory in its strictness. Transubstantiation has become too elusive in its meaning and too doubtful in its philosophy to find adherents outside the Roman obedience. But among Anglo-Catholics, as is well known, the demand for Devotions is insistent and increasing ; theologians who support it are discovering the necessity of devising fresh grounds of doctrine for its justification ; and in the notions of symbolism and meaning they seem to find what they need. In reference to the general doctrine of the Eucharistic presence we have already criticised one of the resulting theories which has been worked out in detail. Many, however, find reason enough for the practice of Devotions in much more general arguments. By consecration in the Eucharist, they say, the elements are " charged with new meaning ",[1] and as they continue to symbolise that meaning outside the rite itself, they may at all times be justifiably used as an external aid to the spiritual worship of the Lord's Person. This plea demands careful consideration.

All arguments for the legitimacy of Devotions depend

[1] I borrow the actual phrase from Canon Streeter (Farnham Conference on *Reservation*, p. 39), who does not base this argument upon it.

upon the affirmation that whatever the consecrated elements essentially are within the Eucharistic rite, that they continue to be outside it. And the converse proposition seems to follow, that, whatever the consecrated element is when used for Devotions, that is all that it essentially is in the Eucharistic rite. If, then, the Reserved Sacrament is simply an external aid to devotion in more or less the same way as a crucifix or an icon, we are led to the conclusion that even in the Eucharist it is essentially no more than that. Thus we are brought back to a doctrine of the Eucharistic presence which is not far removed from Receptionism. One of the chief perplexities of the whole discussion arises from the fact that the interest of many Anglo-Catholics is so exclusively fixed on the worship, not the doctrine, of Catholicism, that they seem willing to adopt the most apparently un-Catholic of doctrines, if only it can be represented as affording ground for the external practice of a Catholic devotion. But it must be admitted that their constant appeal to Catholic experience loses much of its force, if the doctrine hitherto connected with that experience is to be abandoned. The paradox surely would become extreme, if Devotions were to be justified by a well-nigh Receptionist doctrine of the Eucharistic presence.

But this is not the only difficulty raised by the appeal to symbolism in this connexion. If the Reserved Sacrament is a symbol of a purely artificial or conventional type, it is clearly wrong to treat it as in any sense equivalent to that which it represents. To treat the word " love " as though it were equivalent to the reality which it denotes (unless the word on the particular occasion were being actually uttered in some expressive way) would be merely absurd. On the other hand, as we have already suggested, there seems to be no intelligible ground for saying that

the symbolic character of the consecrated elements
outside the Eucharistic rite is really *expressive* at all.
And this is tacitly confessed by the manner in which the
Devotions are practised. Except in the case of Exposition,
a practice which in fact very few Anglicans defend, the
Reserved Sacrament is never perceptible to the bodily
senses of the worshipper. It is indeed surrounded by a
possibly expressive symbolism of altar, tabernacle,
lights, and the like ; but its own presence is never outwardly apprehended at all. Now, if a sacrament is in
its essence an outward and visible sign of a spiritual
reality, it is strange, to say the least, that in a sacramental
worship the sacrament itself should be carefully guarded
from view. In the Roman theory the Eucharistic Body
of the Lord is so far other than a sign that this conceal-
ment may be but an appropriate expression of reverence ;
but it really stultifies the argument that the sacramental
character of that which is in the tabernacle is constituted
by its expressiveness as a symbol. We cannot, therefore,
admit that the insistence upon symbolism or new meaning
in the elements is any real help to the doctrinal justification which is sought for Devotions.

How, then, shall we find our way out of the maze in
which our own criticisms of so many diverse theories
seem to have involved us ? We have the clue when we
take up once more our previous assertion that the
doctrine of the Eucharistic presence must be treated in
the closest connexion with that of the Eucharistic offering.
The Eucharist is the self-offering of Christ as externalised
in human ritual, so that human lives may be incorporated
into its living reality through communion with Him Who
offers and is offered. The action of every Eucharist
begins in the inward and eternal sphere where Christ

is seated at the right hand of God. Christ's action then reaches its first stage of externalisation in His Body the Church, which at a given place and time in the person of its priest solemnly offers the bread and wine in memorial of His passion. The action is thus further externalised and extended into the consecrated bread and wine themselves as representing the offered Body of Christ's manhood. From this furthest or lowest point of externalisation the action of the living Christ returns back and upwards into the members of His Body the Church as they receive Him in communion. In them it brings forth the spiritual fruits of their own self-offering which raises them towards heaven in Christ's power. So the Eucharistic action returns in the end to heaven which was its source. Thus interpreted, it consists of a double movement, first downward and outward, then upward and inward. Thus it re-embodies in ritual and fulfils through the life of the Church that which was first and perfectly embodied in fact through the historical life of Jesus Christ. At every point of the Eucharistic action the whole Christ is present in that through which He acts ; and that through which He acts is at every point His Body as the instrument and expression of His will. And we may believe that part of His purpose is to descend even into the material sphere, so that He may raise those who live in that sphere even as it were from beneath, and enable them to find Him in all things which are made the material of His offering. "Now that He ascended, what is it but that He descended first into the lower parts of the earth that He might fill all things ?" "As the rain cometh down and the snow from heaven, and returneth not thither, but watereth the earth, and maketh it bring forth and bud, that it may give seed to the sower and bread to the eater : so shall My Word be that goeth forth out of My mouth : He shall not return unto me void, but He shall accomplish that which I please, and He shall prosper in the thing whereto I sent Him."

The foregoing gives the sequence of ideas in relation to which we should seek to affirm the doctrine of Real Presence in the Eucharistic elements. And it will readily be seen how such an interpretation of the presence avoids the grounds of criticism which we have noticed in others. Its fundamental thought is this, that the presence is to be sought in the elements not as physical objects, but as they are within the process of a certain action which takes them up into itself, uses them as its instruments, and expresses itself in them. It may be true to say that the presence resides in what is done with the elements rather than in the elements themselves, if it be remembered that in the process of that action the elements are more than merely the instruments of a living spirit beyond them and become actually the expression of the life of that spirit itself.[1] The presence of Christ is not to be localised in a material thing, nor do we assert, as does the dogma of Transubstantiation, that it is the reality beneath what appears to be bread and wine ; but it is to be truly identified with the localised bread and wine, in so far as these constitute the matter wherein through the Eucharistic

[1] We here definitely part company with St. Thomas when he differentiates between the Eucharist and other sacraments by saying that "this sacrament is accomplished in the consecration of the matter, whereas other sacraments are accomplished in the use of the consecrated matter " ; and when he proceeds to deny that any act concerning the use of the matter is essential to the sacrament of the Eucharist (Summa III, Q. 78, Art. 1). According to the view here put forward, the consecration is but the first step in the properly sacramental use of the matter ; and the difference between Baptism and Eucharist is to be found in the distinct use to which, by Christ's appointment and operation, the sacramental matter is put in each case. This does not at all exclude the doctrine of a Real Presence in the Eucharist, which quite distinguishes it from Baptism.

Q

action Christ externalises His offering of Himself to the Father and imparts its living power to our souls.

The Real Presence is not thus affirmed in any sense in which it could conceivably be opposed to the reality of Christ's immanence in His Church and in human souls. For it is affirmed only in closest connexion with the Eucharistic action which apart from that immanence is without meaning or effect. Again it is not affirmed as implying any " real absence " of Christ elsewhere. For the Eucharist is the expressive symbol of the whole process by which the world is made to fulfil God's purpose ; and from that fact the special sanctity of the Eucharist is derived. On the other hand the Real Presence is affirmed so that the communicant is not left at the mercy of his own fitful and insecure consciousness of spiritual things, which, on occasion, may be so little stirred by the expressiveness of the Eucharistic symbolism. We believe that if the Christian wills at all to take part inwardly in the Eucharistic act, Christ truly acts upon him through the outward thing which he receives, and that the inward efficacy of that outward reception may be infinitely greater than his consciousness can grasp.

As regards the effect of consecration, there seems to be no reason why we should not willingly accept the statement that the bread and wine are changed so as to become the Body and Blood of Christ, if it be understood that the terms body and blood denote, not material things as such, but outward things as they are in relation to a spiritual activity which operates and expresses itself through them. The term body is naturally so used in modern speech, and we cannot justly call the use metaphorical, inasmuch as the human body seems to constitute only a particular case of that relation of outward to inward which the word body essentially denotes. A similar use of the term blood is, of course, in a general way quite strange to modern ears ; and the meaning of the phrase "the Blood of Christ" in a mystical context is but vaguely apprehended, familiar as the language of religion has made the phrase itself. It is the ancient identification of the blood with the life in sacrifice which determines the Eucharistic meaning of the word, as it was doubtless the reason for our Lord's use of it in interpreting the purpose of His own death.

At the same time, if we so interpret the effect of consecration, the change wrought in the bread and wine is sufficiently represented as a change of use and meaning, and is not a change in the physical objects as such. It will follow that the change is objectively real only within the process of the Eucharistic action by which the new use and meaning are given and in which they are found. The result of such a doctrine upon the practice of reserving the Sacrament is not difficult to define. It is in every sense of the word a convenient custom that part of the consecrated elements should be reserved for the communion of those who are unavoidably prevented from attending the Eucharist in Church. The communion of these is in reality simply a postponed part of the Eucharistic act[1] ; and in it the reserved elements, without further consecration, have to the full that heavenly use and meaning which the Eucharistic action gives. During the interval in which they are reserved, they remain consecrated, that is, set apart for a most holy purpose, and to use them for any common purpose or in any common

---

[1] Evangelical theologians should notice that dislike of multiplying sick-room celebrations beyond necessity is due in part to the fact that these are from one point of view too like private Masses. The Eucharist is essentially a public rite among Christians, it is *the* sacrament of their corporate life ; and it is much more fitting that those who cannot attend the public celebration should still be partakers of it afterwards, than that private celebrations should be multiplied for the sake of individuals.

way would be, in the strictest sense, desecration. But, though they are set apart for a certain purpose, they are not, during the interval of reservation, in the actual use of that purpose, nor outside that use can they be said to express the meaning which is theirs within it. Their holiness then, while they are reserved, is real but negative. As physical objects they are consecrated, that is, set apart for Christ; but He takes them up into His Eucharistic action, only when that action is in progress. And though the mind will at all times naturally associate the reserved elements with their Eucharistic meaning, they actually express that meaning only in the Eucharist itself. Hence it seems fitting that the reserved elements should be reverently guarded and concealed from view during the time that they lie reserved, and no place could be more appropriate than the altar of the church. But it is hard to find justification here for Devotions expressly directed towards the place where they lie.

We are aware that in much of what has been said we have laid ourselves open to a charge of intolerable dogmatism where dogmatism is least easily forgiven. It is not for us to define the Eucharistic action of Christ; and it may seem hardly less presumptuous to oppose a theological theory to what so many Christians feel to be an imperative need in their devotion. Nevertheless there is sometimes a value in trying to be definite even in things which are confessedly indefinable. The attempt may help the spirit to discern where the true mystery lies. And it is exactly because the theory which we offer is tentative, that we have tried to work it out into all its apparent consequences. It may thus be the more readily and clearly judged at the bar of Christian reason and experience.

CHAPTER X

WORSHIP AND MORALS

NO theory of sacraments, however limited its aim, can be complete without some special treatment of a problem which presses hardly upon the modern mind, namely, the problem of the relation between the God-ward and man-ward aspects of human activity, the relation of worship to life, of religion to ethics.

There are still some, no doubt, to whom it will seem a paradox to suggest that this is a real problem at all. They have been brought up in the belief that the demands of religion and of the moral law are really identical; that the better a man is ethically, the more fully he serves and pleases God, and that the more punctually he fulfils his religious duties, the higher the measure of moral goodness which he will achieve. Religion and ethics help and support each other. They are two aspects of one service, which is the seeking of God's Kingdom, and of one goodness, which is communion with God. What need is there to suggest the possibility of a contrast between them ?

Now we may agree that this account of the matter is in the end profoundly true. Worshipping God and doing good to one's neighbour are indeed two inseparable aspects of one ideal life. The full knowledge of that truth is that which constitutes the glorious liberty of the children of God; and by it Christians are free-born citizens of God's universal Kingdom. Yet they will never understand their liberty, nor use it aright, unless they have learned something also of that great sum of toil and tears whereby the human race has purchased what their Church preserves for them as a birthright.

Hegel has made it a familiar thought in philosophy that human progress must always consist first in taking to pieces some single experience or aspect of experience, and then in putting the pieces together again into a unity which the previous division has enriched. We advance, as it were, from unison, through discord, to harmony; from identity, through difference, to the organic unity in which differences are held together and reconciled.

We have already indicated the operation of some such law in the common opposition between theory and practice, knowing and doing. These opposites are at first born out of a vital process of experience which included the germs of both. The animal and the human infant know and act at once; their action is part of their knowing, and their knowing of their action. The dog's recognition of his master is often a series of violent bodily contortions; and the thought that " this is good to eat " is not separate in the animal's or baby's mind from the initiation of the movements proper to eating it. The animal's habit of fusing knowledge and action together is used by the prophet to rebuke Israel's failure to recognise Jehovah. " The ass knoweth his owner and the ox his master's crib; but Israel doth not know, my people doth not consider." Yet even on the subrational plane of life the instinct of curiosity seems to give promise of a thirst for knowledge for its own sake. And as the human mind develops, and reorganises and redirects its instinctive impulses, its purpose to know its environment becomes more and more sharply distinguished from its purpose to change or modify it, or to evoke certain responses from it. Theory and practice fall apart, and begin to exercise conflicting claims upon human energy. The philosopher and the scientific student dwell on the limitations of the practical man, while the practical man is more openly scornful of the theorist. The one regards action as a means to knowledge ; to the other knowledge is a means to action. Which is right ? Is the truest aim of human life to know the world as it really is, or to make it a better place to live in than it is now ? Somehow we cannot be satisfied with either alternative by itself. Theory and practice must somehow be joined again in the ideal world which we call heaven. There to know God is to serve Him, and to serve Him is to know. There must be a heavenly contemplation which is also a supreme activity. Yet that final harmony will be infinitely different from the first primitive union in which doing and knowing are indistinguishably fused.

Or consider another equally common antithesis, that between goodness and happiness. Originally, no doubt, in the infant's mind the good and the pleasant are one thing—not, of course, that the two are consciously identified, for this is impossible until the ideas of goodness and pleasantness are already distinct, whereas to the infant mind there is but one sensation, which may be called indifferently good or pleasant. Then, as the conscience is born, the good and the pleasant come to be sharply distinguished, and are frequently opposed to one another. Yet we cannot acquiesce in any permanent divorce between them. Men invent various theories in order to bring goodness and happiness together again. The necessity for this reconciliation is the motive of philosophic hedonism and utilitarianism, and also of beliefs in another world or a future age where happiness rewards virtue, and pain is the punishment of vice. All such theories are more or less inadequate ; but some reconciliation there must be. We know that we ought to enjoy most what is really best ; and we are driven in the end to picture to ourselves, as the result of our inner conflict, some sphere of being in which goodness and happiness once more are realised together. Yet how far removed is this happiness of perfect goodness from the primitive experience in which the terms " pleasant " and " good " are names equally applicable to the conditions of a single undifferentiated sensation !

The same general law holds good of the relation between worship and life, between God-ward religion and man-ward ethics. Anthropologists continue to give us divergent conjectures as to the way in which the human race first came to be religious, and as to the original connexion between religious and other ideas. But we may at least plausibly suppose that in the earliest form of tribal society neither religion nor ethics existed in the sense in which we ourselves understand those terms. The germs of both were included and fused together in the whole life of the group determined by instinct and tradition. Man was dimly conscious of the need that he should enter into some kind of relation with an unseen spirit or deity, and dimly conscious also that in some way he must serve and co-operate with other members of the tribe and respect their property. But the two kinds of obligation were not clearly distinguished. Often the god of the tribe is so closely connected with the life of the tribe itself that he seems to be little more than a personification of its continued existence, and his will merely adds a mysterious sanction to the traditional customs whereby that existence is preserved. And, again, the benevolent or punitive action of members of the tribe towards one another has no consciously moral motive, but springs without thought or reflexion from that instinct for maintaining the life of the group which is also the source of what appears to be worship of the unseen.

Gradually religion and ethics stand out as distinctly conceived motives of action upon the confused background of instinct and custom which was the original stuff or raw material of both. Religion begins as soon as the mysterious sanction of tribal customs is felt to proceed from a personal or quasi-personal will, separate and unseen, which makes certain definite demands upon the tribe for worship, service and sacrifice. Ethics begin, probably at a later stage, as soon as a man is able to judge the actions required of him towards his neighbour as being either good or bad in themselves, as being in harmony or in conflict with a certain law of goodness which claims to govern man's action towards man. The primitive moralist is thus enabled to criticise the demands of social custom, and to follow them or to rebel against them from motives different in kind from those of mere conformity, prudence or self-assertion.

Now it is a strange but undeniable fact in human history that no sooner are religion and ethics realised as distinct motives, than they begin to fall apart, and a certain opposition and conflict between them is increasingly manifest. Early religion as a rule has but little connexion with the ideas of right and justice which are the foundation of morality. It depends on the notion that man's life is in the grip of mysterious unseen powers whose favour must be won, whose wrath averted, and towards whom the attitude of unquestioning self-abasement is imperatively required. True as it may be that most primitive peoples are found to possess some dim and half-forgotten notion of a beneficent creator, still the operative idea of godhead among them is an idea of awful and mysterious power, rather than of goodness. Often such ideas of godhead are developed apart from goodness altogether. It is generally true of pagan religions that the morality of the gods is on a lower and more childish level than that of the worshippers. Gods excel men in power and immortality, not in goodness. They jealously exact certain kinds of propitiatory worship and gifts from man, and visit omission with the most dire penalties. Whole systems of sacrifice and ritual are invented to placate them. Not seldom their character is conceived of as really malevolent ; and it is now known that in Central America a whole civilisation was ruined by unspeakable abominations of slaughter carried out in the name of religion. In practically all primitive cults, a certain specific kind of fear or dread of a mysterious power is the dominant emotion. As Otto has so convincingly shown, the attitude most universally characteristic of religious worship is essentially non-moral and non-rational. Holiness belongs to deity ; but the idea of the holy in primitive religion connotes mysterious awfulness rather than moral purity.

All theists will, of course, maintain that man's moral ideas and ideals have a divine origin. But it may be gravely doubted whether, at least as a general rule, they spring directly from his religion. Ideas of right and justice arise out of men's dealings with one another in the social life of the community. Society cannot exist without a government and order which recognises certain claims and enforces certain obligations. As these claims and obligations cease to rest merely on instinct and custom, and are made the object of a more or less rational criticism, they are found to involve principles of right and justice whereby governments themselves may be judged. But primitive morality is closely bound up with the observance of the laws of the community as regulating men's social relations with one another. The standard of moral right may condemn certain laws as bad ; but on the whole it has its origin in law, and the moral reformer or rebel almost invariably makes his appeal to the principle of some older law, real or imaginary, which subsequent innovations have set aside. All these considerations of law, justice and morality stand more or less apart from the system of worship or cultus which constitutes religion in the narrower and more special sense.

Yet the essential separateness of religion and ethics, real as it is when we regard human history, is only one side of the truth after all. Man cannot acquiesce permanently in any divorce between them, and he has never allowed the separation to be complete. There has always been close interaction between religious and ethical thought ; and, if some religions have been almost wholly devoid of ethical value, ethical ideas in their higher forms have generally claimed some sort of divine sanction. From the beginning religion has been essentially connected with the social life of the human group ; and when man has asked himself the question, Whence came the notions of lawful right and justice whereby society is held together ? it has commonly seemed natural to him to turn for an answer to those mysterious and awful powers which he has learned to worship as divine. Thus the notion of a divine author and upholder of a moral law is grafted with more or less completeness and success upon the notion of awful and worshipful mystery which is perhaps the proper and original idea of godhead. From one point of view the Old Testament appears as just one long-continued essay in this work of reconciliation. It is this aspect of its meaning which gives ground for the extreme opinion that the story of the Old Testament is the record of a conflict between two quite different

religions, the older religion of a mysterious deity manifested in the terrors of the thunderstorm and propitiated
by sacrifice, and the newer religion of the divine Law-
giver Who demands not sacrifice but righteousness.
This opinion clearly points to an essential truth ; it errs
only in supposing that the two religions ever existed as
two clearly distinguished entities in the mind of either
priest or prophet, and are not rather abstractions whereby
the modern mind enables itself to grasp the significance
of a more or less confused progress and conflict of ideas.
However that may be, the post-exilic authors and editors,
starting from Ezekiel, clearly achieved an imperfect
conflation of older beliefs, which are easily traced in the
earlier portions of the Pentateuch and the historical books,
with the newer thought about God, which constitutes
the main message of the prophets from Amos to
Jeremiah.

It is interesting to compare and contrast the story of
the Old Testament with the evolution of religion in ancient
Greece. The primitive tradition that Zeus destroys
perjurers with the thunderbolt represents a very early
attempt to moralise the mysterious awfulness of deity.
The sin of perjury gives an obviously convenient occasion ;
for the troth solemnly pledged to man in the name of
God is of all human acts that which most evidently unites
God-ward with man-ward relations, religion with ethics.
But the moralisation of the idea of God never proceeded
far in the popular and official religion of the Greek world.
And in Athens of the fifth century B.C. moral ideals were
so far in advance of that religion, that Socrates and Plato
had practically to condemn it wholesale, and to preach
a different deity altogether as the author and guardian
of the moral life.

The main point to be emphasised for our present purpose is this. At every stage above the lowest and beneath the highest an alliance between religion and ethics is by no means to be taken for granted. On the contrary their union is always imperfect, and they are frequently found to be in opposition to one another. Morality is experienced as a law requiring of us certain action, often painful to ourselves, for the good of our fellow-men, our neighbour, our descendants, the nation or the race. Religion requires of us worship, self-abasement or self-surrender, towards a mysterious spiritual power more and other than human. And, whatever efforts we make, we cannot completely unify the two obligations involved. The best reconciliation achieved apart from Christianity is to suppose that God, Who demands our worship, is Himself the author and upholder of the moral law. But this supposition raises further questions. If moral life is essentially what God requires of us, shall we not serve Him best, not by worship, but by seeking the good of our neighbour ? " I will have mercy, and not sacrifice." If so, worship becomes a mere means to moral life. But then it is not really worship, and so religion is sacrificed altogether. If, on the other hand, we impose worship as a God-ward duty additional to the man-ward duty of a moral life, the two obligations, not being unified, cannot but compete with one another. For the religious consciousness cannot be satisfied with apportioning some part of life only to God, and, if once it be admitted that worship is specifically God's part, it will draw us towards that essentially inhuman type of religion, which, somewhat after the manner of the lean kine in Pharaoh's dream, swallows up its rivals, the kindlier social activities of life, and, having done so, appears no less gaunt and ill-favoured than before.

Christianity shows us a more excellent way. Let us see

what light the revelation of God may throw upon our problem.

In the first place, love worketh no ill to his neighbour ; therefore love is the fulfilling of the moral law. But if love fulfils the law, it also does much more than keep the commandments. It aims not at *keeping* anything, but at creating a new condition of social life for men, at bringing in the kingdom of heaven. As we noticed in a previous chapter, the difference between loyal observance and adventurous creation makes just the difference between the ethic of the Old Testament and that of the New. And thus in love morality has passed beyond itself. How do we know that we can be successful either in creating a new order of social life or in becoming new creatures ourselves, if this is what the morality of love indeed requires of us ? We need faith. And if faith is justified, moral goodness must be more than just an ideal set forth in the laws which a divine governor has ordained ; it must in the end be sought as belonging to the very spirit and life of the universe, which supports and empowers those who lend themselves to be instruments of its creative activity. In such a belief alone can we find strength and courage for our moral task. But the belief is no mere means to moral achievement ; it does infinitely more than inspire us to work for our neighbour's good. It brings us near, and demands our surrender, to a mysterious, unseen and pervasive power, which is fulfilling itself in the new world it enables us to long for, and in some measure to create. Thus our moral nature itself is made to feel the need of worship, not as a means to doing good, but as an element in the goodness of the new world which it is seeking. For this is the world of love, and it can only be created or enjoyed in self-abandonment to the spirit of love itself.

Secondly, love is the fulfilling of all laws of sacrifice and worship. In worship from the beginning man has been feeling his way towards some kind of communion with the mysterious powers of the spiritual world. And more and more clearly he has been made aware in so doing that God's claim is not merely upon his but upon him. It is more than a claim upon his conduct, his actions, his social behaviour ; it cannot be met by the observance of any law. It is this mysterious something more, this absoluteness of the divine claim upon human life, which was first expressed in the thought of the dreadful holiness of God, and supplied the motive for the propitiatory ritual of sacrifice, even when that motive, perverted through the neglect of moral and rational illumination, plunged religion in cruelty and gloom. The religious consciousness, in its purest and truest form, has always known that no merely moral achievement can enable man to stand unashamed and confident before his maker. Man cannot plead before God as he would before a human judge ; nor can he satisfy His demand with anything less than the surrender of his life. Such is the religious conviction which gave us the book of Job. To point out its essential character and significance is the great contribution which Otto has made to theology.

But if God be love, the reflexion of the divine love in man's soul may help him to achieve the apparently impossible, to see God and live. For the fulness of love includes self-surrender even to death, and yet does not find in death the end of life. If man could love God with the love which God has for man, he could offer his life as a true and sufficient sacrifice, which would open for him the gate of heaven. And, in so far as he was inspired by that love, he would, even as he worshipped its source, more than fulfil every claim of moral law ; for truly to worship the

God Who loves men is to work for the joy of every soul which He has made. But how shall man be made partaker of that love ? The Christian answers, " I thank God, through Jesus Christ my Lord ". The Cross is the perfection at once of sacrifice towards God and of saving help towards men. The prophecies of it are in the long and blood-stained records of sacerdotalism, no less than in the burning words which have expressed the moral zeal of the prophets themselves. Not with the fire of that zeal only did our Lord come, nor only with the water of purity, but also with the blood of sacrifice. In His love, divine and human, not Jew and Gentile only, but prophet and priest, moralist and mystic, are fashioned together into one new man. The claims of worship and of ethics are no longer rivals, but complement each other. And the reconciliation is found, not in the affirmation that the God Whom we worship is also the Governor who decrees our duty towards our fellow-men, but rather in the discovery that the true worship of God and the true service of men are alike possible only in the power of the one Holy Spirit of love, Who leads us through both to the world in which the communion between Creator and creature is eternally perfect.

Yet what a world of difference there is between such a union of the service of God with the service of men and that original, primitive experience of the human race in which the two services have never been opposed, because they have never been distinguished. We may discover in the end that the truest worship of God is the service of our fellow-men, but only because we have discovered also that the highest service of our fellow-men consists in utter self-surrender to God. And there would be no glory in the union, if it had never been possible to oppose religious holiness to moral goodness. These must be apprehended as distinct before they can be harmonised. It would mean comparatively little to say that God is good, if the proposition had been all along simply analytic and not synthetic, in the Kantian sense of those terms—if, that is, good itself had never been known as other than a property of God. It is because the ideas of God and of goodness have been separated in human thought, that we can prove the glorious freedom of the knowledge that the dread mystery of Godhead is but a veil for the majesty of love. It is because the face of heaven has so long been dark, that St. John's cry has its ring of triumph, " God is light, and in Him is no darkness at all ". Truly with a great sum the freedom has been bought. The horrors of all perverted religion, culminating on Calvary, are the price. Yet, if the price paid is enough to redeem the world, τετέλεσται, and all is well.

But how can all this be translated into terms of earthly practice ? We are finite creatures living in a world of space and time. We must in practice assign part of life to worship, part to our dealings with our fellow-men. It may be that the God-ward and man-ward activities in the end are one through love, and that in heaven they are realised together. But on earth they must be felt as separate. How, then, can we think and live in the truth of their unity ?

It is indeed a tragic fact that those who are most sincere and active in their religious duties, and spend most time and trouble in fulfilling them, do sometimes fall below the level of comparatively profane persons in neighbourly kindness, human sympathy and philanthropic effort. It is no mere chance, but a sign of our Lord's penetrating observation of men, that in his parable of neighbourliness those who passed by on the other side were very religious men, and he who in this matter kept God's law was a

R

Samaritan. The term which in recent times has had most nearly the same connotation as Samaritan is Bohemian. The punctilious Christian, hardly less than the punctilious Jew, is apt to lose sight of the Bohemian virtues. And, moreover, we are often inclined to forget that Pharisaic rigorism is not the only type of false religion which our Lord condemned. He was only a little less severe upon the shallow and emotional piety of the man in the street. The truth is that religious feelings, no less than religious forms and rules, may always become a danger to spiritual life. There is no greater mistake than to suppose that all is well with a man just because he is zealous and regular in worship, or that, to put him on the true road to heaven, you have only to bring him to a beautiful church and make him feel the mystery of the divine presence in the Mass, in the Tabernacle, or at the mission service. Our ecclesiastics, especially laymen, are often prone to argue that anything which leads men to express ardent devotion to Jesus has thereby proved its heavenly worth. The Gospels leave little doubt that Jesus Himself would not agree. Nothing moved Him to greater horror than an adoring devotion towards Himself, which signified nothing more than a sentimental emotion. Such fervid praises as " Blessed is the womb that bare thee ", "Blessed is he that shall eat bread in the Kingdom of God ", met with a singularly cold reception ; and we are given to understand that some to whom He will profess " I never knew you " are among those who have called most persistently upon His name.

Yet, of course, all this does not prove that worship is not the highest activity of life. The fact that *corruptio optimi pessima* does not impair the value of the best. To realise the dangers of religion need not drive us to exchange the warmth and colour of Catholic devotion

for the somewhat grim conscientiousness of an ethical
society, or to substitute a co-operative commonwealth
for the Kingdom of God as an outlet for effervescent
emotions. The better way is to conceive all prayer
offered on earth as partaking of a sacramental nature.
Private prayer, the worship of the heart, is indeed the
most truly inward and the least outward of all human
activities. But it partakes of the outward, in so far as it
occupies time ; and again, in so far as it occupies time, it
constantly symbolises and effects the true meaning and
purpose of all that fills other times in the life of him who
prays. This is true even of the wordless prayer in which
the soul strives to life up itself, its thoughts and doings,
its desires and capacities, as an offering to God. Indeed
it is only so far as prayer has these relations of symbolism and instrumentality to what is beyond itself, that it
is sane and healthy and sincere. It is exactly when the
worshipper cultivates worship strictly as something apart
from the rest of life, that it becomes the narcotic rather
than the stimulant of his soul. And it is at least as easy
to confuse narcotics with stimulants in the spiritual
sphere, as it is in the physical. "Those who sleep,
sleep in the night, and those who are drunken, are drunken
in the night ; but let us, who are of the day, be sober and
watch." Drunkenness is but sleep disguised, to whatever
prodigies of action the drunkard may dream himself to
be stimulated ; and there may be some enthusiasts for
prayer who are scarcely less deluded than he. But
Christian prayer is watchful. And because its eye is really
open towards God, it is never really closed towards the
world. Prayer indeed can be its true self only when
it is in direct relation to that which is other than itself.
For it is itself the God-ward aspect of all activities, and
the time of prayer is that sacramental time, the meaning

and effect of which must be spread over all others, until the union of all is perfect in eternity.

If we can but remember that in Christianity the holiest things are the most truly representative of what is common, we shall not be snared in the false religions of ascetic rigorism on the one hand and of emotional self-indulgence on the other. And the representation of the common in the holy is, we believe, the first principle of sacramental theory.

APPENDICES

A. A Modern Theory of Eucharistic Sacrifice

In the text of the foregoing chapter no mention has been made of a modern type of theory, which relates the Sacrifice of the Cross to the Sacrifice of the Mass in a different way from that of any of the doctrines so far discussed. In the Roman Church this theory has been worked out fully in Père de la Taille's great book *Mysterium Fidei*; and among Anglicans, Mr. W. Spens has independently arrived at similar conclusions, which he has briefly set forth and defended in *Essays Catholic and Critical*. This theory agrees with the view which we have already taken, that in the Eucharist there can be no actual immolation. It therefore does not follow in their strictest sense the words of the Tridentine Decree (Sess. XXIII), in which it is stated that our Lord, " *celebrato veteri Pascha, quod in memoriam exitus de Aegypto multitudo filiorum Israel immolabat, novum instituit Pascha*, seipsum ab Ecclesia per sacerdotes sub signis visibilibus immolandum *in memoriam transitus sui ex hoc mundo ad Patrem* ", etc. But, on the other hand, it tries to give more justification for calling the Mass an actual sacrifice than is explicitly afforded by the doctrines of St. Thomas and Cardinal Vasquez. Its method is to distinguish two integral elements in one sacrifice, and to suggest that the Last Supper and the Mass supply the one element, while the death on the Cross supplies the other. Fr. M. C. D'Arcy,

S.J., an English exponent of Père de la Taille's theory, writes as follows : " A propitiatory sacrifice consists of a visible public act—that is, a liturgical act—and that act has two constituents—a formal offering of a victim, and a slaying or immolation of that victim. . . . The Last Supper and Calvary make one identical sacrifice, in which the oblation is formally made at the Supper while the real immolation takes place on Calvary. . . . That the Mass is a sacrificial act is clear, for all the requisites are present—Priest, Victim, and oblation in a visible rite. But now straightway the question arises, How is a victim present ? There is no act of immolation, no new blood-letting. As the Council of Trent asserts, the Mass is an unbloody sacrifice. The answer is shown to us in the Last Supper. There our Lord, by means of the bread and wine, represented the immolation to come. Behind the appearances were his true body and blood, so that the Passion was represented symbolically by the separate consecration and the Victim really offered. Similarly, in the separate consecrations at Mass there is a symbolical immolation which serves as a visible liturgical action necessary for a true sacrifice. But that action is only symbolical or mystical ; no new *real* victimising of the flesh and blood of Christ takes place."[1] Mr. Spens's statement is to very similar effect, though his language is at once less theologically guarded, and much more congenial and intelligible to Anglican ears. According to him a solemn ritual, which invests a death with sacrificial meaning, is no less an essential element in sacrifice than the death itself. Hence he concludes that " the Last Supper and the Eucharist are not separate sacrifices from that of Calvary, but supply a necessary element in the sacrifice of Calvary, by expressly investing our

---

[1] *The Mass and the Redemption*, pp. 47, 49 and 67.

Lord's death before God and man with its sacrificial significance ".[1]

The objections to this theory are two. It seems over-formal and elaborate. And the suggestion that the Eucharist or the Mass, even when considered as repeating the Last Supper, can supply something which Calvary by itself would lack, seems hard to reconcile with the Christian tradition or experience. To say that Calvary and the Eucharist each supplies an element in one sacrifice is to make not one of them, nor each, but neither, to be a perfect, complete and all-sufficient sacrifice in itself. There seems to be much force in Dom Vonier's contention, when he writes : " To save the oneness of the Christian sacrifice the strange hypothesis has been put forward in our own days that the Eucharistic sacrifice is not so much a representation of the Sacrifice of the Cross as an integral portion of the Sacrifice of the Cross. The Eucharistic sacrifices, both at the Last Supper and now, are being con-sidered as so many stages in the one great all-embracing sacrifice whose culminating act was on the Cross. It is not my mission here to criticise theological opinions. It is certain, however, that to consider the Eucharistic sacrifice as being in any way a portion of the universal sacrifice is a profound reversal of the traditional rôle of the sacrament. A sacrament is not part of the drama, however great that drama may be ; a sacrament is essentially the representation of the completed drama. The historic drama must be complete before sacraments are possible. Sacraments are the monuments of the finished thing only, not the introductory scenes or the last acts of some great historic deed. If the Eucharistic sacrifice were in any way a portion of the universal sacrifice it would represent nothing except itself. . . .

[1] *Essays Catholic and Critical*, p. 436.

Is not one of the basic principles of the Eucharistic sacrifice to be found in the very completeness and finality of the Sacrifice of the Cross ? If Mass gave anything to the Cross it would cease to be a sacrament, as it would cease to be a representation. Mass is the memory or the monument of Christ's passion. Is it not the very purpose of a monument to stand for the complete victory, the heroic deed, the final triumph ? We do not erect monuments to failures or things half-achieved. To take away something from the completeness of the Sacrifice of the Cross on the one hand, and on the other hand from the completeness of the Sacrifice of the Mass, is not to join them into one organism, but it is to destroy them both. In this matter you cannot make a whole with two halves, because sacrament and nature are totally different. They become one through that very difference, as I have already said, because the one is the total representation of the other's totality of reality. The traditional view of the Church is that the Sacrifice of Calvary was complete and perfect in the genus sacrifice ; the Eucharist adds nothing to it ; but it is truly the " brightness of its glory and the figure of its substance '."[1]

Without going further into the question how far the implied criticisms of other theories are just, I could accept almost the whole of the above passage as a forcible statement of the same doctrine of the Eucharistic sacrifice which I have been trying to defend.

B. The Meaning of Transubstantiation

In the past two main arguments relied upon by Anglican apologists against Transubstantiation have been these : (1) that it supports a gross and carnal notion of the

[1] *A Key to the Doctrine of the Eucharist*, pp. 137 *sqq.*

Eucharistic presence, and (2) that it conflicts with the plain evidence of the senses. It is clear that until the definitions of the Council of Trent had firmly established themselves in Roman Catholic theology, there was considerable justification for these attacks. As early as the ninth century, Paschasius Radbert, while strongly insisting on the spiritual character of the Eucharistic mystery, had written that " though the figure of bread and wine remain, yet these are altogether a figure, and after consecration we must believe that there is nothing else than the flesh and blood of Christ ". "This ", he goes on to say, " is certainly no other flesh than that which was born of Mary, suffered on the Cross, and rose from the tomb." Such was afterwards the doctrine generally accepted ; and the celebrated Berengarian controversy carried opinion towards forgetfulness of the spiritual side of Paschasius's teaching. At the Council held in Rome in 1059 Berengar was made to sign a document in which he declared himself to " hold the faith which the Lord and venerable Pope Nicholas and this holy synod have by evangelical and apostolic authority delivered to be held and have confirmed to me, namely that the bread and wine which are placed on the altar are after consecration not only a sacrament but also the real body and blood of our Lord Jesus Christ, and that with the senses (*sensualiter*), not only by way of sacrament but in reality (*non solum sacramento sed in veritate*), these are held and broken by the hands of the priests and are crushed by the teeth of the faithful ". At the same time Berengar was made to repudiate contrary propositions as heretical. It was in the latter part of this century that the word *transubstantiatio* first came into use. And in spite of the far more spiritual sense which was given to the term by scholastic philosophers, the Marian persecution in England

R 2

was marked by a return to formulæ which were at least open to the charge of teaching a carnal mode of presence. The assertions that Christ's *natural* body and blood are present in the sacrament are of common occurrence at this time. Bishop Bonner made it an accusation against John Warne that he believed no substance of Christ's *material* body and blood to be in the sacrament. Finally, Sir John Cheke, in recanting before Cardinal Pole, was made to recite almost the actual declaration forced on Berengar.[1]

On the other hand it is entirely clear that the Anglican objections mentioned do not hold against the strict theory of Transubstantiation elaborated by the Schoolmen, perfected by St. Thomas Aquinas, and made by the Council of Trent the basis of the official teaching of the Roman Church. For in this theory it is made abundantly clear (1) that the Body and Blood of Christ are not present in the Sacrament, either as in any way occupying space,[2] or according to their proper and natural mode of being[3]; and (2) that the consecrated elements do truly retain every reality of bread and wine which it is possible for any bodily sense to perceive, and that therefore the appearance of bread and wine are in no sense illusory or deceitful.

But may we go on to affirm that this doctrine of Transubstantiation teaches the presence of Christ in the sacrament after a *spiritual* manner? This is an exceedingly difficult question to answer with accuracy. It is indeed

---

[1] I take all the foregoing facts and quotations from Darwell Stone's *History of the Doctrine of the Holy Eucharist*.

[2] I take this to be exactly what St. Thomas meant by the phrase *nullo modo localiter* (Summa III, Q. 76, Art. 5).

[3] Cf. Summa III, Q. 76, Art. 6. *Christo autem non est idem esse secundum se et esse sub hoc sacramento, quia per hoc quod dicimus ipsum esse sub hoc sacramento, significatur quaedam habitudo ejus ad hoc sacramentum.*

clear that the intention of the doctrine is to teach what must be called in a general way a spiritual conception of the sacrament. It is also true that it teaches a spiritual manner of presence, if we define *spiritual* in purely negative terms as meaning non-spatial, non-natural, non-carnal, and the like. But if we take the expression " spiritual manner of presence " to mean positively " presence after the manner of a spirit ", the case is different. Neither St. Thomas nor the Council of Trent affirms anything of the kind. St. Thomas does not speak of presence after the manner of a spirit, but rather of presence after the manner of a substance (*per modum substantiae*), and he goes on to explain that just as the entire nature of a material substance such as air or bread is under every particle of air or bread, so the entire Christ is under every particle of the sacramental species. The only reservation which he makes to this analogy consists in his teaching that the Body of Christ is not the subject of the spatial dimensions of the species in the same way as the substance of bread had been before the consecration ; and that therefore, whereas the substance of bread might be said to be in the accidents locally (or spatially), because we may speak of *its* dimensions, this would not hold good of the Body of Christ, into which the substance of bread is converted. " *Unde nullo modo corpus Christi est in hoc sacramento localiter.*"[1]

It may be presumed that the Council of Trent had in mind a similar doctrine to St. Thomas's. And Dr. John O'Neill tells us that it was the anti-Thomists (i.e. the later Scotists and others) who explained " the presence of Christ's Body in the Host after the analogy of the presence

[1] This teaching is taken from Summa III, Q. 76, Arts. 3 and 5 I have paraphrased the Latin in one or two places, so as to bring out what I take to be the author's meaning.

of a spirit in space ",[1] though, of course, they held this theory to be consistent with Transubstantiation as defined by the Church. Bellarmine (*De Eucharistia*, Lib. I, cap. iv) certainly seems to regard the teaching of a spiritual mode of presence as a dangerous, though legitimate, gloss upon the orthodox theory. He writes as follows: "*Adverbia quae dicunt modum existendi corporalem non dicuntur de Christo in Eucharistia, licent dicantur de ipso, ut in caelo residet : alia vero nihil prohibet dici. Ratio est quia (ut saepe diximus) non habet Christus in Eucharistia modum existendi corporum, sed potius spirituum, cum sit totus in qualibet part. Itaque dicemus, Christum esse in Euchar- istia vere, realiter, substantialiter, ut concilium recte loquitur, sed non dicemus corporaliter, id est, eo modo quo suapte natura existunt corpora, nec sensibiliter, mobiliter, etc. Immo contra dici posset esse spiritualiter, ut Bernardus dicit in sermone de S. Martino ubi affirmat in sacramento exhiberi nobis veram carnis substantiam, sed spiritualiter, non carnaliter ; tamen non videtur haec vox multum frequen- tanda, quia periculum esset, ne traheretur id ab adversariis, non tam ad modum, quam ad ipsam naturam significan- dam ; propter quod item periculum non videtur valde usurpandum illud, non esse corporaliter, nisi addatur continuo explicatio.*" It seems, therefore, that Cardinal Newman was travelling altogether beyond the doctrine of Transubstantiation as such, and putting a definitely non-Thomist interpretation upon it, when he wrote that " He (our Lord) is in the Holy Eucharist after the manner of a spirit".[2]

The difference seems to be more important than is usually supposed. If we take Transubstantiation in its

---

[1] *Cosmology*, vol. i, *The Greeks and Aristotelian Schoolmen*, p. 190.

[2] *Via Media* (1877), ii, 220. Quoted by Dr. Stone, Farnham Con- ference on *Reservation*, p. 59.

strict or Thomist sense, and apply to it a rigorous
criticism, it appears to delocalise only too completely the
presence which is the inward reality of the Sacrament. For
" presence after the manner of a substance " turns out
to mean no more in the end than " presence after the
manner of a logical abstraction ". The whole process of
separating substance from accidents is a process of
thought, not of fact ; and we are led towards a " subjectivism " which even the Receptionist avoids. " *Nullo
modo localiter* " then becomes true in a sense which St.
Thomas never intended, and the whole basis of Catholic
devotion to the Sacrament disappears. If, on the other
hand, we take the phrase " presence after the manner of
a spirit " for our guide, we affirm something which St.
Thomas doubtless did intend, and which every worthy
believer in the Real Presence recognises as true, viz.
that our Lord's gift of Himself is present in the Sacrament,
not at all as occupying space, but somewhat after the
manner in which the immaterial realities of the natural
world, human mind or spirit, are said to be present *at*
or *through*, rather than *in*, particular places, such as those
occupied by the human brain or body. But evidently
this conception is in no way helped, rather it is gravely
hindered, by demanding that the substance of the material
elements must be removed, before they can become the
shrine of such a parousia.

Why is it then that the main body of Western Catholicism has obstinately clung, so far as official definition is
concerned, to affirming the substantial rather than the
spiritual mode of presence ? One reason no doubt is
the self-defeating desire to interpret literally the words of
One Who ever bade men seek truth not in the letter but
in the spirit. But perhaps another influence also has been
at work, as the passage quoted from Bellarmine may

almost seem to suggest. The substantial mode of presence seems to connect the presence of the Lord with the things or physical objects *as such*, and so to justify extra-liturgical devotion, whereas the spiritual mode of presence is less naturally regarded as a presence fixed in the objects as such, but rather suggests a presence coming through the objects as they are used in the action of the Eucharistic rite. It is in this latter type of presence that I have tried to vindicate belief.

It seems to me that those who are so scrupulous never to localise the Lord's presence, are making arbitrary distinctions, and fail to realise the meaning of sacraments in Christian experience. Since in sacraments, after a sacramental manner, we are obliged to *temporalise* the presence, why should localisation appear abhorrent under the same conditions? Nay, I am willing to believe, if a critic will have it so, that St. Thomas's " *nullo modo localiter* " goes too far. What seems to me in principle wrong is to connect divine presence objectively with outward or material things apart from the two relations of expression and instrumentality. I connect divine presence objectively with a sunset, because it is divinely beautiful. In a different and more intimate manner I believe divine presence to be connected with the material signs of sacraments, and most of all with the Eucharistic elements, because in and by them Christ is not only expressed but also acts upon me. But this special association of divine presence with sacraments seems to hold only *in* the appointed expressiveness and instrumentality of the sacramental action. I cannot persuade myself that the special association of divine presence with a material thing *set apart for* sacramental use is other than subjective, that is, created by my thought. It may be that in this I am guilty of precisely the same mistake which I have just imputed to others. I can but confess that this prejudice, if prejudice it be, has deeply influenced all that I have here written.

INDEX

I. INDEX OF SUBJECTS

Αγια τοῖς ἁγίοις, 115
Atonement and omnipotence, 79
sqq. ; philosophical meaning,
84 ; and Sacraments, 101 *sqq.* ;
and Church, 123 *sqq. See also*
Cross, and Incarnation

BAPTISM, 108 ; and Fatherhood
of God, 168 *sqq.* ; adult and
infant, 168 *sqq.* ; instrumental
and symbolic aspects, 169, 173
sqq. ; and original sin, 170 *sqq.* ;
justification of infant baptism,
175 *sqq.* ; symbol of unity, 178 ;
and Confirmation, 181 *sqq.* ;
and Eucharist, 185 *sqq.*
Beauty, nature of, 20, 25 *sq.* ; of
art and nature, 27 *sqq.* ; and
expression, 30 *sqq.* ; and moral
goodness, 32 *sqq.*, 40, 51 *sq.* ;
and theism, 35. *See also* Cross,
and Jesus, life of
Body and Blood, Eucharistic
meaning of, 208 *sq.*, 226 *sq.*

CHARACTER, Sacramental, 109, 187
Church visible and invisible, 132
sqq.
Confirmation, 108, 181 *sqq.*
Consubstantiation, meaning of,
205 ; and omnipresence, 206
Creating and making, 21 *sq.*
Cross, the, as philosophical principle, 82 *sqq.* ; and evolution, 85
sqq. ; and happiness, 87 ; and
beauty, 87 *sq.* ; and the intellect, 88 *sq.* ; and the moral life,
90 ; and psychology, 91 ; com-
pletes Incarnation, 93. *See also*
Atonement and Eucharist

DUALISM, whether postulated by
ethics, 46

EUCHARIST, the, 109 ; and Bap-
tism, 185 *sqq.* ; and Last
Supper, 187 *sqq.* ; and Sacrifice,
196 *sqq.*, 210 *sq.*, 245 *sqq.* ; and
Presence, 204 *sqq. See also*
Real Presence, Reservation,
Transubstantiation, etc.

ETERNITY AND TIME, 52 *sq.*
Evil, problem of, 36, 38, 49 *sq.*,
79 *sqq.*
Expression and significance, 26 *sq.*
See also Beauty and Symbols

GRACE, not limited, 110 *sq.* ; how
given, 112 *sqq.* ; *ex opere
operato*, 130 n., 213 *sq.*, 219

HOLINESS, nature of, 106 *sqq.*, 234
Holy Order, 108 ; " power "
and " authority " of, 142 *sqq.*
See also Validity, Reunion, etc.

IDEALS, inwardness of, 19 *sqq.*
Immanence, and transcendence,
16 *sq.*, 44 *sq.* ; and Incarnation,
101 *sq.*
Incarnation and philosophy, 55
sq. ; stated in terms of value,
59 *sq.* ; extension in sacraments,
101 *sqq.* ; double meaning of,
102 ; connexion with Atonement, 78, 102 *sq.* ; and Church,
123 *sqq. See also* Jesus, life of
Institution of sacraments, 119
sqq. ; of Eucharist, 187 *sqq.*
Instrumentality and significance,
12 *sqq.*
Instruments, nature of, 5 *sq.*, 47 ;
and instrumentality, 6 *sqq.* ;
artificial and natural, 6, 16 *sq.*
Intention, doctrine of, 130 n., 157
sq.

257